MILLENNIUM
8

First published in 2001
jointly by

Gracewing
2 Southern Avenue
Leominster
Herefordshire HR6 0QF

Millennium Romae 2000 A.D. MM
1 Largo Angelicum
00184 Roma
Italy

ISBN 0-85244-438-9

By kind permission of the Edizioni Studium - Roma
First Italian Edition published 1992

Printed by Rotostampa S.r.l.
Via Tiberio Imperatore, 23 - 00145 Roma

Rocco Pezzimenti

THE POLITICAL THOUGHT OF LORD ACTON

The English Catholics in the Nineteenth Century

Gracewing.

Millennium Romae

PARCERE SUBIECTIS ET DEBELLARE SUPERBOS

2000 A.D.MM

On completing these pages, I would like to offer special thanks to Professor Mario D'Addio, who particularly urged me to write this work and has given advice and followed its progress with great attention. I would also like to thank my friend Brian Williams, Professor of Modern European History at John Cabot University, Rome, for his kind and valuable collaboration during my bibliographical work in Cambridge, and for the English translation of the work.

A cordial word of thanks also to the staff of the British Council in Rome, and especially to Ms. Sylvia R. Bolognese, for enabling me to make use of international book loans, without which this work would have been impossible. Finally, I have received invaluable help from my friend Prof. Livio Mariani in the re-reading of the text.

Contents

Part I

THE GENESIS AND FORMATION
OF LORD ACTON'S PERSONALITY

*1) What should be understood
by "liberal Catholicism"?* 9

2) The years of formation 23

*3) The influence of Döllinger
and the publication of the Syllabus of Errors* 27

4) The Catholic renaissance in England 33

5) The return to England: reasons for isolation 43

6) The "Rambler": reasons for a failure 47

*7) Relations between Newman and Acton:
the Catholic press* 69

*8) Relations between Newman and Acton:
the temporal power* 79

9) The University project 109

10) Readings and reference points 117

Part II

LORD ACTON'S POLITICAL THOUGHT

1) History in ethical perspective 131

2) Lex Continui 139

3) Inaugural Lecture on the Study of History 145

4) History from the point of view of eternity 155

5) The political lessons of the Middle Ages 161

6) Liberalism, Catholicism and democracy
(the notion of limitation) 165

7) Federalism 181

8) Nationality and nationalism 189

9) Liberalism, democracy and socialism:
liberty and equality 195

10) Marxism 203

11) What future for democracy and socialism? 207

12) A note on J. S. Mill 211

13) Characteristics of Lord Acton's liberalism 215

14) A note on Burke:
concerning the French Revolution 239

Conclusion 245

Appendix I 249

Appendix II 253

Notes 257

Bibliography 273

PART I

THE GENESIS AND FORMATION OF LORD ACTON'S PERSONALITY

1) What should be understood by "liberal Catholicism"?

Lord Acton is not easy to define as a historical figure. This is not only due to the rich variety of his existential experience but also because his literary output does not provide us with even one single example of a well-defined work brought to a conclusion. His writings are at times "occasional" while at other times they are highly ambitious in human terms, as witness the project for a *History of Liberty* – to such an extent that they may even have remained almost entirely in the realm of intention. Professor Herbert Butterfield, one of the greatest experts on Acton, says this about his unfinished works: "The truth is that Lord Acton had engaged, as his notes show, in a truly colossal undertaking: although he wrote little, he nevertheless gathered material on such a vast scale that it would have served for a number of works on different subjects. In fact he did not limit himself to studying the subject of liberty from a general historical viewpoint, but studied every major problem in all its details, amassing notes and stacks of quotations drawn from the sources".[1] This sketch presents us with an extremely meticulous historian who was led by the circumstances of his life to seek out the depths of the heart more than to write. This is borne out by the fact that various experiences interweave in the life of Lord Acton, who always remained (whatever the reservations of certain scholars) a Catholic and a liberal in a period when these two terms were unable to find any synthesis – not only for cultural reasons, but also because of international politics.

No work on the historical and political thought of Lord Acton can be considered clear or exhaustive unless it first clarifies the terms of a somewhat thorny problem: that of liberal Catholicism. There is no easy answer, when we remember that even defining liberalism itself is certainly not a straightforward task.[2] There are so many components which go to make up what presents itself as a "vision of the world" which, however, despite its variety, nevertheless has concrete, and thus describable characteristics. Such a description is necessary if we want to escape from the state of incomprehension into which even historians and experts on liberalism themselves often fall. In Mateucci's opinion, "the reason that there is no accord on stipulating a common definition of liberalism is threefold. In the first place the history of liberalism is closely linked to the story of democracy... In the second place, liberalism has been present in various countries in very different historical periods... in the third place, it is not even possible to speak of a historical diffusion of liberalism. To this must be added a certain indeterminacy in the historical reference-points of liberalism: from time to time it may indicate a party or a political movement, a political ideology or a metapolitics (or even an ethic), a particular institutional structure or the political reflection which this has stimulated".[3]

If this is the case, it must be an even more difficult task to talk about "liberal Catholicism", which seems to many to be a difficult combination to understand at all. And yet, on closer examination, things are not so complex after all. There are certain aspects which enable us to throw light on the intricate problem. Matteucci himself admits, for instance, that some part of the discussion about liberalism must take its inspiration from the enormous influence which the English liberals have exercised over the whole continent.[4] The present work, which deals with a such a liberal Catholic as Lord Acton, thus moves within the natural ambit of liberalism: it takes it as a source of comparison and is enriched by it.

Liberal England no longer lives in its splendid isolation, but seeks to relate itself to the rest of Europe, from which it had inherited many problems since the Napoleonic era. As De Ruggiero rightly observed (in a work which has already become a classic of liberal historiography), "perhaps the most salient characteristic of England in the nineteenth century lay in its tendency to move towards Europeanization, which meets up with the contrary trend on the part of continental peoples to study and imitate England, resulting in a mutual understanding and adaption, and a greater affinity of problems, mental forms, sentiments and institutions".[5]

De Ruggiero also sees in the English religious movement of the nineteenth century (in which the Catholic element was certainly not merely a minor part), a characteristic element of British liberalism, to the point of seeing in English religion, divided between Anglicans and Nonconformists, Catholics and Dissenters a sort of backbone of English liberalism.[6]

There would thus have been some reciprocal influence between England and the Continent: from the British Isles, the transformation of society brought about by the French Revolution was observed, while on the part of the Continent there was an examination of the long-established gains of the British political system. These two elements are basic, to such an extent that, for example, in the light of the first, Conzemius describes "liberal Catholicism... as the effort made by Catholicism to adapt to the transformation of society brought about by the Revolution".[7] In this way the Catholics seem to plan reformist intentions which, although they are almost always found within the context and tradition of the Church, aim not only to renew society in its external aspects, but also seek to bring about what was then termed "internal renewal of Christian civilization", even in the typical presuppositions of historical and theological thought.[8]

This way of defining liberal Catholicism seems to me in fact less then clear, because in this way it is presented as one of the many aspects of liberalism, and clearly opposed to liberalism in its secular and anti-religious manifestations. And yet this is not the case. A series of commonplaces have come into use in connection with this concept which have sought to see, in every expression of Catholic thought in the nineteenth century, aspects almost invariably seen as conservative, or best, cautiously moderate. And yet even the documents judged to be most hostile to liberalism contain reflections of great interest which can help us towards a definition of liberal Catholicism.

We can take one example which has long since become classic: the Syllabus of Errors. When examined closely, it is clear that liberalism understood as a political system capable of opposing absolutism was certainly not condemned. What was condemned was in fact what we might term philosophical, and in some senses, moral liberalism.[9] And it could hardly be otherwise, for as quite a few Catholic thinkers of the nineteenth century point out, (and Lord Acton stands out among them), in the long-past Middle Ages Christian philosophy, by considering even the possibility of tyrannicide and studying themes such as those of consensus and the limits of obedience, laid down the bases of modern liberalism.

In this light, liberal Catholicism begins, little by little, to take shape. It is the product of history, that Western history in which classicism was permeated and reinvigorated by Christianity. Lord Acton's speculation confirms this to such an extent that for him, without an adequate reflection on history, it is not possible to understand the real value and meaning of liberalism at all. It has rightly been observed that "he thought that he could obtain directly from historical reality a criterion for justifying his apologia for the rights of liberty and the duty to resist arbitrary power which is incumbent on all mankind, including the believer".[10] Historical reality, we should note, is not to be considered under the abstract ideal categories typical of the dialectical method,[11] but understood as a constant moral effort which always accompanies those societies which in one way or another have been affected by Christianity. In short, *liberalism*, over and above all its distinctions, is basically the *product of a civilization*. In this viewpoint, any coupling which seeks to link the noun "liberal" to any Christian adjective is pleonastic, because *on the historical plane*, outside this context liberalism does not exist. The adjectives become necessary later, when a certain kind of liberalism, seeking to subjectivize the moral criteria and beginning to frame anti-religious arguments, is opposed to those which have no intention of impinging on what concerns morals and theology.

A liberalism which is concerned with moral, religious and even theological problems was seen by the majority of Catholics merely as a way of thinking capable only of resulting in religious indifferentism. On the political plane, the issue seemed different, however, since every striving towards perfection of freedom could be included in a tradition of civilization which had received its vital lymph from Christianity itself.

As time went on, however, the question of liberal Catholicism underwent a series of developments of such a kind that quite a few exponents, even in the hierarchy, ended by speaking about liberty, at least on the level of a quest, and even in the theological field. This seems to be a story of our own days, but here too Lord Acton seems to come to our aid when he "describes the liberal Catholics as those who wish for liberty not only *for* the Church but *in* the Church".[12] This problem is still much debated even today, and has not infrequently created some friction. But it is a problem which for Acton, as we shall see, has more than anything else a theoretical value, for on the practical plane – and his own life fully demonstrates this – the last word always lies with authority (it goes without saying that this is only valid for moral and theological questions). The last word because in the meantime the search goes on for various opinions and their debate forms part of the context of catholic theology.[13] Newman himself also appears to be in agreement here.

Over and above these problems, which at times assume the tone of a dispute, and which we can say were nevertheless limited in relation to the great debate which concerned Catholicism almost everywhere in Europe, it must be stated, however, that the latter is presented, by all its major exponents, as the finest outcome of the civil history of Europe, to such an extent that it actually defines its civilisation.

While admitting this, we would not venture to say that the label of "liberal Catholic" presents us with a stereotype, repeated everywhere it is found. On the contrary, liberal Catholicism presents such a variety of personalities, of forms and of episodes that it is one of the richest aspects of the history of the last century. It is for this reason that in order to study it, we need to trace its most essential lines. Here we may agree with Conzemius, for whom there are three distinct elements to be borne in mind:[14] 1) Liberal Catholicism should be studied by keeping in mind the fact that the national contexts little by little give it particular orientations. 2) Liberal Catholicism often shows the defects of classical liberalism in general in the sense that, while it proves capable of notable expositions on the theoretical plane, in practice it often proves incapable of realizing political designs. 3) Although there is some element of incomprehension, liberal Catholicism remains in general fully within orthodox bounds, and for this reason it cannot be considered as an anticipatory glimpse of modernism.

A fourth motif can be added to these – a negative one, because it shows up an element of great weakness. The liberal Catholics, although they were seeking unity of intention and action behind a great debate, in reality failed in this objective because of rivalries which were only rarely personal, but more often national and political. The example of England and Lord Acton illuminates this observation quite clearly. "The liberal Catholics, in fact, exalted the Anglo-Saxon virtues which pleased the new classes, but which … the Irish immigrants rejected. Not only were such values alien to their traditional culture, but for the Irish, they symbolized the patrons and bosses who oppressed them. Consequently, they had little sympathy for the liberal Catholics".[15] We should also remember the grave crisis through which the Holy See was passing, with the approaching loss of temporal power. This problem, with clear implications for international politics, often caused Catholics to look with suspicion especially at those states such as England, which were opposed to France and Austria in the delicate game of the European equilibrium, and also at the internal balances within the nations. It is these facts, these political contingencies, which after having forced Catholics to take up gradually differing positions according to the socio-political context, also led to talk of different versions of liberal Catholicism. But all this is related to episodes which then gradually faded away: we may cite another English case – with a government committed to supporting the Italian cause, it was impossible to exercise weight and influence inside the committed and educated classes in England to demonstrate the dangers that the loss of the temporal power would involve for the Church. This means that the intrinsic value of liberal Catholic thought passed beyond the immediate time period within which it matured, because it was expressed, and so had to be examined within a range of considerations which went beyond the simple historical point of reference; at the same time it provided a framework for history itself, in which the internal and external elements, transcendent and immanent, were interwoven and at times hard to distinguish.

History, as the liberal Catholics conceived it (Lord Acton and Newman in particular, but also Rosmini), is not tied to any dialectical determinism; it does not offer predetermined targets, because it is first and foremost the story of intelligence and freedom, and secondly does not recognize any earthly resolution which can be considered determinative. It has been rightly observed that in the liberal Catholics who studied history there is a faith, sometimes overstated, in the final triumph of truth through freedom. But this optimism derives from the fact that for Catholic thinkers, divine grace is always present, and aids human liberty.[16] A further conviction is to be found in some of them, quite clearly expressed by Newman, that beyond circumstance and change, the Church is a kind of prodigy which is able to overcome everything by transforming and raising itself.[17]

History, however, is to be seen not just as a path to salvation, but also as one of moral improvement. This, which may seem to go without saying, is of maximum importance, especially in England where, as a result of industrial development, history was being reduced little by little to a path towards an ever-growing prosperity and a progressive liberation from need. Not that these gains were to be rejected, but they needed to be integrated with a progressive moral development, so that humanity should not exhaust its efforts in economic action. This conviction was a common notion of the whole of English liberalism after the great age of reform. Everyone, including certain conservative circles, was convinced that prosperity – or better, the advantages of the few and the industrial growth of the nation, could not fail to weigh heavily on the undefended shoulders of children, women and immigrants,[18] for the benefit of whom the (Catholic) Church in England acted in its welfare activities.

To place oneself on the side of the excluded was also to take up a specific cultural position. The English middle classes were not identical with those of the Continent. "The English industrial classes do not have that worship of tradition, of custom, of heredity, by which Burke described the characteristics of the liberal landed aristocracy ... These industrialists are various rationalists of the technical and business worlds ... Modern industry is, like all modern creations, the daughter of rationalism".[19] Against this mode of thought, there is the whole critique of certain religious circles, where this position of a radical liberalism was unacceptable – a radicalism which at bottom wanted to clean the board of the whole of the past. But there was also the whole dispute with the liberal Catholics, for whom as we have seen, freedom, being the product of an entire civilization, could not be abstracted from tradition. It is perhaps here, and especially in England, that the great matter of disagreement between "radical" liberalism and "Catholic" liberalism lies. The first has "a love of the particular and the concrete, and a very English hostility to over-general principles".[20] The second actually bases its peculiar character on the universality of certain principles which English and Western history in general have taken on board over a long time, in a historical process lasting many centuries. Behind the latter conviction there was the stability and objective security of certain institutions: behind the former lay the risk of an individualist position, entirely directed towards the search for a form of utilitarianism as an end in itself.

The notions of radical liberalism, however, met with a sad fate in England. English liberalism (and here perhaps we should not distinguish between classical liberalism, either secular or of religious inspiration, but rather merely speak of liberalism *tout court*), is well aware that every right presupposes an authority which sanctions it, and that this authority is the product of an exhausting path which absolutely no one can ignore. On the contrary all forms of radical liberalism forget that "the fact is that the individual does not always follow the logic of his own interests with full consistency, and indeed that he may be led to follow a misunderstood utility, in conflict with that of others, and in the final instance ruinous even for his own particular interests".[21] On the contrary, liberalism based on tradition, is in constant search for an equilibrium. A balance between autonomy of initiative and pursuit of individual usefulness, with the authority of a state which must see to it that the interests and the needs of the majority do not end up by being motives for unresolvable and increasingly serious conflicts. Liberalism understood in this way watches over conflicts which it judges never to be completely terminable, but which it tries never to render irreconcilable by resolving them gradually in a concrete and "measured" fashion. Basically this position, defended by a number of moderates, does ensure that certain steps forward are taken in history, while the other more radical position, because it ignores history, causes steps backward to be taken, for in cancelling history itself it wanders into utopia.

This position of moderate liberalism was to become typical of a large part of English Christianity, at least among the lower and middle classes, in the 30s and 40s of the nineteenth century, until it began to diversify in the later years of the century. "And this thrust from below", as De Ruggiero has rightly observed, "had the result of shattering the indifference and apathy even of the higher clergy. The contrast between the exemplary life and sincere evangelical activities of poor young priests, and the mindless and self-indulgent life of the exploiters of the Church is painfully noted by the mass of the faithful in a period of fervent Christian revival".[22] It is in this climate that the great religious crisis of Oxford took place. Apart from the converts, it also produced a notable series of people who were influenced throughout their lives by this inimitable experience. Among these was Gladstone himself. This is the explanation for the complexity of a movement which to some denotes a certain ambiguity, but which it would perhaps be more correct to describe as a rich and diverse variety of positions.

Gladstone is indeed an outstanding example of this complex period. A principal exponent of English liberalism, he is the proof that the liberal conception is the product of Western civilization, and finds its essential and defining component in Christianity. Although he could not be said in any way to be one of them, he was present at Oxford during the crisis of the Oxford converts, and he knew almost all their leading figures. He was undoubtedly struck by the extraordinary personality of Newman, for whom he conceived a profound respect which lasted all his life.[23] His friendships, his collaborators – one may include Lord Acton – are the proof that the religious motives behind his liberalism were considerable. While he remained a firm member of the Anglican Church, his attitude towards Catholics was not only sympathetic and tolerant, but also positive, as, for example, when it came to dealing with the delicate question of Irish immigrants. In questions concerning education, too, Gladstone[24] went against Anglican public opinion in proposing non-discriminatory educational projects.

His ecclesiastical policy was also against discrimination. In fact, although in his earliest moments of political activity, Gladstone showed himself to be very close to Anglican orthodoxy with the doctrine of the unity of Church and State, after a short time he distanced himself from it. His "liberalism" led him to be favourable to emancipation, not only for Catholics but also for Jews, convinced as he was that the real value of religion is that of being the foundation of autonomy of conscience and civil liberties. Thus to separate the Anglican Church from the State, for a deeply religious man like Gladstone, did not mean a profession of atheism or sceptical indifference. On the contrary, it was the firm conviction that the authentically liberal development of a state could not do without full religious liberty.[25] To repress and suffocate the freedom of religion was, for Gladstone, the worst civil calamity that could happen, because it generated a climate of distrust and fear which has nothing to do with a liberal society.

Gladstone's attitude towards religious liberty cannot, however, be judged as "paternalistic". On the contrary, it is evidence that real liberalism is the product of a civilization in which religion has played a determining role. Gladstone often made it clear that his attitude was typical of a genuine Englishman, who could not ignore the value of civil liberty.[26] We can agree with De

Ruggiero's argument, according to which "English liberalism is not summed up entirely in the Liberal Party: it has its complementary expression in the Conservative Party, which is renewed in contact with its adversary".[27] English liberalism is thus also a total expression of the political struggles of its parties, supported by a civil society which had found its best inspirations precisely in the different religious motivations.

It should also be said that the favourable response which the demands of the Catholics met with in England at a certain moment was reflected in an international climate which favoured mutual comprehension between the different confessions and between believers and "secularists". There are two important questions which concerned the Church and the Catholic movement in general in the 1820s and 30s. First of all it should be remembered that despite the fact that the Roman Curia was passing through a period of strong conservatism, the Papacy never openly supported the Holy Alliance (Russia, Austria, Prussia) which, whatever its intentions, was seen as an expression of religious confusion, and as a levelling down of the various confessional beliefs. How could three sovereigns be in close agreement when clearly one of them was an expression of Catholicism, one of Protestantism and the third of the Orthodox Church? There is also a second and very important reason: in the "hot" years of 1830 and 1831, Catholics played a fundamental role alongside the liberals in the obtaining of Belgian independence.[28] It is true that in a conservative view it is easy to justify the commitment of the Catholics because it was a matter of taking part in a struggle against one of the traditional strongholds of Protestantism, the Kingdom of Holland, but it is also true that that revolution brought about a state ruled by a constitutional monarch, to the achievement of which the Catholics had made a notable contribution. This aspect had a considerable influence on English public opinion which viewed the Catholic reawakening with sympathy.

In the following decade, with the election to the papacy of Pius IX, it seemed that enthusiasm and comprehension towards Catholics might grow still further, but it was again the international situation which complicated the role of Catholics in many European states, and also in England. More than the publication of the Syllabus, and yet more than the subsequent dogma of Infallibility, it was the slow decline of Austria in the whole of central Europe that caused the ecclesiastical structure to rigidify, and with the contemporary growth of Italian unity there was a weakening of a traditional defender of the Papal States.[29] Needless to say, such a condition, the results of which were completely uncertain, resulted in those Catholics who at that moment showed liberal sympathies being viewed with suspicion, and their life began to meet with some difficulty everywhere. This was so particularly in England, where the whole of public opinion, hostile for a whole variety of reasons to Austrian power, was overwhelmingly favourable to Italian unity.

The importance of this point has perhaps not been yet fully evaluated. The isolation into which many exponents of liberal Catholicism fell led to the rapid development of the idea that there could be no compatibility at all between Catholicism and Liberalism. The adversaries of the Church made every effort to show that within it there was no possibility for the development of liberty. Within the Church, many looked with suspicion on every liberal notion. Thus a reality which had until recently appeared evident to many came to be ignored – i.e. the fact that if the tradition and civilization of Christianity is set aside, it is impossible to speak of liberalism. Few seemed to survive in this climate, but among those that did, Lord Acton matured his grand design in these years – unfortunately not fully realized – of writing a history of liberty with the specific aim of showing how it is impossible to speak of liberalism while ignoring the history of Christianity. Acton's position is of the maximum importance because – in contrast to those of Gioberti and Rosmini and others – it comes from a layman and thus in the English context, one who carried greater weight.

To this motive must be added the fact that in England, apart from the Catholic renaissance "the liberal de-Anglicanization of public life created room for the English Catholics".[30] This phenomenon, which developed above all in the latter years of

Gladstone's leadership, points to the fact that a genuine liberal policy could not be in any way hostile to Catholicism, considered as one of the character-forming elements of English history. It is certainly true that many people contributed to changing this attitude, and among them Newman most of all, when they tried to demonstrate that Catholics were good subjects of Her Britannic Majesty, on a par with Anglicans and followers of other religious bodies or faiths. But it is also true that the political situation itself, and the customary farsightedness of Gladstone, contributed to this change of direction. It was he who, for example, in understanding the explosive situation in Ireland, evolved a policy in favour of the "emigrants from the Green Isle", even though he always remained convinced that more courageous decisions must be taken vis-à-vis Ireland – and in this he anticipated to some degree what would happen in the twentieth century. Gladstone's long-sightedness, however, derived, as we have mentioned, from his own cultural background, and from his friends, among whom Newman and Acton stand out. It is truly surprising to find that at the end of the century, Leo XIII, when he spoke about the situation of the Catholics of Poland dominated by the Russians, could maintain that everything was made more complicated by the fact that the oppressors, in this case, were devoid of a man such as Gladstone. But could the Russians ever have had a Gladstone? Could that cultural background, those liberal institutions, ever have existed in a tradition which had never distinguished the political from the religious, and which was thus deprived of the necessary premises for the birth of the most elementary principles of liberalism? The Pope's rhetorical question was the confirmation that a liberal prime minister such as Gladstone was unthinkable and inconceivable outside a history which had seen the triumph of the path of liberty – thanks, in fact, to the contribution made by the faithful. It was just another confirmation that liberalism is one of the best products of Western civilization, to which Catholicism has made a decisive contribution.

2) The years of formation

The situation of the liberal Catholics around the middle of the nineteenth century could certainly not be described as good; out of favour both inside and outside the Church, they were unable to make much headway with their ideas. The situation of the English liberal Catholics, however, was even more difficult. For them the situation was less favourable than elsewhere; their numbers had become very thin, and the church authorities watched over them with greater rigidity because they did not want their activity to compromise in any way the happy outcome of the restoration of the hierarchy in England.

This minority was opposed by the whole of English Catholicism which, around the middle of the nineteenth century, had two main tendencies which were certainly complementary to each other, whenever they wished to collaborate, but which remained nonetheless mutually suspicious. On the one hand, the converts who followed Newman concentrated around the educated and thoughtful circle with its centre at Oxford. His friends enjoyed that atmosphere of tranquil, accessible study, made possible by the pacific and friendly spirit which characterised the clerics of the early Victorian period.[31] On the other hand there were those dedicated to action, whose leader was the vigorous Henry Edward Manning (many Catholic activities were also appreciated by the British government: one has only to think of the work of the Sisters of Mercy, and of those of Our Lady of Norwood[32] in the field hospitals during the Crimean War).

These two tendencies, although they were sometimes shining in their zeal, did not show themselves to be specially open to the liberal spirit, both because they had no reason to put themselves in conflict with the Holy See at such a delicate moment and because they had no wish to compromise the dialogue with the English Catholic tradition, by nature conservative, and with the more sympathetic areas of Anglicanism. If we add to this a certain mentality of that "splendid isolation" so typical of the Victorian age, from which many of the English Catholics were certainly not exempt, it can be understood why the English Catholic Church remained closed to certain influences which, in contrast, were creating some fervour among French and German Catholics, and even quite a few Italians. This is the context into which Lord Acton and some of his friends, with great difficulty and amid substantial incomprehension, tried to insert themselves.

John Emerich Edward Dalberg Acton was born in Naples in 1834, of an ancient English family which as a result of "adventurous" circumstances had moved in the previous century first to France and then to Italy. His maternal family too had a noteworthy tradition in European history. The Dalbergs were among the leading nobles of the Holy Roman Empire. The standing and fame of the relations of the young Acton were to be increased after the early death of his father, on the occasion of his mother's second marriage to Lord Leveson, whose aristocratic family had a long tradition of involvement in English diplomacy and politics. His step-father was to hold important offices in the governments of Lord John Russell and William Gladstone.

Apart from the important connections which this complex family could offer him, Acton also acquired a broad cultural background and spoke and read a number of languages. This truly unusual circumstance accompanied him throughout his life. We need only remember that a few years later, even in different contexts he could never use the same language: he chattered in English with his son, in German with his wife (born in Bavaria), in French with his sister-in-law, and in Italian with his mother-in-law.[33] The perfect knowledge of these languages made it possible for him to read books of history, theology, philosophy and literature in very impressive numbers.

At the time of her new marriage, Lady Acton had agreed with her husband, who was an Anglican, that her son John should be brought up as a Catholic. And this was done; Acton was educated by the most notable personalities of Catholic thought of the last century. He studied, in fact, for a brief period in Paris with Monseigneur Félix Dupanloup, for a long time in Oscott, the English Catholic College whose president was Bishop Wiseman, and he completed his studies with Professor Johann Ignaz von Döllinger in Munich:[34] three different directors, with completely differing objectives and forms of training.

"Dupanloup was involved for a while in one of the most interesting Catholic experiments in modern times; the attempt to restate the relations of Church and State so as to satisfy the requirements of political liberalism".[35] This aspect was to become one of the basic themes of Acton's thought. In 1843, John was sent to the Catholic College of St Mary, Oscott, where he was to spend several years. This was an important period, when the youth acquired a very rich vocabulary, according to some, already that of an adult,[36] a broad vision of many problems and that love for reading which was to grow even greater in the following decade in Germany.

In the 1840s, while he was still at boarding school, the famous movement of the Oxford converts began to develop (and this, as we shall see later, was one of the causes of the Catholic revival in England). Acton heard the comments of his teachers on it, and above all he noticed the ultramontane attitude of Wiseman, hostile to liberal ideas, and fearful that the Oxford converts would do more harm than good to the reconciliation of the English State to the Catholic Church. It was precisely this certainty of Wiseman, who envisaged that the Church would grow and progressively "clean up" human affairs that conferred on the young Acton that singular love of history which would begin to develop during his stay in Germany.

When he had reached sixteen years of age, Acton arrived in Munich to study under the guidance of Professor Döllinger. These were intense and formative years. The relationship with his new teacher was to last a long time, even though it was often interrupted by a number of interesting journeys (Acton would be in the USA in 1855, and in Russia in 1856 for the coronation of Csar Alexander II); these journeys would later be the subject of careful reflection. With Döllinger he was to visit Italy in 1857, and between them a sincere and lasting friendship, even if finally a critical one, developed.

3) The influence of Döllinger
and the publication of the Syllabus of Errors

Although we make no claim to have analysed Döllinger's thought, we cannot ignore the role which the German theologian played in forming the personality of the young Acton during the years of his stay in Germany.

As a result of the developments in German historical thought, Catholic theology in Germany felt the need to undertake new studies in order to respond with increasing precision to the needs of modern man. Among the most active in pursuing this aim was certainly Döllinger, who for many years enjoyed the support of numerous followers. The German scholar remained within the fold of orthodoxy for many years; the disputes with the ultramontanes then began to create the first suspicions that led to a hardening of attitudes between the parties after the publication of the *Syllabus*. The latter "provoked in Döllinger the impression that in Rome it was intended to eliminate all space for discussion within the Church, heading for an open breach with the intellectual world".[37] Thus Döllinger proposed to collect, by a very detailed study, all the documents capable of weakening the claim of infallibility. It goes without saying that in those very years Acton was acquiring his taste for historical studies and his meticulous attitude to research, and was gathering useful information for his never-realized project for a history of liberty.

Döllinger's position, like that of the Church itself, had its own justifications. The theologian "expressed a need for dialogue and for openness which is proper to someone who has overcome many trials and has the faith of the prevailing reason in a

27

rationalist era: he is, furthermore, profoundly conscious of the power of scientists in the new society, and holds that the Church too must take cognizance of this, even if only for pastoral reasons".[38] The Church, for its own part, found itself at loggerheads with an agnostic State, and thus assumed a defensive position that explains the conflict with progressive theology. This conflict became more acute when the new theological trend, after the publication of yet another study by Döllinger, "denounced the legendary character of a number of traditions relating to the Popes of the Middle Ages".[39] These views were rapidly taken on board by the Italian anti-clerical movement, and by those (and Acton was among them) to whom the cause of Italian unity was dear.

Döllinger had also exercised a certain influence on the English "converts"; these, however, after the submission of Newman to Rome in 1845, had distanced themselves from the German thinker, who only had Acton on his side.[40] The latter attempted to show the English that the new historical method, adopted in Germany by Döllinger and his followers, could have had a profound influence in England.[41] But this attempt, apart from being unsuccessful, possibly caused Acton to become further isolated. There are a number of elements which point to this fact. In 1864, following in the steps of Döllinger, Acton took a stand against the *Syllabus*, and above all against the section entitled *Errores qui ad liberalismus hodiernum referendus*. In the same year, there was a major upheaval in Acton's life, because the latest number of the *Home and Foreign Review* appeared, marking the end of the collaboration between Acton and Catholic journalism in England.[42] Acton, deeply convinced of his position[43] preferred isolation to open conflict, and awaited events which would prove him right. His conviction was also based on a circumstance which is not always mentioned: the closing of the doors to liberalism was much desired by the Jesuit fathers who at that moment carried their fullest weight in the Roman Curia (an aspect of matters which history was rapidly to change;[44] the end of the temporal power was to prove an effective remedy).

Acton's isolation – or it might be better to say his voluntary standing aside – was momentarily suspended during the First Vatican Council. The intention of the Council, in Acton's opinion, was on the same lines as that of the Syllabus, which "remained unchanged by the decisions of the Council".[45] Acton, who resumed his writings just at the time of the Council, in his new residence in Rome was to insist strongly on the dangers which could derive from the proclamation of the dogma of Infallibility which, at times, he judged to be another hard blow against liberal ideas.

Probably behind Acton's position there is the more or less open pressure from the English government, which was deeply concerned about the protectorate which France was exercising over Rome,[46] and about transalpine meddling in Italian political affairs. The doctrine of Infallibility was, in Acton's eyes, for many ecclesiastical circles and not only in Italy, a hidden defence of the temporal power of the Popes. The latter appeared to liberal Catholics (one might cite Manzoni, for instance) to be in open conflict with the times. "Seen from this point of view, Acton's intervention in the matter of the Council involved an affirmation of his political beliefs rather than his doctrinal creed... It may be defined as the affirmation of a liberalism which he conceived to be in peril".[47] A peril demonstrated by history, if we think of the way in which the hopes of Italian liberal Catholics were extinguished.

If we examine the attitude of Lord Acton towards the work of the Council, we can see clearly how he was able to distinguish the religious, and therefore enduring, moments in the life of the Church from the secular, and thus transitory, ones. His ethical vision of history led him to reject the temporal claims, to some extent because these placed the Church in a position of submission towards France and aristocratic Austria, which could certainly not be considered champions of liberal ideals.[48] Recently history had shown, on the contrary, that the two continental powers had very decisively repressed the manifestation of any form of liberal energy.

For Acton, as long as the Church did not emerge from this agonizing and dangerous situation, it would not be able to confront the problems of the modern world, which were above all those of reconciling the secular spirit of the times with that of religion, freedom with authority, and reason with faith. In Acton there was almost a frenetic desire to see the Church free itself and become purified from all earthly attachments, in order to dedicate itself to that ministry of human advancement which meant injecting into history that ethical content which would move it towards other than earthly ends. This conviction is demonstrated by the fact that once the doctrine of Infallibility had been proclaimed, Acton sought to demonstrate its spiritual value with regard to questions of faith,[49] in order to defend it from the attacks of the liberal world, and in order to continue a dialogue with the authorities of the Church.

A good Englishman, Acton always believed that one day the Church might yet take an interest in the new constitutional principles which had emerged in the modern world, and which had made their first appearance in British constitutionalism.[50] The division of powers and the multiplicity of intermediary powers operating in civil society, according to him, found their most complete *raison d'être* in the Catholic philosophical tradition. It may be here that we find the explanation of the patience with which Acton bore with the many incomprehensions between his thinking and the positions of the English hierarchy. Led by his own historical and Christian vision to look beyond the present, Acton was convinced that mutual incomprehension would be overcome sooner or later.

"I am alone in London, sad, unhappy" Acton used to say from time to time. Sad at the incomprehension showed by the hierarchy towards his ideas and towards modern culture in general. Sad because he loved the Church. "I cannot bear that Protestants should say the Church cannot be reconciled with the truths or precepts of science, or that Catholics should fear the legitimate and natural progress of the scientific spirit. These two errors seem to me almost identical, and if one is more dangerous than the other, I think it is the last, and that it comes more naturally to me to be zealous against the Catholic mistake than against the Protestant".[51] These noble words show the malaise of a soul which feels a strong need to remain included within the Church, but feels equally strongly the need to understand humankind of his own time, to share and aid its just expectations.

Acton's intentions were viewed badly by some members of the English hierarchy,[52] who seemed to be almost embittered by the immaturity of the times and the deleterious psychological assault to which the Holy See was subjected; completely wrapped up in the Roman problem, it was unable to live in the serenity needed to face up to new problems. The times could not be said to be ripe, but Acton's faith was indeed mature when he stated: "I will sacrifice the existence of the Review to the defence of its principles, in order that I may combine the obedience which is due to legitimate ecclesiastical authority with an equally conscientious maintenance of the rightful and necessary liberty of thought".[53] These words served to calm the English Church, but they isolated Acton even more, and made him less and less serene. It has been said – I think with some reason – that catholic intellectuals such as he, Rosmini and others, unfortunately lived a generation or two too soon. This prematurity had the sole advantage of creating patterns of incomprehension and damaging isolation, which often even limited the full development of many deep reflections engaged in by those who were certainly the most profound intelligences of Catholicism in the last century. It should not be forgotten, for example, that Acton judged Rosmini to be the most intelligent Italian cleric of his time.[54]

4) The Catholic renaissance in England

Before analysing the difficulties that Acton met with in re-establishing a place for himself in the English Catholic Church, and examining the reasons for his isolation, it will be as well to give some discussion to the Catholic renaissance in England. This phenomenon got under way around the middle of the nineteenth century, thanks to a series of not always predictable circumstances which altered the social structure of England.

As a result of particularly dramatic internal conditions, many Irish people were forced to emigrate to England, facing the local Catholic Church with a need for unprecedented changes. English Catholicism, living in isolation as it had been up to then in circumscribed surroundings, was mainly aristocratic in character, and felt itself to be stimulated to come to terms with the reality of the working class, and to create new parishes to cater for the thousands and thousands of workers of Irish origin who had strong links with the Church of Rome. Consequently English Catholicism, which since the time of the Reformation had been upheld by Vicars Apostolic as in a "missionary country",[55] felt the need to adapt itself structurally and in other ways to the new needs of the moment.[56]

It was in this period that the work of the future Cardinal Wiseman began for the normalization of relations between England and Rome. The undertaking did not prove easy: incomprehension and reproaches of various kinds complicated matters. The susceptibilities of the anti-papists had to be placated, but when this failed, the same distrusts which arose within the English Catholic world had to be overcome. The demands of the

Catholic tradition did not sit well with the new needs of immigrant Catholics. Thus "the land-owning nobility, jealous of their ancient privileges, looked with suspicion on the constantly growing role that the Irish element was playing in the life of the Catholic Church, and above all they reproved priests coming from Ireland for their political intervention in a direction distasteful to conservative interests".[57] To complicate matters even more, a further element entered the situation: perhaps the most important of this religious revival in England: the converts.

Around the end of the 1840s and the beginning of the 50s, there was a veritable wave of conversions, more important still because they came from intellectual and respected circles like those of Oxford. Cardinal Wiseman, who was the key figure and the hinge around whom the new conversions turned, when speaking of converts like Newman, Ward or Manning (a former Anglican archdeacon who shocked public opinion by making a public abjuration), said humbly: "I am inclined to recognize that in everything, except in the fortune of possessing the truth, ... we are their inferiors. I have said for a long time to those who surround me that, if the theologians of Oxford enter the Church, we must be disposed to retreat to the shadows and take second place".[58] Unfortunately not all had the wisdom and the humility of Cardinal Wiseman, and many of these converts encountered not a few difficulties in fitting in, especially among the Catholic clergy who, certainly not in matters of zeal, but in mental openness and cultural education, were in fact quite inferior.

This lively but by no means idyllic situation was perceived by Newman himself, who was the subject of various misunderstandings, which fortunately faded after the publication in 1864 of his *Apologia pro Vita Sua*.[59] Before this date, Newman had seen quite a number of initiatives end in failure. In 1851, for instance, welcoming the invitation of the Irish episcopate, he would have accepted the Rectorship of the University of Dublin, which was not long afterwards to prove a total failure. Newman in fact saw the university as first and foremost an environment in which men of the world were prepared for the world, and not simply as a seminary and monastery[60] as it was understood by the Irish ecclesiastical world, which could never succeed in overcoming the basic suspicion it nurtured towards English Catholicism and in particular towards the most recent converts.

However, it is not as if the situation within the fold were any easier. Among the Catholics themselves there were plenty of causes of conflict. Many influential members of the hierarchy, despite the interest aroused by the Oxford converts, were against young Catholics frequenting the university environment. Manning himself admitted that he was "most perturbed at the thought that, being in contact with Protestant circles, even the English Catholic élite might risk becoming 'similar to the French, Catholic in name but in fact indifferent, lax and liberalised'… and he encouraged … a decision by the English bishops who, on 13 December 1864, virtually unanimously, had advised Catholic students not to attend Oxford".[61] The protests of a few who sought – in vain – for support from Newman proved to be without effect; Newman himself had been disillusioned by the Irish experience, and sought to avoid further damage, and to bring the situation to maturity in the slowest and least drastic way possible.

Relations with the Crown were also a matter of no small concern to English Catholicism. Queen Victoria and the Prince Consort found themselves, in fact, in a very special position. They were related to Catholic sovereigns and princes over half of Europe. This fact, instead of making their notions about the English Catholic movement any easier, ended up by making it more rigid, to avoid giving any concessions to those who even minimally suggested the possibility of weakening the Established Anglican Church. This conclusion is reinforced by the fact that Queen Victoria always regarded the Oxford converts with suspicion, as she condemned the acceptance of Catholicism by cultural figures, because, to her way of thinking, the Church of Rome with its "backwardness" and its prejudices was far away from the culture of the nineteenth century. (It goes without saying that this was probably one of the most troublesome problems as far as Acton was concerned). Over and beyond these considerations, Catholicism seemed to the Queen to compromise, or at least weaken, the national cause. The Crown seemed therefore to make more and more appeal to Anglican principles, and above all Queen Victoria maintained the prestige of the monarchy as a bulwark of the Protestant faith.[62] This faith, according to circles close to the Crown, had inspired the material and industrial progress of the United Kingdom, and thus drove the majority to regard the Catholicism of the "poor" Irish with a certain suspicion if not with downright hostility.

It should be added that immediately after the development of the Oxford Movement, there was an increase in apprehension and fears over the Chartist disorders. The fear of revolution was added to that of an increase in the number of "papists", seen as a real threat. Public opinion demanded a clear and unambiguous position on the political and religious level, which would preclude any possibility of compromise with the Roman Church. The standard-bearer of this position was to be Mr Gladstone himself, who would wed liberal principles to the Anglican standpoint. This could be said to be the real reason for the success which he enjoyed in around fifty years of political struggle.

It is in the same climate that another element in the Catholic renaissance in England should be viewed. In the autumn of 1850, Pius IX nominated Nicholas Wiseman as Cardinal Priest, with the title of Santa Pudenziana, and Archbishop of Westminster. But what really counted was that this act resuscitated the English hierarchy. The move provoked a fierce wave of reaction in England. In London, public demonstrations were held, and effigies of the new Cardinal were burnt in the streets. Lord John Russell, who was then Prime Minister, dealt decisively with the agitation, to prevent the opposition from exploiting it. The Duke of Norfolk supported the public agitation. Another Catholic peer protested against the Edict of the Court of Rome, and in 1851, a draft law for Ecclesiastical Titles was approved. It set a fine of £100 for any Catholic bishop who might assume the title to a territorial see.[63] Fortunately, although approved, the law was never applied and it was abolished twenty years later.

The sincere and profound repugnance of English conservative and anti-catholic circles, which had deep historical roots, after its moment of bitterest feeling, which coincided with the proclamation of papal infallibility at the First Vatican Council, waned rapidly for two concomitant reasons: on the one hand the end of the temporal power and on the other the dwindling of conversions. Both of these causes made Catholicism more acceptable to public opinion. However, the anti-Catholic prejudice, although it had grown feebler, did not manage to assuage the anti-papal sentiments which were most strongly felt in ultra-nationalist circles. Because of this, during the whole Victorian period, Catholics met with many difficulties in obtaining work, finding lodgings, and in the general matters of everyday life.

To external difficulties we must add internal ones which the reorganized English Catholic Church might never have suspected a few years earlier. One of the main difficulties was that of not only accepting but integrating into the ecclesiastical structure and other Catholic environments, all the converts who had followed Newman. Another burden of responsibility weighed on reawakening English Catholicism: that of organizing the faithful who were moving quickly into the industrial towns. The commitment of the Catholic Church literally changed its face, often giving rise even to disputes (present even today in embryo) in cities such as Liverpool, Newport, Birmingham, etc. In this latter work Wiseman, as Vicar Apostolic of the district of London, played a particularly outstanding role.[64]

If the problem of following, organizing and evangelizing the faithful in the great cities seems large, and capable of mobilizing substantial energies, that of accepting the converts was certainly no less difficult. Indeed, in many ways it was more delicate still. We can think, for instance, of the fact that when the Oxford converts approached the Catholic Church, they began to circulate in London social circles, and their focal centre ended up in the university, as indeed many of them had hoped it would. The second wave of conversions, that of the late sixties, created many problems. Catholics they were, indeed, but animated by a genuine liberal spirit, and the Oxford converts of the 1860s were characterized by a sincere repulsion from the *Syllabus Errorum*, about which it was only the charisma and humility of certain figures (notably Newman) that prevented a dramatic fracture inside the English Catholic Church.

Even though it may have been indirect, there is no denying that it can be said that Lord Acton also had his own influence on the Oxford converts. We need only mention that one of the sincerest opponents of the Syllabus among the converts was Richard Simpson, former editor of the *Rambler*, but above all unquestioned and inseparable friend and collaborator of the English historian.[65] It should be added, however, that even with the latest converts in the 1860s good sense did prevail in the end. Quite a few realised that to radicalise their position would only serve to damage the Catholic Church which, for its part, had to work hard to make itself accepted by public opinion and by a constantly suspicious political structure. Only a few took a rigid stand on their positions. The isolation of these latter, unquestionably the most radical, made it possible for English Catholicism to place quite a few of its best elements in positions which had been denied them since Stuart times. Thus more than one leading Catholic held important posts in the diplomatic corps and the judiciary. And in the colonies Catholic Governors were nominated[66] while the importance of Catholic forces within the Conservative Party began to grow. We must agree with Cardinal Manning in stressing the great strengthening of the English Catholic community.

The confidence and satisfaction of the Cardinal must have been given credibility by a sincere and devoted, at times even frenetic, participation by the grass roots of Catholicism, in a way that has rarely happened, here or elsewhere, in the contemporary period. Mathew effectively stresses that the spontaneous and free-handed generosity of the poor had been building churches and schools week by week: the churches were always built stone by stone with the small wages of the faithful, and this fact goes part of the way to explaining the intense attachment to the parish unit, which remained their spiritual centre. The old priests with their strong influence, in the fine old Irish tradition, received the reverence and affection of a people who wanted to feel themselves in the hands of strong, secure leaders.[67] The great mass of

English Catholic workers in the big industrial cities were a cause of serious reflection for many observers.

Alongside the English and Irish clergy, a fundamental role, and certainly not one to be underestimated, was played by the so-called missionary priests. Among these, a noteworthy place is accorded to Fr Aloysius Gentili and Fr Domenico Barberi. It is to the first, a member of Rosmini's Istituto della Carità, that the establishment of the Rosminian Order on English soil is credited. To the second, a Passionist father possessed of a rare spirit of mission, must go the credit for having received Newman into the Roman Catholic Church. Apart from these two, we should add the work of the Capuchins, the Friars Minor, the Jesuits and the Redemptorists as witnesses to the by no means casual renaissance of English Catholicism.

While this was going on in the cities and ports and commercial and industrial centres, there were no less interesting developments in the rural world. When we come to the mass of the upper bourgeoisie of the countryside, the absence of adequate participation in political and administrative life seems even more surprising. Their emergence to practical political liberty had been gradual since 1688; the use of that liberty had been intermittent. A few of them had risen to high ranks in the army.[68] This is quite an important consideration, if we remember that these had been the families which had maintained the Catholic faith in England from the sixteenth to the nineteenth centuries. At times they had acquired political and military titles, but more often they had been forced to sell them, and thus the Catholic renaissance led in these circles to a really much-needed sense of confidence and encouragement.

In short, English Catholicism seemed to be strengthened, and even though it was not markedly homogeneous it understood the importance of unity around its own clergy. It also possessed a profound religious sense, a notable devotion and attachment to the Sacraments to the extent that many people, beginning from this established fact, said that Catholics, with their devotion to the life of prayer, lacked even an elementary understanding of social problems. It seems that in fact the Church was led to move cautiously in this context, because once it had found its way back with full rights into the religious and civil life of England, it could certainly not appear as a destabilizing element without running the risk of compromising its undeniable successes in a very brief time. This was the reason why then as later, English Catholics always developed their parish life more fully,[69] with more and more effective forms of participation.

It is now possible to understand why English Catholicism "was wholly and in all ways consonant with the traditionalist outlook which in France had been dubbed *ultramontanism*. What we have referred to as the Irish element followed this line completely, but it was soon followed too by a number of the most conspicuous Oxford converts, such as F. W. Faber, W. G. Ward and Manning himself".[70] This position, however, as can easily be understood, was based on different reasons in England from those which prevailed on the Continent. In fact it was a bulwark, or a measure of orthodoxy in the face of Protestantism and Anglicanism. This intention was also quite well interpreted by those Oxford converts who "undertook to present Catholicism as a *respectable* religion, and the only one capable of guaranteeing the continuity of the Christian message against the irreligious spirit of modern society, characterized by the development of science and technology, and by philosophical and political thinking centred on the values of freedom and the absolute and unqualified exaltation of humankind".[71] Even though his intentions may have been different, this was one of the questions which Acton felt most strongly about. Rather than taking a defensive stand, the English historian would make every effort to demonstrate to his contemporaries that cultural achievements – whether in science or philosophy, politics, economics or social matters, could never come into conflict with Catholicism which, by its very nature, was drawn to welcoming every "discovery" which brought fuller benefits to the life of mankind, both on the spiritual and the material plains. Only within Catholicism could a theory find its full completeness and natural harmonization.

The will to defend Catholic orthodoxy in the face of Protestantism, and particularly of Anglicanism, explains the position of the English Catholic Church towards the exponents of its own liberal wing. Liberalism had in fact been espoused by the Anglican world, a union of the inheritance of the Whig tradition and a deep loyalty to the English Crown and hence to the State Church. This stance, which became that of the Liberal Party, also tended to welcome into its ranks those dissidents from the Catholic world[72] who in their turn had shown themselves to be in conflict with the Church of Rome and with the English Catholic hierarchy. Some writers have thought to include Acton among these, as his liberal stance and influence on Gladstone were well known to all. It is no mere chance that Acton was accused, together with some of his friends, of belonging to the "Catholic Left". But it is necessary to add, as we shall find again and again in this work, that despite certain moments of dissent Acton never thought of leaving the Church. He preferred instead to retreat into silence, or, to put it better, he preferred to wait – convinced as he was by his outstanding historical learning – for time to wear away certain misunderstandings and make certain statements obvious. While in his youth he had been impetuous and at times inopportune (for example in his attitude to Papal infallibility), he was gradually acquiring that serenity which in the latter years of the century would render him one of the most respected historians.

Lord Acton's stance confirms once again the state of malaise in which liberal and catholic intellectuals found themselves in the second half of the nineteenth century within the English Catholic Church. The latter, in the person of several high ecclesiastics like Newman, for instance, could understand and partly sympathize with them, but were unwilling to break up a very delicate position of balance which had cost centuries of waiting and suffering. The actual provisions of 1829, if applied according to the letter, risked compromising some of the most significant achievements. It is true that from 1829 onwards, the Catholics had the right to vote, to sit in parliament and to occupy almost any of the high offices of state. However, as a concession to anti-Roman sentiment, it was forbidden for the bishops to adopt the titles of sees already used by the prelates of the Established Church; religious services were forbidden outside the churches themselves and private homes. By another provision, restrictions were imposed on the freedom of the religious orders and on their growth.[73] Most of these provisions remained dead letters, but the Catholic hierarchy always felt their weight bearing on their activities.

5) *The return to England: reasons for isolation*

The isolation of English Catholicism was somewhat typical of British culture in general. On the historiographical plane too[74] it still had a very insular character. If we think for a moment of the vast historical learning of Lord Acton, so typically continental in character. we can understand why his difficulties over acceptance became progressively greater. It should also be added that Acton, with an enthusiasm typical of the young and of men of faith, burst into England with hope and conviction after his studies in Munich. He hoped that "the English Catholics would be able to become the leaders of world Catholicism. And he was convinced that … England was especially adapted for the role of leader of the Catholics in the political field, because its constitutional doctrine and the teaching of Burke represented the political ideas which were most congenial to Catholicism".[75] It is not hard to understand that these attitudes led to soul-searching by conservatives of all allegiances: non-Catholics in general because they rejected this re-launch of Catholicism on English soil, and the Catholics themselves because they did not want to compromise Catholic orthodoxy with liberal ideas. Both motives combined to contribute still further to the isolation of Lord Acton.

Both as a Catholic and as a Liberal, Acton enjoyed a really enviable situation. Born in Italy, for reasons of parentage, friendship and personal interest he could travel with great ease to Rome to discuss, and adopt positions in, the heated discussions of those days. Moreover his friendship with Gladstone and Lord Russell (first Foreign Minister and then Prime Minister) made it possible for him to read the private reports sent to Rome by the British government.[76] This truly privileged position also caused Acton to meet with several problems with the ecclesiastical authorities, not least because in these years he took up a strong position in favour of Rome as capital of a modern and liberal State. This standpoint should not lead us to assume that Acton wanted to see a state supremacy, or state intervention in ecclesiastical affairs (such a position was certainly in conflict with his genuine liberal spirit); on the contrary, "according to Acton the state in Italy is not such as to be able to carry on a *healthy* policy in matters ecclesiastical, for abuse of its power over the Church is to be feared".[77] It was therefore a matter of mutually counterbalancing two powers which, as long as they were in a position of equilibrium, could contribute positively to the cause of the Italian people.

There is probably a purely tactical motive in this standpoint of Acton's. To take a stand in favour of the unity of Italy, and of Rome as capital, meant showing England that Catholics were in tune with the modern needs of emerging states, alongside which the forces of liberal England were also aligned. Even his acceptance of German theology perhaps has a some reference to this idea. Acton, moreover, knew quite well that for the English spirit, clerical Italy represented the ecclesiastical organization steeped in superstition, while Germany represented the pure spirit of search for truth.[78] The idea that this viewpoint was also dictated by tactical motives finds some confirmation in the fact that despite his sympathies for the new Italian state, Acton was never enthusiastic – as we shall see later – about the national theories which he sometimes saw even as in conflict with the most elementary liberal principles.

Two further elements can be adduced in support of what has been said. In the first place: despite the fact that Acton had repeatedly criticized the hierarchy, both in Italy and in England, he never took an open and clear stand against them. On the contrary, he preferred on many occasions to give in on some of his points rather than leave the Church: one may cite, for example, the suspension of the *Home and Foreign Review*.[79] Secondly, Acton was very sensitive to the fact that English Catholicism was a minority, which to obtain credit and respect would have to commit itself to a field capable of involving the majority of public opinion.

The desire to make English Catholicism into a propelling element of British political life is to be explained by the fact that, for Acton, being a Catholic was a matter both of personal pride, and above all of a conviction that Catholicism, *because it had remained separated from, or at least counterposed to,* political power, (we may point to the difference in this respect from Anglicanism) could be a real guarantee of liberty. Because of this, in the last resort Acton always preferred submission to the Church. For one thing, Acton was a pious and practising Catholic, for whom separation from the Church would have been extremely painful, Acton also knew how to distinguish between the mortal and fallible ecclesiastical organisation, and the eternal and true Church.[80] It was thus that, as a layman, he sometimes attacked the ecclesiastical structures even though he was not so ready to accept such attacks from clerical sources. In criticizing he was above all responsible for his own soul, while clerics such as Döllinger risked corrupting the souls of others as well.[81] It should not be forgotten that perhaps specifically to avoid revealing the repressive aspect of the Church to English eyes, Acton wrote very little, with the aim of avoiding polemics.

What should have been his masterpiece, *The History of Liberty,* remains inexplicably a work which excited great expectations but was never completed and indeed scarcely even drafted. "For almost thirty years the rumour circulated that he was compiling a massive *magnum opus* on an almost universal scale; i.e. a study on the evolution of humanity, under the form of a *History of Liberty*. This work is one of the great legends of English historiography; it has been described as the most famous book never written ... On the other hand, he did not in fact follow the modern fashion of choosing a particular sector of history in order to become a specialist in it ... he gathered together at one and the same time materials on the most diverse periods, in the manner of a great scholar".[82] It would almost seem as if this great work was never completed because the author was incapable of controlling the enormous amount of material he had gathered. But in reality this is not so. Many have sought to see in this refusal the desire not to provoke ecclesiastical censure,[83] but there is probably yet another reason, more intimate, but no less important.

Acton saw, in human history, the unveiling of the spiritual and moral life of the individual. Just as Fichte saw in history the progressive development of freedom, Acton found there the slow and toilsome but nevertheless continuous growth of the ethical dimension. Since he possessed a "quite severe moral measure",[84] he was affected by a truly rare scrupulousness of judgement which led him to think much before he gave his opinion. To enter into the private context and the moral sphere of humankind was, for him, an action to be undertaken with the maximum of prudence, because it meant entering into judgement on that freedom of conscience in which no one could take up on himself the faculty of intervening. The true roots of Acton's "moral liberalism" are to be found here; we only have to remember that on the basis of these presuppositions, Acton justified his struggle against the worship of the state. For him, a liberal state only has "the task of assigning duties, and of tracing the lines between good and evil only in its own sphere".[85] Entry into the private sphere of the individual is almost unnatural, and hence inhuman.

6) The Rambler: reasons for a failure

Evidence of the motives described above can perhaps be found in the examination of the experience of Acton, together with a group of other Catholic intellectuals, in the review, the *Rambler*. This attempted project sums up much of the difficulty which Acton met with as a writer after his return to England. The *Rambler*, founded in 1848 by a number of converts who wished to approach the problems posed by modern criticism in a scientific fashion, also proved to be a review capable of capturing the attention of the educated world outside the Catholic Church.[86] The intentions were good, but the review, which fell under the influence of Richard Simpson[87] became immersed little by little in a rancorous and pointless dispute which also concerned traditional Catholic methods of teaching.

The intention of the group which produced the review, to which Acton also belonged, was to accept critical method even in religious history. The collaborators were convinced that the Church had everything to gain and nothing to lose from this new scientific method.[88] Acton had derived these ideas from his friend and teacher, Döllinger, during his stay in Germany, but this standpoint had already become almost accepted opinion in the European liberal circles and had also penetrated among those theologians "who were interested more in the life of dogma than in its metaphysic ... Catholic theologians, who were in close contact with their adversaries in the universities, rapidly understood the need to follow them on to the new ground where they were fighting the battle, so as to oppose them with their own weapons: in other words with the facts, texts and documents, and where

47

necessary revising those positions which might prove to be incompatible with the facts".[89] We should remember too that Catholic theologians not only had to reply in the debates to liberal historical criticism, but were also obliged to keep abreast of all the historical studies which their Protestant colleagues were undertaking.

However, the fears of the English hierarchy did not depend simply on the internal situation, but also on the fact that the introduction of the scientific spirit into historical studies had begun in the German universities, where Catholics, Lutherans and rationalists had sunk their common interests in subordinating their passions to scientific objectivity.[90] For the English Catholic world it was a matter of defending their orthodoxy even more firmly, as they entered once again into contact with the Anglican world, always suspicious towards Catholicism. It should be said that Acton himself complicated the relations between the review and the English Church by his attitude. By his historical studies, conducted in Germany and in contact with a master such as Döllinger, he showed a "particular kind of superiority",[91] which made the relations between the parties even more tense.

Not even a character as strong as Newman, who in 1859 tried to act as a mediator between the parties, succeeded in saving the review from crisis. Despite the fact that for several months he acted as editor of the review, he was incapable of dispelling the doubts of the English hierarchy, who could not accept the increasingly liberal outlook of the *Rambler*. Thus in 1862, after a public reproof, the review was suppressed. In the end the situation had in fact become decidedly more tense. The editors, accepting Acton's statement that he would in the future be described as "a man who had renounced everything in Catholicism which was not compatible with freedom, and everything in politics that was not compatible with the Catholic faith"[92] now openly expressed their ideas concerning the temporal power of the Pope, complicating the activities of all those churchmen who, in contrast, were striving to create an "image" of the Roman pontiff who was at the basis of the dispute between the two religious confessions. We should remember that it was in these very months that the debate began on the question of the validity of Anglican Orders, on which it became necessary for future pontiffs to take a stand.[93]

And yet it could be said that in theory the possibilities for development of the Catholic press were very different. However, good intentions were shipwrecked since as time went on, the progressive intellectuals involved in the review realized that they had been practically consigned to isolation because they were not liberal enough to satisfy the English form of liberalism, and not "completely" Catholic enough to seem safely orthodox to the Catholic hierarchy.[94] Even so, the press was an indispensable instrument, above all for converts, or for the innovating elements such as Acton; and it had to be a "special" press, which was able to handle the most distant and diverse cultural standpoints. It was in fact among these very converts that the venture of the *Rambler*, founded in 1848 by John Moore Capes, had begun.

The review obviously began life amid a number of difficulties, among which the economic problem was far from insignificant. However, it managed to take off quite quickly because of its founder's clear position. Capes had in fact been ordained as an Anglican, and after his conversion he showed ability in carrying along and winning over even the most refractory Catholic circles with his enthusiasm. Furthermore, he was able to introduce into his review that devotion towards the Church of Rome that was a reason of pride and identity for all, but especially for the old Catholics who rediscovered, in this line of thought, the *raison d'être* which had led them to stand fast during centuries of discouragement and incomprehension, and not infrequently persecution.

In its very early numbers, the review dealt with several fairly important problems which went under the name of "Social Catholicism", and which paradoxically were completely ignored in the years which we could call the years of dispute. With his moderation but also with his firmness, Capes had posed himself the delicate problem (it must be remembered that we are here in the spring of 1848!) of the relations between the poor and rich classes.[95] Convinced that this controversy risked dragging society towards revolution, Capes was of the opinion that the Church must engage itself in resolving the possible conflicts in a pacific way, but within the context of those democratic rules which were yet to be fully developed. "Capes was inclined to believe, with some regret, that democracy was inevitable, and he sought to prepare the lower classes for it by bringing to them the benefits of education and religion".[96] This also explains the great commitment of the review, and of its individual founders and collaborators, to the foundation of Catholic schools and missions among the poor.

Another element dealt with by the review from its first numbers was the interest in those teachings and those thinkers known under the name of "liberal Catholicism", which were beginning to find favour on the continent of Europe. It was to be this very attention to the new European Catholic culture that would involve personalities such as Acton in the review. But it would appear that this attention to European Catholic culture also shows up the inferiority complex of English Catholicism, which in its own country was forced to admit an absence of any genuine form of Catholic literature.[97] This explains why, despite the very limited number of copies, Capes and his collaborators made all kinds of financial sacrifices to spread a review which in the beginning had the aim, among others, of creating a space for Catholic intellectuals which they had never enjoyed before.

This question affected the most varied forms of the cultural and artistic life of the nation. To cite an example which today may seem paradoxical: the expansion of Catholicism created the need to build new churches. The "Old Catholics" preferred that they should be built in the Gothic style, because they saw in this a continuity with and conformity to the national style. The converts, on the other hand, wished for models and styles which had developed in the Catholic world in the modern era, with decorations which would inspire the most genuine forms of Catholic devotion.[98] The Gothic was seen as a mediaeval style, which for the converts should be abandoned because in the modern age, it was identified with the State Church. The new Renaissance and Baroque styles, on the other hand, were the expression of a Catholicism which had developed its own post-Tridentine Reformation.

In the spring of 1854, Capes asked Simpson to become assistant editor. The post was refused by Simpson, who, however, from that moment onwards contributed to almost every number of the review, and worked to make the publication become the organ of the Catholic Left.[99] The description is perhaps a little exaggerated, but it is true nonetheless that, with the collaboration of Simpson, the review took on a far more aggressive style, and began progressively to be viewed with suspicion by the hierarchy. It should be remembered that right from his first contribution to the *Rambler* Simpson showed that he was convinced that the Catholic Church had nothing to fear from the results of contemporary science in particular, and from culture in general.[100] This conviction was to become one of Acton's favourite themes.

Simpson's ideas, regardless of any question of their validity, were defended in a way which was irritating and often inappropriate. Soon Cardinal Wiseman was forced to name a commission of three theologians to examine Simpson's doctrine. The dispute grew gradually, thanks to a series of other articles, and from that time onwards for a few years the hierarchy, partly to avoid useless controversy in the face of British public opinion, abandoned the review to its destiny, i.e. that of becoming the organ of the liberal Catholics. It may be for this reason that the influence of Richard Simpson is much greater than his writings would seem to justify.[101] In fact he was an element of catalyst around which there gathered characters such as Thomas Weckerell, Sir Peter Le Page Renouf, and naturally Lord Acton, who sought to reconcile Catholicism with the liberalism of the nineteenth century.

When the change of direction by the *Rambler* became clear to all in the autumn of 1858, Capes resigned the editorship. It was then that the review passed into the hands of Simpson and his collaborators, and it was also then that, as the first non-convert, the youthful Acton became part of the direction; at that time he was barely 23 years old.[102] With the issue of February 1858, Simpson became the regular editor of the review, and Acton his closest collaborator.

Despite his youth, Acton made an immediate impression with his personality, to the point of acquiring a more important role than that of Simpson. The latter, a loyal and deeply committed friend, rapidly came to share the leading role with him, adapting himself to a position in the front rank, but always in the shadow of one who should normally have been his disciple. Acton was not naive, and he quickly realised that he was isolated, with Simpson and a few others, in a truly gigantic undertaking. A further negative element was added to the suspicion of the hierarchy towards the review. Acton came from a European education particularly linked with French and German Catholicism, and this placed him in a position of superiority vis-à-vis his collaborators, but one of disfavour amongst the English Catholics who wanted at the same time to safeguard tradition and orthodoxy. For Acton, on the contrary, it would be possible, in a logic of continuity, to find a sure place for liberalism within tradition. However, this undertaking would require the political education of the Catholics, and such a task of education also belonged,[103] in his opinion, to the review.

As early as the beginning of 1859, Acton published an article "Political thoughts on the Church", in which he expounded his political views. "Acton argued that the Church cannot be indifferent to politics, for its mission is to transform the lives of men as well in the public as in the private sphere".[104] The English historian was to remain constant in this idea throughout his life. For him, it was the notion of conscience itself which asserted the need for personal liberty. It followed as a logical consequence that the Church should not tolerate any government where liberty was unknown. One of Acton's greatest displeasures, in fact, was to observe that it was precisely in the countries with a Catholic tradition (Austria above all, and this explains his sympathy for Italian liberation) that freedom was attacked and suppressed.

The educational intentions of the review went far beyond political problems, but were intended to embrace the widest possible cultural range. As we have already pointed out in the case of Simpson, Acton too was convinced, for example, that the Catholic Church had more to gain than to lose from the advancement of science. But he was also convinced that apart from – and perhaps even more than – the hierarchy, the old Catholics, far too suspicious of novelty in general, would be suspicious of such a notion. The consequences of an attitude of this kind could be seen by all: "If non-Catholics had often misinterpreted science, Catholics were often ignorant of it; and this defect, more than any other, prevents Catholic writers from having any influence on the educated Protestant public".[105] Acton, like Simpson himself, found it intolerable that circles hostile to the Church should be able to reproach Catholic thinking with being antiquated, and unadapted to the times; nor was he able to accept the breach between the scientific spirit and religious conviction which was to be found in many English Catholic circles – and, as Acton himself could well testify, not only English ones.

The year 1858 was an extremely important one for the review, because it was the year in which both the Catholic hierarchy, with its fears of new ways of thought, and the liberal Catholic staff, placed their hopes – obviously with different intentions – in Newman. (We shall deal with his specific relations with Acton in the next section; here we will only explore the future Cardinal's position in relation to the problem of the Catholic press.) It is interesting to note that in this period the position of Newman with regard to Acton was conditioned by a clear intention: to give full value to the person and talents of the future historian while smoothing over some of those occasionally radical positions which could compromise his work, and force him into an isolation from which there was no escape. Newman did not succeed completely in this intention. We may remember that in 1858 Acton had begun to work in the full favour of Cardinal Wiseman, but by the summer the latter had already become highly suspicious of possible dangers and divisions which some of Acton's articles which appeared in the *Rambler* might generate among Catholics.

A proof of Newman's benign and moderate attitude towards Acton can be found in the fact that the churchman sought to give the liberal Catholics the possibility of collaborating with another magazine – *Atlantis* – (two numbers of which were published each year), founded in Dublin during the attempt to institute a Catholic University there. Acton, who at once sought to make the review into a quarterly, was favourable to the attempt because he thought it was preferable to have another new liberal Catholic organ, and one which had few links with the hierarchy. This, as can easily be imagined, must also have been the intention of Newman who, despite his moderation, had the intention of avoiding compromising the Catholic hierarchy in a dispute which could have degenerated into endless polemics, and perhaps into a sensational rupture.

Despite the efforts and attempts at mediation undertaken by various parties in 1858, it was sadly clear to everybody by the beginning of the following year that the *Rambler* had set out on a road from which there was now no turning back. The management of the review was making itself known little by little as a law unto itself in English Catholicism, thus compromising the unity of the Church. This problem caused no little anguish to Cardinal Wiseman.[106] Moreover, specifically in opposition to the principles expounded in the *Rambler*, the most conservative element in English Catholicism was "stressing" the principle of authority in the Church, and boosting the development in England of the "ultramontane" party. The latter enjoyed considerable influence in the controversies going on with the liberal Catholics, because of the prestige of its representatives. These consisted mainly of converts who had had a considerable effect on British public opinion by their gesture; it did not understand them but it did respect and esteem them. The Church looked to such people as W. G. Ward and Father Faber with growing sympathy after they obtained the support of the future Cardinal Manning and of Cardinal Wiseman himself, who found in this group backing and support for his opposition to the direction of the Review. In the immediately preceding years, the group of Simpson and Acton had progressively become the owner of the review, so that it was now very difficult, if not impossible, to reduce it to silence. The hierarchy, in the names of Cardinal Wiseman, Archbishop Errington, and Bishops Ullathorne and Grant, was more determined than ever to find a solution, though they were hoping nevertheless right to the end that it should be as painless and unsensational as possible. In these circumstances, the best person to resolve the case was held to be Newman.[107] Precisely because he enjoyed the confidence of the liberal Catholics, he was invited by Ullathorne to bring the *Rambler* back on to the path laid down by the hierarchy at pain of censure. Newman immediately informed Simpson of the hierarchy's intentions, and because of the esteem which everybody in the review accorded him, everything seemed to become easier, so much so that Simpson placed himself entirely in the hands of the future Cardinal. He offered Newman the complete ownership of the magazine, with the maximum freedom to do whatever he considered most suitable with it.

Newman experienced a moment of difficulty. Accepting the responsibility for the *Rambler* involved quite a few problems for him, not least in the relations with other Catholic publications such as *Atlantis* and the *Dublin Review,* with which he had collaborated and with which he would now be entering into competition. He also knew, though, that if he wanted to save the *Rambler* and its ideas, there was no other road available.

After a few consultations and a number of tacit responses from Cardinal Wiseman himself, he formally accepted full control of the review, with Acton, Simpson and Capes, who were, however, to remain proprietors and contributors. The solution worked well, as Newman was a full guarantee of orthodoxy both in studies and research.

But even Newman's balanced position was due to have little success. The international events of the 1860s became critical for the Church, and the problem of its temporal power kept international relations fairly tense. The review, and thus its leading exponents, were bound to take up a position on such a delicate issue. It is strange to note that in 1860 (the year when Garibaldi's Thousand went to Sicily, and the problem of Rome as capital of Italy became a crucial one), Newman's position is in fact far more radical than Acton's. The position of the future Cardinal appeared "insufficiently clear" to the ultramontanes, and thus it was accepted that Newman was more concerned with the spiritual life of the

Church than with its temporal problems. Acton seemed more moderate; for him the temporal power seemed necessary, if only to defend the independence of the Holy See, which otherwise would be at the mercy of Italian nationalism.[108] It should be stated at once that even though Acton's position on the temporal power was to undergo transformations, his suspicion towards Italian nationalism (and indeed towards nationalism in general) remained unchanged. Even though Acton had very little regard for the Papal administration, he was equally untrusting of a large part of the forces of liberalism and the Risorgimento, who seemed in his view to be too contentiously anti-clerical, and thus incapable of guaranteeing the liberty of the Catholic Church when, on some future date, Rome would become the capital of Italy.

Acton's doubts and perplexities were shared, though for different reasons, by a majority of English liberal Catholics. There was in fact need for great caution on the Roman question. Even those among the contributors to the review who because of lack of trust in Italian nationalism defended the temporal power (though with gritted teeth) were forced to tread carefully in doing so. For reasons of international policy, English public opinion and politicians were favourable to the proposal to make Rome the capital, quite aside from the religious issue. And this in fact would mean the abandonment of Rome by the French troops, and hence the modification of the hold of a rival power. Moreover, the liberal Catholics, and Acton above all, were convinced that to bring the Roman situation to a crisis would have worsened their position within the Church even further. A humiliated Pope, reduced to impotence, might have left Rome for Spain, southern Germany, or Austria, with the logical consequence of stiffening the attitude of the Church and making it even more reactionary in direct contact with firmly illiberal surroundings and situations.

But apart from political motives, the "management" of Newman also met with severe difficulties on the cultural plane. In 1859, Darwin's *Origin of Species* was published. This fact seemed to mean that "the conventional formulations and interpretations of the Christian religion were to be challenged by the new theories of natural science and biblical criticism".[109] Since the

Protestant world was taking a "certain" position (not that of the liberal Catholics) the editorship of the review thought that it was impossible to ignore such an important fact, but rather to confront it with the greatest seriousness. Newman, for his part, was close to the position already taken by Simpson and Acton. He believed that "Catholics need not fear the discoveries or the theories of science".[110] This became the conviction, and the battle cry of the *Rambler*, which demanded free discussion and a free debate on scientific questions. Catholics opposed to this possibility seemed to the contributors to the review to be ignorant of the scientific problems with which Catholicism, since time immemorial, had had little familiarity. The need was again felt for the liberal Catholic publication to assume a teaching role, in order to convince even the most stubborn that orthodoxy had nothing to fear from science, and indeed everything to gain.

It fell to Simpson to write about the work of Darwin, and given the delicacy of the question, it could be said that what he produced was a truly impartial essay. Simpson took the position that could be described as "in the Galileo tradition"; he sought to define the relations between science and faith in the clearest possible terms. The field of scientific analysis is that of phenomena; the field of faith is the world of the spirit.[111] By defining proper limits to the respective spheres, all conflict would be avoided, partly because the liberal Catholics began from the premise, typical of much Catholic philosophy, that there could be no conflict between faith and reason, above all because the latter especially was subject to constant research, and hence to constant correction. Newman's position was even clearer. The passage of time was tending to make him more moderate, or perhaps wiser, and for him it was a matter of upholding the right to free research. Only such an open position could allow Catholics to face up seriously to the scientific questions, and thus guarantee that well-informed believers would be present in such a delicate and important discussion. This was Newman's constant position, not least in his writings on the problems of a university education.

In his article on "Religion and Faith", which appeared in the *Rambler* in July 1861, Simpson maintained that without free scientific research the result would be the imposition of dogmas which, on the contrary, might receive some support from science, though clearly this could not be a confirmation, since dogma is, by nature, superior to science. The latter is concerned with facts; faith goes beyond the facts themselves. However, this distinction was not an end in itself but concerned a rather larger problem which was then taking shape, and at the end of the 1860s was to become a major element of great friction: infallibility.

In his article Simpson already gave a hint of many distinctions to be made within the problem. The infallibility of the Church is restricted to those questions which are solely religious, and to those religious questions which concern other problems. When they are not matters of faith or morals, but of political history or science, Simpson maintains that they should not be held back by the decisions of the Church.[112] Behind these considerations can be seen a much greater problem. There was in fact in prospect a whole reform of philosophical and theological studies to put the students of religious institutes and seminaries into a position where they could understand the problems of their time. Behind these ideas, which the *Rambler* made its own in 1860–61, the person of Acton can certainly be seen. Educated in the Catholic college of Oscott, he knew more than anyone else the weakness of Catholic education, and he sought in every way to remedy it. He also knew that in many institutes, a clergy poorly prepared in the problems of the modern age was generating an equally uneducated and unprepared laity, thus destined to play a secondary role in civil society.

The ideas of the review were thus the cause of a new and deep rift with the hierarchy. In 1861, even the personality of Newman had little weight in calming the disputes which had already created an irrevocable gap between liberal and ultramontane Catholics. Neither were the placatory arguments of Acton of much avail. He continued to maintain that all the conflicts between science and religion, between Church and State, between fallibility and infallibility, were due to the fact that their respective fields of competence were not being respected, and the "spheres" of God and Caesar were seeking to blur the distinction between them in order to resolve one another's problems.[113] Acton's idea remained unheeded.

The problem arose again in June 1861, when all the forces of English Catholicism found a point of agreement in the need to found an "Academy of the Catholic Religion". But this initiative proved to be an *ignis fatuus* because of the impossibility of finding unity among the English Catholics. For when Acton proposed, with regard to the regulatory principles of the new Academy, to remove it from the direct control of the hierarchy in order to guarantee it a greater freedom of action and research, a new breach was created. The outlook of Manning and Ward prevailed, and the forces of liberal Catholicism ended in disarray.

While speaking of conflicts and divisions between the two Catholic factions, a brief mention should be made of something which also helps to explain the final outcome of the dispute. The liberal Catholics were isolated and their numbers were small; this also explains the reason for their weakness. English Catholicism was all on the side of the hierarchy. The latter was so worried about the *Rambler* group because it exercised a great influence on British public opinion at a very delicate moment for the Catholic Church. The contributors to the review, knowing their own precarious situation, also made an effort which could be described as apologetic. Acton wrote an essay: "The Protestant Theory of Persecution",[114] and Simpson wrote numerous articles on the Catholic martyrs of the Elizabethan period. However, this had little effect on the restoration of unity, or indeed on eliminating conflicts.

With regard to Acton, it should be said that there was another matter which began to make his relations with the Church difficult in this period. He began, in fact, to strike up that friendship with and mutual admiration for Gladstone that was to have so much importance in the English historian's life when, isolated from almost everyone, he experienced moments of great solitude. This explains why, in fact, the disputes between the English hierarchy and the *Rambler* were more often political than philosophical or theological. It is odd but symptomatic that in the same spring of 1861, in a letter to Simpson, Acton took up again the delicate question of the relations between Church and State, saying that it had always troubled the best minds among Catholics, and that the case of Dante[115] was possibly the best example of this.

But as the example of Dante in fact demonstrated, it was difficult to draw distinctions in the matter of the boundaries between politics, religion, philosophy, theology and so on. For this reason it was unthinkable that the hierarchy should remain neutral in such a delicate situation, just as it was unthinkable (and Acton was aware of it) that Newman should put himself into conflict with his ecclesiastical superiors if the latter threatened to censure the review.[116] The future Cardinal, despite his sympathy for, and the closeness of his own ideas to, the contributors of the *Rambler*, was more deeply concerned with avoiding possible schisms than struggling to the end for the freedom of the review. Acton knew all this; he could also understand Newman's delicate situation, but he did not resign himself to the fact that the only organ of English Catholicism, which was read in the Protestant world also, should sacrifice its line or risk being suppressed.

In the summer of 1861, the relations between Newman and the management of the review (especially with Acton and Simpson) were passing through a very delicate stage. The churchman, even though he believed that historical development would make things clear and demonstrate the truth, held that it was always right to defer to the authority of the Church which, in his opinion, was a guarantee of legitimacy.[117] It was likely that the *Rambler* would remain even more isolated if it did not adapt itself to Newman's advice.

In the autumn of the same year, it seemed to everyone that the fate of the review was sealed. Even the publisher, James Burns, who incidentally had close ties with the hierarchy because of other matters, showed very great hostility, and after a stay in Rome this turned into a refusal to proceed with the printing of some numbers. There were few other occasions in their lives when Acton and his friends experienced such a sense of their solitude. It may seem paradoxical, but it was in fact Acton who, in this intricate and difficult situation, succeeded in avoiding the loss of a sense of reality. The closing of ranks by the hierarchy was seen, after the first moment, as a positive factor. On the one hand the Church finally felt that it had been freed of a difficulty which had created more than a few internal problems; on the other hand the liberal Catholics could seek another, independent, publisher and carry on their activities calmly and perhaps also more profitably. A double hope thus inspired the editorial group of the *Rambler* to make a new start with their venture. But as soon became apparent, new misunderstandings were about to arise, and made the situation even more irremediable.

The venture of the *Rambler* came to its close half way through 1862. There were too many elements of friction. For a variety of reasons, the liberal Catholics wanted to transform the review into a Quarterly, but this turned out to be in competition with the *Dublin Review*, a publication directly controlled by Cardinal Wiseman, who certainly did not intend to put himself on the same plane as Simpson and his friends. Even less did the Cardinal want to put himself on that same plane by allowing a review controlled by the hierarchy to circulate in the same period in competition with one which was completely independent of it, and on frequent occasions, in conflict with it.

Competition between the two reviews, however, was not pleasing to the *Rambler* group either. For their part they recognized that they could not push the situation beyond a certain limit. Moreover, someone like Acton "did not wish the Liberal Catholics to assume the responsibility for perpetuating Catholic factionalism".[118] Acton was, above all, convinced that this spirit of faction would damage English Catholicism, and thus he ended up by taking a conciliatory line, or at least one which avoided as far as possible damaging the image of revived British Catholicism. It was probably for this very reason that the liberal Catholics decided to transform the *Rambler* into the *Home and Foreign Review*, specifically to give themselves greater freedom and not to employ the name of a review which for years had been tied to the happenings and wishes of the ecclesiastical hierarchy, and was still greatly associated with the latter.

Before going on to examine what happened to the new publication, we may pause for a moment to examine a letter from Acton published in the final number of the *Rambler*, and directed to someone who supported a view then frequently heard: that the physical sciences are the great enemy of religion. "Acton asserted that a conflict between the facts of physical science and the dogmas of the Church was impossible, for the facts alone could not contradict religion. The danger came from the moral sciences; the solution was to confine each science to its own sphere, operating according to its own principles".[119] This conviction was from now on to become a rallying cry for Acton, convinced as he was that this limitation of the respective fields of enquiry would above all have facilitated theology, freeing it from all those "obsolete opinions" which, with their presumed scientific character, had more than once caused it to lapse into contradiction. It seemed almost – though the English historian never admitted this explicitly – that the Church must free itself from the Galileo complex which still made it fearful of taking up a position in scientific disputes which it often merely condemned as damaging and dangerous. For Acton, on the other hand, the truth (of which the Church makes itself the interpreter), if it is genuinely such, need never fear arguments and disputes. These, when they occur, serve only to illuminate the truth more clearly. Study, in any field or discipline, if conducted with honesty and rigour, is always a source of light.

The new review, despite the fact that it had a new title and a new format, did not manage to escape from the control and criticisms of the hierarchy. The latter, even though it did not feel any longer that it had any direct involvement, could nevertheless not accept that Catholic intellectuals should act, at such a delicate moment (the Roman question was becoming more and more complex as the 1860s wore on), with different intentions from its own. In this very period Wiseman had caused the English Catholic Church to adopt a more and more ultramontane position.

On his journey to Rome in 1862 for the canonization of the Japanese martyrs, he had assured the Pope of the full backing of English Catholics on the question of the temporal power.

The new publication also sought to present articles which only indirectly dealt with religious questions, in order to render the situation less troubling. But the attempt was doomed to disaster. As well as Cardinal Wiseman's judgement, that of Bishop Ullathorne was particularly severe.[120] At this juncture everything seemed to become more difficult. Ullathorne was Newman's direct superior in the hierarchy, and this meant that the *Home and Foreign Review* lost its most illustrious supporter within the ecclesiastical world. Newman in fact acknowledged his complete submission to his Bishop, and through him to the Catholic Church. The fact was described by Acton as "simply absurd",[121] but it should be remembered that later on, the English historian himself was to end up by taking a similar approach.

Bishop Ullathorne's rebuke brought about one of the most critical moments of English liberal Catholicism. Newman, Simpson and Acton, though for very different reasons, all felt great bitterness, which caused them moments of great isolation. The position of the future Cardinal was perhaps the most delicate. Faithful to the Church and to his superiors, he had nevertheless original – and orthodox – ideas which the future would reveal to be fully justified. But, moderate by nature, he opted for the way of patience, and of waiting; he trusted to his writings and his prestige to lead the English and eventually the Universal Church to overcome that unjustified suspicion towards some of the disciplines and principles of liberalism.

The position of the two laymen was different. Simpson, for his part, knew all too well that a whole series of suspicions were attached to him thanks to certain articles published in the *Rambler* – suspicions that the new review had not succeeded in dispelling. For this reason he decided to write a book.[122] He wished to assume his own personal responsibility for what he had written in the past, with the aim of exonerating the other contributors – but at the same time he wanted to reply to certain criticisms by Bishop Ullathorne. Simpson's attempt was noble, in its intention of eliminating any possible suspicions about some of his friends. He did everything possible, in fact, to show that no one else had had a hand in his writings.

The pamphlet was a great success. Newman was very pleased with it, thinking that it might well heal a situation which had by now become untenable. But his hopes were disappointed. Bishop Ullathorne was not at all satisfied with Simpson's essay. It appeared to him confused and to some extent contradictory. Religious, Hegelian, scientific and pantheistic notions were interwoven in it, making the content unintelligible, according to the Bishop. In fact, however, Ullathorne had probably understood Simpson's ideas quite well, and knew that above all else the essay was a response to his criticisms of the review, put forward some time earlier. The fact is that the essay of Simpson did not obtain the hoped-for effect, and in fact complicated the situation even more.

Apart from Newman and Simpson, the only one who remained of the most conspicuous group was Acton. He was completely aware of having taken the path of isolation. The two–year period 1861–62 perhaps constituted the greatest crisis in his life.[123] The lack of power of a person as worthy of respect and balanced as Newman within the hierarchy was a *coup de grâce* for him. Even so, in this profound desolation, Acton matured further. He explored new depths in his ethical studies, aware that the witness to certain principles, when it is purified of personal interests, always achieves its end. He continued to contribute to the review, though he was convinced, like all the rest, that the life of this new journal too was doomed. Despite this conviction and this interior solitude, it should not be thought that to continue to contribute meant for Acton doing so in a superficial way. In fact he made sure of a number of contributions from the continent, and gave his backing to that admiration, showed by all contributors, for contemporary culture which made the *Home and Foreign Review* one of the most admired journals of its day.

The review showed a special interest in overseas politics and took up specific positions towards them.[124] Acton himself dealt with burning questions. His attitude to the American Civil War is the most questionable of these. He clearly supported the Confederation, and never took up a position against slavery. But it is in European politics that Acton's position are most clearly revealed, and most consistent with his thinking. He rejected the nationalism of Prussia and made it clearly understood that the German question would have a logical and positive outcome only in federalism. Although he pointed out some defects in the Austrian system, he nevertheless remained impressed that several nations, even in the absence of liberty and constitutional guarantees, could succeed in living together (as we shall see, nationalism was never admired by Acton, who in fact criticized it sharply). With regard to France, and the French Emperor Napoleon III, his judgement was always harsh. The French Emperor had put an illiberal and even reactionary stamp on history . Even more complex are his judgements on the Italian situation. Acton was no admirer of the temporal power, but he did not, either, have any sympathy for Italian nationalism, especially if it were to be guided by the Savoy monarchy which was inspired by Cavour's anti-Church policies. To follow in this direction, in Acton's view, would not lead to a free Church in a free State, but to the predominance of the latter over the former, and would give rise to a conflict without any predictable end.

It was on this very question that the *Dublin Review* also entered the fray. The latter review was directly controlled by the hierarchy, and evidently there was a polemical relationship between the two.[125] Very often the *Dublin Review* was a kind of critical manifesto against the *Home and Foreign Review* – so much so that the latter, with its perplexities over the Roman question and with its ambiguities (we should remember that Acton actually proposed the transfer of the Papacy to England or to Ireland!) lent itself easily to the sarcasms and criticisms of the ultramontanes.

The two-year period 1862 to 1864 saw the fate of the liberal Catholics deteriorate irremediably, with the issue of the *Syllabus of Errors*; they ended up reduced to silence. In 1863 Acton had also committed the "error" of praising the "new era of theology" during a congress of scholars held at Munich. Summarizing the introductory address of Döllinger, Acton praised Germany as the ideal home of the new theology, and showed his conviction that "German scholarship was destined to revitalize Catholic thought and prepare the way for the reunion of the churches. German theology, employing the weapons of modern science, does not shrink from the results of scholarship, and is unafraid of error".[126] This very clear taking up of a position in support of Döllinger made the review's position even more precarious and also threatened Acton personally. The German theologian, not greatly admired in Roman circles, was seen as suspect by the ultramontanes, who even expressed doubts about his orthodoxy. The position of the ultramontanes was strengthened and supported after a papal letter was sent to the Archbishop of Munich. This letter implicitly condemned the independent position of Döllinger, as it encouraged Catholic scholars to take an attitude of greater deference to the ecclesiastical authorities.[127]

A short time before the publication of the Papal Letter of March 1864, Acton, writing to Simpson, had said that he was disposed to submit himself to the authority of the Church where it was infallible, but had also stated that he considered himself free in those fields where infallibility made no sense.[128] This conviction, in the light of the position the Holy See had taken up, proved to be very hard to defend. It seemed clear, in fact, that the implicit condemnation of Döllinger's theses also applied to the review which had praised and welcomed similar notions. Acton made no secret to anyone of the fact that after the publication of the papal letter, it would be very difficult indeed for a good Catholic to go on writing for the *Home and Foreign Review* without having serious problems of conscience.[129] It was clear that Acton felt that he had been wounded to the depths of his soul, and he considered the idea of isolating himself still further, perhaps specifically in these circumstances.

The review ceased publication with the following number, in which an article entitled "Conflicts with Rome" appeared, signed by Acton but almost certainly edited by Simpson. The English liberal Catholics were flying the white flag. The basic motives for this were those which Acton held dear: in the first case, of distinguishing the infallible truths of religion from those sectors in which infallibility had little to say. He also insisted on the need for rigorous research in the field of science as in the field of history, philosophy and politics, since genuine Catholicism had nothing to fear from the progress of studies. If the Papal Letter suggested that it had only implicitly referred to certain controversies, Acton's article, on the other hand, made it clear, quite explicitly, that the liberal Catholics felt themselves wounded by the present concerns of the Roman Curia. However, Acton did not go beyond this. He did not want to fall into the error of bringing English liberal Catholicism to be explicitly rejected. He preferred to stand aside, trusting to the path of ideas and at the same time, becoming obedient. To dig his heels in and seek to continue to write articles would have led to an incurable breach with Rome which, remembering their own past, the English Catholics rejected as the worse evil,[130] convinced as they were that better times would, sooner or later, arrive.

The trials of English liberalism provided an example for all liberal Catholic movements throughout the rest of Europe. Their defeat was final, and without appeal, in the 1860s. Certainly the political events in the Papal States made no small contribution to this result, in the sense that after the taking of Rome, the Pope would feel himself constrained to take even more clear-cut and drastic positions. But the fact remains in any case that the rather feeble efforts of the liberal Catholics were abandoned; they were left to their own resources, and did not even have the strength to organize themselves in parties or movements capable of going beyond these moments of crisis. 4 December 1864 was the date of the end of their dreams. On that day, along with the publication of the Encyclical Letter *Quanta cura*, the *Syllabus of Errors* was also published. These papal documents, clearly in line with the Papal Letter addressed to the Archbishop of Munich and published on 5 March, took away all support even from the most willing to co-operate, and advised them to resign themselves.

Oddly enough, when the *Syllabus of Errors* appeared, Acton was in Rome. He decided not to say or write anything, but chose the path of silence, which immediately cost him some displeasure. The English Catholics resident in Rome prepared a document of congratulation to the Pope, and asked Acton to sign it.[131] Acton refused. He did not wish to write anything against the Pope, but nor would he write anything to support him. This gesture of his isolated him even from his own Catholic compatriots who resided in Rome. For him it was another moment of great unhappiness, in which he decided to concentrate his efforts in other directions: those of study and education.

67

7) *Relations between Newman and Acton: the Catholic press*

Even though after the failure and closure of the *Home and Foreign Review*, the relations between Newman and Acton went through a difficult period (for reasons which we shall deal with below), it is nevertheless the case that in the middle of the nineteenth century there was between these two men one of the most fruitful collaborations that the Catholic Church had known in this whole period. The differences in character, tradition and culture between them were notable, but "they were agreed that only in a religious culture could freedom flourish".[132] While this was their common conviction, their ways of going about realizing it and presenting it to public opinion were very different. Newman was more cautious; he succeeded, as Acton did not, in winning esteem, a ready audience and even an authoritative weight in distant circles, more often than not in those hostile to the Roman Church. Often, in the moments of deepest crisis or confusion, everyone awaited the judgement of the future Cardinal who, with the careful weighing up of someone who was not seeking his own interests first and foremost, strove solely to serve the truth, to reconcile disputes and to heal the fractures which had caused all kinds of misunderstandings.

The two had already found a fixed point in their friendship at the beginning of the 1850s, when they met at Oscott College. For both, the immediate future of English Catholicism would be decided on the cultural level, and they were also both agreed that it was necessary to take up the challenge which was facing the church from various sciences and various sectors. In their view the Church had nothing to fear from such a challenge, because the Truth, simply because it was the truth, would always end by triumphing. This is the reason why in the fifties, the young Acton was literally fascinated by Newman's idea of creating a Catholic University because after a long period of isolation, English Catholics needed to be educated in the major problems of religion, politics and culture of the nineteenth century.

The co-operation between the two for a number of years in the press and in the diffusion of Catholic reviews is to be seen in the light of this intention. In the 1850s Newman particularly admired Acton's talent and educational background. He was the only one to understand the importance that the youthful scholar could acquire at the educational level in England. Acton's mental outlook and his cultural education were European, in the full sense of the term, and the young man could bring to England that fresh breeze of novelty which would be of value to English Catholicism, not only to revitalize it but also to provide comparison with other experiences of faith. Above all, relations with Germany interested Newman in that period, and Acton, with his friendship, would be able to ensure and explain these relations, given his perfect knowledge of German.[133]

The wide cultural horizons possessed by Acton were probably also useful for another purpose: that of waking up a hierarchy in which Cardinal Wiseman was a leader of admittedly saintly character, but of quite restricted cultural outlook. It may only be a supposition, but it is worth noting that Newman, for more than twenty years, was vigorously active in the role of intermediary between the hierarchy and the liberal Catholics. And no one can deny that he showed a sincere sympathy towards the latter, which often led him to encourage their undertakings and their dreams, even while correcting their "absurdities".

It should be remembered that if Newman and his most intimate collaborators had not felt a certain sympathy and esteem for Acton and his ideas, the young scholar not only would not have been able to begin his collaboration with the *Rambler*, but would not even have been able to bring about that transformation in the review which took place on his arrival.[134] The review, in fact, when Acton arrived, was in the hands of a group of converts. They were certainly able, and desperately anxious to show their orthodoxy, but hardly open to those novelties typical of German theology, which Acton was presenting. He certainly exercised a great fascination (demonstrated by the fact that such an authoritative figure as Simpson, fourteen years older than his future friend, should have voluntarily "submitted" himself to him). But his success, even in the context of English Catholic publications, cannot be explained without assuming that Newman took on the task of convincing the converts. The latter, too, needed to be educated by Acton – perhaps not on the level of their orthodoxy, but on the political plane, and with his ties with the Continent, he could meet their demands. Furthermore, in the early days of Acton's contributions to the *Rambler*, it was thought that the young contributor was capable of demonstrating that the Catholics were an element of stability in the English political system, for it was Acton's firm conviction that Catholicism was, by nature, favourable to the parliamentary system, and to moderate forms of monarchy.

It has been mentioned that Acton's German friendships were a notable gain for the review, but also a notable source of anxiety for the hierarchy. In connection with this, an episode at the end of 1858 can be taken as symbolic. In the December number of the *Rambler* there appeared a letter from Döllinger, translated by Acton, entitled "The Paternity of Jansenism". The letter certainly shocked Cardinal Wiseman, who made it clear to someone that he was worried that it could give rise to scandal of some sort.[135] Newman was informed of the matter, and he then passed on the fact to Acton. It is important that immediately, from then onwards, the two were agreed that it was necessary to modify the exclusively theological character that the review had had up to then. This intention seemed to both of them sufficient to ensure greater freedom to the publication in dealing with historical and political subjects, and to give it greater freedom in research. If theological subjects were to be abandoned in this way, the hierarchy would also feel more at ease.

Unfortunately Acton's youthful enthusiasm invalidated this intention. In the February number of the *Rambler*, (this was in 1859), an article appeared with the title "The Catholic Press", in which there was an untrammelled outburst about the situation of the Catholic intellectuals. The tone was certainly hostile, and this fact, after the translation of the famous letter on Jansenism, rendered Acton's situation in the eyes of the hierarchy even more difficult. They actually sent an ultimatum to Simpson (at that time managing editor of the review) and asked Newman to elucidate this incident which might degenerate dangerously. If the *Rambler* was saved, it was once again due to the moderation, good sense and charisma of the future Cardinal, who had, however, to take on the responsibility and the burden of the review. A few days after the dispute, Newman could write to the English hierarchy, in the name of his superior, Bishop Ullathorne: "Mr Simpson most frankly put the whole question of the *Rambler* in my hands, and expressed his wish to abide by my decision".[136] This was probably one of the most delicate moments in the life of Newman, constrained as he was to act as intermediary between two worlds which were far apart and yet both believers in the same Catholic church and in tradition.

In May the first number under Newman's "management" came out. It had been prepared with great care, because the intention of its new director was that of not giving readers the idea that it had broken with the past, but was actually moving on quietly in continuity. But it was also necessary to reassure the hierarchy, because a Catholic review in open conflict with its own ecclesiastical authorities could not have had the circulation and the hearing which all its contributors wished it to have. It was in fact Newman's presence, and even the guarantee that he offered, that allowed Acton and Simpson to continue to write for the *Rambler.* Cardinal Wiseman did not trust them, and he even demanded their exclusion. In order to resolve the issue, the first article by Newman in the review for which he had become responsible was entirely aimed at softening the position of the hierarchy, and correcting some of the more extreme among his collaborators. His intention was, in short, to proceed step by step, seeking to be effective without provoking irrevocable breaches.

The *Rambler* went through a real transformation: it changed format, became a bi-monthly instead of a monthly, changed its direction, and so on. This renewal can be explained by Newman's desire to give new vigour to the magazine but above all by the plan to make the "new series" appear as a bridge which could connect the liberal Catholics and the Ultramontanes, and at the same time reconcile freedom of research with faith and respect for institutions.

A genuine spirit of liberality characterized Newman's direction. Even though he felt a certain sympathy towards the France of Napoleon III, he accepted articles which criticized the policy of the French Emperor. Although the name of Döllinger had created so many problems, he invited him to clarify the famous question about Jansenism.[137] This liberality was regarded with a certain suspicion by the English hierarchy, which although it had been initially pleased by the successes met with by Newman in bringing the former editors to heel, were now deeply embarrassed, precisely because of the prestige enjoyed by the future Cardinal, by the fact that it might now prove necessary to bring him into line with the English bishops. Among other things, Newman was a convert, and as such had a great following among the intellectuals who had been converted in such a sensational way a few years earlier.[138] This further complicated the issue for his ecclesiastical superiors, who – if they had brought down Newman, apart from the negative repercussions of the act in itself, would have only two other possible solutions: either to suppress the review or to leave it to its former directors, among whom Acton was now emerging as the leader. These two alternatives demanded patience and delay.

Newman himself may have taken advantage of his own public persona. Probably convinced of the fact that the *Rambler* would either come out under his direction or not come out at all, he published an article in the July number entitled "On consulting the Faithful in the matter of doctrine" (an article which was not included by the author later in his collected works). The content of this essay, quite a delicate matter in those years, provoked new and even more bitter dissensions. Bishop Brown of Newport actually troubled the Prefect of the Propaganda Fide Committee because he held that Newman's writing was tainted with the danger of heresy. Cardinal Wiseman was upset by the event, and promised the Roman authorities that he would try and shed light on the whole episode.[139] The head of the English Catholic Church reserved the case for his own authority.

There was a search for the least painful method of getting Newman out of his awkward position. The role that he had sought to fulfil as an intermediary between the ultramontanes and the liberal Catholics could no longer be played, even though it was now impossible to find any substitute capable of understanding the viewpoints of both parties. Newman was irreplaceable in this matter, because throughout his life as a convert he could not be categorized either as a liberal Catholic or as an ultramontane. At this point, however, one thing was certain: once Newman's withdrawal from the review had been obtained, no one else could exercise any substantial influence on the liberal Catholics, and no one else could bring them into dialogue with the ultramontanes. The latter could certainly claim victory, while the former headed towards their inevitable decline.

It is difficult for anyone not familiar with the salient moments of Newman's conversion to understand his ready abdication in the face of the hierarchy. The future Cardinal had submitted to the Roman Church after a long period of meditation, study and solitude. He knew perfectly well that one of the fundamental precepts of Catholicism was obedience, and his stay in Rome had strengthened this conviction. Like many great souls, he had decided to "submit his intentions to the authority of Peter". When he returned from Rome to "his beloved England, he brought with him a papal brief from Pius IX which authorized him to open the Oratory in his native land, and to be its head".[140] The pontifical document was issued at the very moment when the Catholic hierarchy was being revived in Britain. Newman sought always to be subject to this hierarchy, even when he did not agree with their decisions, because in the hierarchy he was to find a sure refuge against those who lost no opportunity to circulate calumnies against him which threw doubt on the sincerity of his conversion. It was perhaps to reply to these unfounded suspicions that he felt the need to write his *Apologia pro Vita Sua*.

Thus it may be easier to understand why, although he had always appreciated certain characteristics of liberalism, these were never allowed by Newman to become a source of controversy with the English Catholic hierarchy and with Rome. When Newman received the news that he was to become a Cardinal, at the beginning of 1879, with the polemics by now a distant memory, he still did not miss the opportunity to stress: All the gossip that has circulated for so long about my being only a half-Catholic, or a scarcely disguised liberal Catholic, so as not to be trusted, are now ended. And it is in fact with that in mind that I did not dare refuse the offer. I have always sought to place my cause in the hands of God and to be patient: and He has not forgotten me.[141] His patience had been demonstrated most of all in the esteem of his superiors towards whom, even when their ideas differed, he had always shown the maximum respect. And it is in this that we see the real difference between Newman and the contributors to the *Rambler*.

In order to understand why relations gradually became cooler between Newman and Acton it is always necessary to remember that the former occupied a clerical position, while the latter was a layman. Among other things, according to the future Cardinal, to conduct liberalism out of its political context and inject it into a religious one could prove extremely dangerous. Newman was basically loyal to this conviction, which he showed unambiguously on the occasion of his first address as a Cardinal. His words are very clear on this point, and show above all a theological concern: Liberalism in religion is a doctrine which teaches that there are no positive truths, that one creed is as good as another: this is a teaching which is gaining ground day by day. All this is in contrast with the recognition of any religion as true, since it proclaims that all are to be tolerated, because all are matters of opinion.[142] Such a position, for a man who had sacrificed his life for what he perceived as *the* truth, was absolutely unacceptable.

It should be noted that Newman, in this address, also showed up the dangers of radical liberalism – the kind which, with its anti-clerical spirit, entered into areas and disciplines which were not its own. But he did not mean, even so, to underestimate the positive aspects, and the historical significance, of liberalism. In fact he stated quite clearly, still on the same occasion, that it is necessary moreover to consider that liberal theories do not lack their elements of goodness and truth, when they proclaim the precept of justice, that of internal truth, of sobriety, of the well-being of the individual, of benevolence, which all form part of its well-known principles, and also of the natural laws of society.[143] The trouble with these good principles, in his view, lay in the fact that they sought to erect themselves into an ultimate criterion of truth, presenting themselves as the final and all-embracing solution for humanity.

In this address (which includes some discussion of political issues), Newman showed quite clearly the need for acknowledging the superiority of religious problems over others, because only the reasons of faith could give a reply to the ultimate expectations of humanity. Newman feared that religion could become an intellectual luxury, or a mere manifestation – however glorious – of human history. His thoughts on liberalism lead us to the conclusion that for him, it should be an element viewed in positive terms, but definitely circumscribed,[144] and this was quite different from the view of Acton who saw it, in contrast, as a product of Christianity.

It has been said that for Newman liberalism, like any other political theory, was incapable of giving a final response to human existence. This consideration deserves a moment of attention, because it helps to understand another difference between Newman and the opinion current among the majority of liberal Catholics. For the convert, the ultimate response comes only from God Himself, because the value and the very essence of life is wrapped in an aura of mystery, and not even theology (useful though it is) can give full and exhaustive answers. We must have a profound respect in the face of God, and His mystery, which is our mystery also. And it could not be otherwise, given that for Newman, theology itself could only investigate the subject of its study with instruments that were almost always inappropriate and incapable of "solving" the mystery itself.[145] This conviction of Newman's might of course seem simplistic, but to appreciate it fully one must remember that in the wake of Acton those rationalistic theological claims of which Döllinger was a leading exponent had entered England, and their result was (in Newman's view) to minimize the sense of the transcendent and of the mystery which for a neophyte and a convert must have been of the utmost importance. For Newman, theology must be an aid, a stimulus and a justification for the spiritual life; it should serve to regenerate spirits, to strengthen them towards the goals of sanctity, the ultimate visions and goals of the human soul directed towards God and living in His Church.

8) Relations between Newman and Acton: the temporal power

In the 1860s another issue brought together, but also divided, the liberal Catholics: the temporal power of the Pope, from which the problem of Infallibility was later to develop. In order to understand the positions of the English protagonists of the age, at times somewhat obscure, and at other times apparently straightforward, we have to remember the background against which this problem unfolded. We have to understand, in other words, what the Papacy meant to English public opinion, because many of the positions taken up by the *Rambler* group were dictated less by theological or dogmatic principles than by the anxiety to avoid any further breach with a public opinion which for some years now had been entertaining a renewed interest in Catholicism. It seems clear therefore that for liberal Catholics, rather than insisting on principles which were basically accepted, it was a matter of not abandoning the dialogue by adopting intransigent positions.

Before talking about Papal infallibility, it was necessary to ask how the English viewed the figure of the Pope himself. An important magazine, the *Saturday Review*, in April 1858 summed up the opinion of the English about the Pope in this way: "The Pope is, to one considerable class of Englishmen, a sort of incarnation of all evil. To another he is the head of a body which fascinates the imagination. But to the great mass of the people, he is an obscure and mythical personage, invested with obsolete spiritual pretensions, and the temporal head of what is generally supposed to be a very ill-governed Italian principality".[146] As can be seen, the English had a by no means edifying image of the Papacy. Above all, the group of converts, who until a few years earlier had shared the same opinions, were concerned that the Roman question could divide souls still further rather than drawing them together. This also explains why, on the problem of infallibility, the neophytes, although they had no doubts in principle on the matter, hoped that the subject could be shelved until a more propitious moment.

The ultramontanes took up a diametrically opposed position. Manning, since the opening lines of one of his essays, had insisted that the temporal power was willed by God; that it had meant the Christianization of Europe, and that its end would signify the decline of European Christianity.[147] It followed that to oppose the temporal power of the Papacy was to oppose God Himself. The Roman question, which began to appear critical after the Franco-Piedmontese war against Austria, thus became another element of friction, apart from the social, political and cultural ones, between ultramontanes on the one side and liberal Catholics on the other. It should also be remembered that the difficult task of mediation by Newman between the hierarchy and the review actually began in this difficult international context, with the outbreak of war. It was extremely difficult, in these circumstances, to take up a position without offending someone. At that moment, everyone in the *Rambler* group had his own highly personal and original ideas. For instance, Acton was torn between the need to change the political situation in the Italian peninsula and his suspicion towards Italian liberalism, which he judged to be too anti-clerical, and thus incapable of respecting the just freedom of the Church. Apart from this, the antipathy felt by Acton towards Napoleon III (we could really speak of hatred), and his undeniable attachment to Austria, contributed to making his position even more uncertain.

Newman's position in these disputes was certainly the most diplomatic of all. When he wrote or spoke about the war in Italy, he was clearly in favour of unity and national liberation, but when he had to take a position on the Papacy he ended up by surrounding himself with an embarrassing silence. However, basically, and in contrast to Acton's obviously more conservative position, Newman suggested for Rome the idea of a neutral city, capable of guaranteeing a minimum of independence for the Church.[148]

Newman could take up a more "free" position than Acton because, in contrast to the latter, he was above the struggling parties, and he had neither special reasons for rancour against Napoleon III (the greatest anti-liberal, as far as Acton was concerned) nor special preferences for Austria and the culture expressed in the German language. Acton, on the other hand, took up a clear position in the *Rambler*, in an article entitled "The Roman Question". This essay can be seen as a sort of apologia in favour of the temporal power. In order fully to understand the apparently eccentric position of Acton, account must be taken of the fact that in the Italian crisis, there were many different motives at play. Among these, the one which seemed most clear to the young Acton was the firm determination of the revolutionary and anti-clerical forces to eliminate the Church. Austria, having proved that it was the only power capable of resisting revolution, had once again confirmed its Catholic tradition and its fidelity to the Holy See. Acton admitted with great clarity even the notable defects of the Papal State, but he showed equally clearly that the revolutionary forces had no intention of correcting the contradictions and political and administrative backwardnesses of the Church, but merely the aim of suppressing the Church as such.[149]

Acton's conviction was based on the fact that the way the two contesting sides saw liberty was in fact entirely different: "the Catholic notion, defining liberty not as the power of doing what we like, but the right of being able to do what we want".[150] From this it emerged that the anti-Catholic vision of the State would end up by imposing a demagogical spirit, from which would come the tyranny of the majority: for Acton as for De Tocqueville, this was the first danger to be avoided. Just because of this principle, it was necessary to uphold the temporal power of the Church. It had arisen from conditions of greater danger and confusion. But, it would be rendered useless, in a changed international condition, if respect for the religious beliefs and for their basic assumptions had so impregnated the conscience of the people so as to make any political safeguard pointless. The temporal power, in short, remained for Acton a necessity that was linked to historical contingency.

Towards the end of 1860, Acton went on a journey to Munich. It was a somewhat delicate moment. Newman was troubled by the position taken by some of the contributors to the *Rambler* (he had not been pleased with the "Roman Question" article). Public opinion was holding its breath, for opposite reasons, over the outcome of the political crisis in Italy. In Germany, even an avant-garde mind like Döllinger's was troubled by the situation. The Pope, in his opinion, should prepare to leave Rome for Spain or Germany. The end of the Papal State appeared imminent. And yet, at this very difficult moment Acton's position on the temporal power was changing. At the beginning of the following year, in the full flood of debate on the Italian situation, he preferred not to utter a word.[151] He felt tormented: his anti-French and anti-revolutionary ideas were not sufficient to stamp out his rightful inclination towards a radical political change in Italy, demanded from many sides.

Acton's position and Newman's were slowly drawing closer again.[152] Although he was still opposed to certain theoretical notions of the revolutionary ideas, Acton, showing a solid political realism, recognized the impossibility of maintaining the Papal power. But just because the position had become critical, Acton seemed to acquire circumspection and prudence, possibly suggested by Newman's own attitudes. For various reasons the latter preferred to remain silent in these disputes. The two chief exponents of English Catholicism, however, spoke of the Roman question in their letters, and it is symbolic that in one of these,[153] Acton shows his overwhelming change by actually criticizing Döllinger on the necessity of guaranteeing the temporal power of the Pope. By doing this, Acton argued, the German theologian was making himself the defender of the Restoration, like the most reactionary exponents of the *Curia Romana*. It was in fact in this period that the English hierarchy showed clear signs of notable intolerance towards the liberal Catholics and their "controversial" review.

A moment of exhaustion, after the Italian crisis of 1860–61, seemed to have taken hold of English liberal Catholicism; possibly (though the conclusion may seem paradoxical) it may have had no other expectation than that the hierarchy's decision should become operative. Moreover, the contributors to the *Rambler*, having failed to make any impression on the ultramontanes, gave up their aim and decided that it would be better to devote themselves to a clearer and indeed more systematic exposition of their own ideas. It is certainly no accident that it was just in this period that Newman was completing the draft of his famous *Apologia*. Nor was it a coincidence that at this same period Acton began thinking seriously of his great historical work, which he was never to bring to a conclusion. Both projects required moments of reflection and a meditative spirit which for too many years had been set aside by the polemical tones and suspicions animating revived Catholicism in England. The intervention of the hierarchy thus ended up by being seen as a logical approach for exhausted and disillusioned adversaries who, nevertheless, were anxious not to give up the chance of launching their message, even though by other means.

Even in such a delicate moment of reflection and study, Newman and Acton had a guiding influence which led them, even though indirectly, to collaborate with each other's works. While Newman was composing the *Apologia*, Acton wrote to him: "Take the opportunity of speaking not only *pro domo*, but *pro ecclesia*".[154] Such an encouragement proves that, even though one may not be able to define the exact way, the influence of Acton on the *Apologia* was considerable, and possibly even determining. When Newman, in the last chapter, abandoned the personal note and passed to a general defence of Catholicism, he surely had in mind the advice of his young friend.[155]

However, all this should not lead us to the mistaken conclusion that there was complete comprehension between Newman and Acton. There were certain elements of divergence between them which would lead them, later on, to a cooling of their friendship. Apart from a difference of temperament, there was a difference of background between them. In a famous letter from Acton to Simpson, this difference emerges with great clarity. "Now Newman has great sympathy with our cause, inasmuch as he is enlightened and liberal and highly cultivated; but I do not believe he really understands our theory, and certainly would not admit it".[156] What did Acton mean by this letter? He was probably referring to the problem which was troubling him more than any other in this period. He was seeking to introduce into English Catholicism that critical spirit of German academic life which he knew personally. All this was aimed at guaranteeing in England too that *impartiality in scientific research* which was so essential to him in responding to the errors of his time. Newman, in principle, was in agreement with Acton. But he became extremely cautious when it was a matter of applying such a spirit of research to religious questions. Although not denying reason the right to search for truth, Newman was nonetheless convinced of the fallaciousness of reason in matters of truth, and for a convert, this was certainly not a matter of small importance. For him the only way to overcome fallaciousness and error was that of recourse to a divinely inspired Church, capable of overcoming all scepticisms and placing itself above passions.[157] The Church is the Providence of God. This in turn made the path of research difficult for Catholic intellectuals, but for Newman it also guaranteed their freedom. In order to understand this apparent paradox, we must remember that for the future Cardinal, true freedom is to be distinguished from false and presumed freedom: the first is guaranteed only within the context of the Church, which with its message is the actual expression of liberty. Certainly Newman, although he was deeply convinced in his heart of this interpretation, was forced to make many efforts when faced with certain "all too human" representatives of the Church, who certainly did not appreciate his conviction. But these, even in their small-mindedness, were contingent aspects in the path of the Church. Time would ensure the triumph of the Truth; it was necessary to arm oneself with hope and constancy, sure that the divine guide would sooner or later always prevail over the restricted limits of the human mind.

Meanwhile, another element of dissension between the isolated liberal Catholics and the English Catholic hierarchy was taking shape in the second half of the 1860s – the question of Papal infallibility. After 1870, the dispute became a matter of triumph for the ultramontanes and of isolation and silence for their opponents. It was not, however, so much the outcome of the struggle which disconcerted the liberal Catholics as the fact that the outcome of the first Vatican Council had further alienated all those Protestants, especially English ones, who after the revival of English Catholicism had shown a desire for union with the Roman Church. The phenomenon was very conspicuous at this time: after the spiritual upheaval provoked by the conversions, quite a few Anglican circles had begun calling into question the actual reasons for their faith. English "Protestantism", at least in its Anglican form, was passing through a moment of serious crisis. The Catholics were convinced that too intransigent an attitude would compromise this drawing closer. For this reason they opposed the proclamation of the principle of papal infallibility at that moment, even if, in their hearts, the vast majority of them were convinced of the principle itself. This principle, moreover, was adding to the polemics already produced by the Syllabus of Errors, and to the definition of the Immaculate Conception, which had led to so much rethinking among Protestants.

While the new dogma provoked so much opposition among those who a few years earlier had regarded the Catholic Church with some benevolence, it also caused many within the fold to reconsider, even, sadly, to the point of leaving the Church. This was the case of Döllinger, Acton's intimate friend, who with all his followers left the Roman Church and provoked what was defined as a schism. The "Old Catholic Church" as the break-away group called itself, gained a wide following in Germany, Holland and some cantons of Switzerland, causing a number of problems for the Catholic hierarchy which, in the German world, was already experiencing many difficulties because of the policy of Bismarck (adhering to his *Kulturkampf*, the latter openly supported the stance of Döllinger and his followers). It goes without saying that this event caused Acton to suffer a great crisis of conscience. Opposed to the proclamation of Infallibility, a friend of the German theologian who had so publicly left the Roman Church, and isolated in his own country, Acton had more than one painful debate with himself about whether to stay within that Church or not. After overcoming certain scruples, Acton remained loyal to the Church, and it is worth noting that at the point of death he stated that he "had never nurtured any serious doubt concerning any dogma of the Church, and that there was nothing which had a value for him equal to that of remaining within the bosom of the Church".[158] And yet Acton must have passed many difficult moments when, immediately after the schism, he observed the success that his German friend enjoyed in England. Döllinger was given high honours at Oxford: Anglican clergy lined up on his side, and even prepared a scheme, which later failed, for the uniting of the various "schismatic" churches.

In England things became more and more complicated when, because of the political opposition of the Irish Catholic MP's, Gladstone's government was defeated, first in parliament and then in the subsequent elections. Irritated, the politician wrote repeated articles against the Catholics, involving even indifferent or distant sections of public opinion in the issue. Gladstone's prestige was substantial, and hence the question became very delicate. Many liberal Catholics found themselves in an embarrassing position, as if they were forced to make a final choice of sides. Acton exceeded himself in skill at this point. He maintained that many of the accusations of the prestigious politician, to whom he felt close, were unjustified, but he nevertheless declared that he was in agreement with him "in reproaching the historical conduct of certain popes... and he allowed a certain satisfaction to shine through at the blow which Gladstone had struck at ultramontanism".[159]

Acton's position would certainly not please the hierarchy which, however, in order to reply to the accusations, had a few able spokesmen whose polemicism rendered them incapable of making themselves listened to. Once again, Acton saw Newman's star in the ascendant. Elderly and alone, the future Cardinal (not awarded the purple until later, under Leo XIII), was already living an exclusive life of prayer and reflection, with the sole intention of being ignored and forgotten. His reluctance had to be overcome, but when it became clear to him that in such circumstances to commit himself was an act of obligation, Newman returned to the scene, admired by all, and by Gladstone most of all, and re-entered the political and journalistic spheres from which he had retired for personal preference and obedience.

The dispute and its outcome are not our concern here. We have paused briefly to examine the issue because behind the delicate contrast between Newman and Gladstone (two friends who liked and admired one another, despite their differences in religious belief), certain important motives are concealed. *First of all*, comes the element which sees in this occasion the last, even though indirect, link (and this is just supposition) which unites Acton to the future Cardinal. If Gladstone, as now seems certain, sent the proofs of his writings before they were published to Newman, it can be considered certain that Acton's presence behind the two figures was decisive.[160] *Secondly*, and in this many other factors are interwoven, Newman emerged from this controversy clearly defined in all aspects of his personality, which won him the ultimate admiration of many and – as always occurs – the criticism and envy of others. The latter "hastened to denounce him repeatedly to Rome, insisting that he should be condemned, and it was mere fortune that Pius IX, despite the aversion that he felt for Newman, while he criticized him ... in a conversation with the Rector of the English College in Rome, always refused to issue any condemnation, indeed not hiding the belief that he had been deceived about him as far as the past was concerned".[161] And it is certainly no accident that that same Providence, and the patience in which Newman had always believed, rewarded him with the election to the rank of Cardinal which Pius IX's successor decided to bestow on him.

Over and beyond his magnanimity, in the confrontation with Gladstone, Newman had some success in an undertaking which even Acton, with all his cosmopolitanism, was unable to achieve. In fact, he had managed to show the English that one could be a good Catholic, a good patriot and a good servant of the nation at the same time and without compromises; Newman himself was the embodiment of this notion. To be a Catholic did not mean setting aside the political responsibilities which the state demanded from its citizens, because the Catholic Church was not a political power to which one was subject, but a path of the spirit to eternal salvation. It is this faith above contingencies, above science, above reason and history which characterizes the personality of Newman. Far more than Acton, he was convinced that in the Church there was an intrinsic wisdom which in crucial moments was capable of guiding the hierarchy, and he was also convinced that *the prevailing scientific spirit was not immune from errors and contradictions, which would sooner or later be exploded,*[162] provoking identity crises in more than a few men of science. To have faith, for Newman, was almost to accept not understanding certain things, such as those, for instance, which characterized the life of the Church at that historical moment. The Church, through its guides, was going ahead in the midst of full materialism and anticlericalism, with the propagation of the dogma of the Immaculate Conception and, even at the very time when it seemed to be destroyed by the loss of its temporal power, proclaimed infallibility. All this in the eyes of unaided reason could seem anachronistic and meaningless, but for a man of faith it was a powerful call to reflection.

Acton, who was still affected by his youthful spirit, was for the moment more taken up by the immediacy of the problems rather than their future perspective. Moreover, the life and survival of liberal Catholicism, which he saw threatened on all sides, were of great importance to him. The immediate contingencies of the Church seemed to him something of a pretext, linked solely to the problems of Italian stability, important as that might be, rather than to the development of universal Catholicism.[163] These are the reasons why the relations and collaboration between Acton and Newman were beginning to weaken even by the end of the 1860s.

When it was realised in 1870 in the midst of the Council that the basic problem on which the bishops were called to debate was that of infallibility (this was the sole problem which the press of the time took seriously), in England the Catholic world seemed to be reunited. Acton was a discordant voice (he was in Rome); Newman was living this moment in a metaphysical frame of mind; the ultramontanism of the hierarchy was triumphant. Other voices were silent. Manning and Ward and other exponents of the Catholic clergy presented, in the press which they controlled, the theological reasons on which the principle which the Council was debating was based, and which it was about to approve.

It would be an exaggeration, however, to say that Acton's isolated position was simply polemical towards the hierarchy and the Roman Curia. In his article "The Next General Council", which appeared in the *Chronicle* in July 1867, Acton, though showing his perplexity at a pronouncement which could increase the divisions between the different Christian professions in Rome, nevertheless made clear (at least in this writer's opinion) the historical reasons for such a pronouncement, showing that he was struck more by the venomous intransigence of the ultramontanes than by the matter itself. They were, he felt, more concerned with principles, however just they might be, than with a dialogue with the "separated brethren" and "those afar off".

Two years later Acton wrote, for the *North British Review*, another article entitled "The Pope and the Council", which proved to be a commentary on a work called *Der Papst und das Concil* which had appeared a little earlier in Germany under the pseudonym "Von Janus". The essay, a work by Döllinger, and the commentary by Acton, mark a definitive break in the relations between Newman and Acton. The future Cardinal asserted that such ideas might be the product of an exclusively liberal spirit, but certainly not of a Catholic one; of a spirit which was unable to discern the true sense and value of the Church, considered solely as a structure of the more or less remote past.[164] A spirit, in other words, certainly not living in the soul of Catholicism.

It should be said that, in view of the future schism of Döllinger (which has already been mentioned) Newman was quite prophetic in this case.

.This severe judgement by Newman, even though not officially known to Acton, was probably taken on board by the latter, because when Döllinger ended his allegiance to Rome, his former pupil did not follow him. Even more isolated, and very definitely set aside, Acton still remained in the Roman Catholic

Church which for him too was the depository of truth. His obstinate dissent prior to the conciliar definition was thus seen solely as the shipwrecked attempt to save the possibility of dialogue with non-Catholics and to safeguard liberal Catholicism. It seems almost as though Acton, having lost his battle, resigned himself to the dictates of Providence. This was the path that Newman had already taken for some time; as can be seen from some letters of this period, he was theologically in line with the Council, but remained extremely doubtful about the timing and manner of the promulgation of the dogma. After a moment of indignation, the spirit of obedience prevailed in him, and the desire to take refuge in Providence.

After the definition of the dogma, its acceptance was quite natural for Newman, as if a voice above the parties had spoken in unmistakable fashion. It should be said, though, that between him and the ultramontanes there was, right to the end, a question of far more than secondary importance: to what point did papal infallibility reach?[165] The question was more than legitimate, for the ultramontanes, in the absence of specific definition, had extended the criterion of infallibility to every pontifical manifestation. It may appear paradoxical, but just at the moment when the relations between Newman and Acton were cooling, the two found themselves very close together on such a crucial point as infallibility.

However, Acton's position was really more complicated. A friend of Gladstone and a convinced liberal, while he accepted the principle of infallibility on the religious plane through faith, he made a great effort for himself and on behalf of his friends to harmonize the new dogma with the liberal criterion of the perfectibility of history.[166] Perhaps the English historian lacked an adequate theological and philosophical preparation which in others, such as Rosmini, had enabled them to deal with the problem of perfectibility and to provide it with an alternative explanation which was certainly more acceptable. And yet he knew that to provide an authoritative justification for religious questions, it was necessary to go beyond contingent and historical reason. He knew that "If reason could demonstrate all truths, there would be no room for faith".[167] In short, he knew that in religious questions there is always room for mystery, and that reason cannot claim to go beyond certain limits if it wants to avoid becoming ridiculous and contradictory. In crucial moments like that of the Council, Acton was unable to harmonize the two terms of a coupling which was indivisible for him: Catholicism and liberalism. But he chose the way of faith, witnessed by the fact that at the cost of silence and isolation, he preferred to remain within the bosom of the Church rather than leave it.

Despite the fact that his opinions were diametrically opposed to the ultramontanes, in his love of the Church and its chief pastor, Acton was in no way inferior to the most strenuous defenders of the Apostolic See. A Church without a Pope is not the Church of Christ, he was to say some years later. This conviction was closely connected to another, according to which the Spirit of Christ operated through his Holy Church, which in guiding men towards true liberty, showed itself to be a divine organization. This explains why the obtuseness of certain members of the hierarchy provoked real crises of conscience in Acton.[168] In the end, however, he found his faith increased when he chose the way of silence and humble incomprehension.

It was thus that Acton, after the period of criticism during the Council, and possibly because of the actions of some figures such as Döllinger, finally adopted an attitude of moderation, convinced that the truth would finally triumph and settle all disputes. The actual relationship between Newman and Acton seemed, some years after the Council, to return to the atmosphere of the past. In a letter at the end of 1874, Acton showed Newman, apart from the notable value that he ascribed to his sympathy, the conviction that the "old" and the "new" would finally be reconciled when certain novelties had been digested.[169] In contrast to many other Catholics who ended up as victims of their own scepticism, Acton had a great hope in the future of his Church, hopes which were never to be dashed.

Despite all this, it may seem something of a contradiction that Acton made it clear in this same letter to Newman that he was quite reluctant to satisfy the expectations of Cardinal Manning, who was asking all English Catholics explicitly for a clear and unequivocal response of acceptance of all the decrees of the Council. This response was never forthcoming. In silence and isolation, Acton had already accepted the path of moderation, but to proclaim this in public fashion seemed to him then almost equivalent to abjuring many of his liberal principles, which would have put him in conflict with the ultramontanes – principles which he certainly did not wish to renounce, convinced as he was that time would show their validity. But this stand only brought disappointment, incomprehension, and a greater isolation and sense of rejection to Acton. Above all, one consideration may be derived from these latest and most delicate post-conciliar issues. They in fact revealed the profound difference that existed between Acton and Newman. The former had chosen the way of silence, convinced that time would even out all the disputes and bring truth to triumph without the slightest degree of shadow. Faithful to the principle that in history a sort of *lex continui* operates (we shall discuss this further in the next chapter) towards a specific end, he considered that the wisest choice was to wait, in the expectation that Providence would not be slow to prove his reasoning right. The latter, in contrast, though he himself had a blind faith in Providence, made no calculation about the future. For Newman, those who accepted the dogmas of the Church only on rational bases and founded on historical reasoning, could scarcely be considered Catholic. In this fundamental difference there reappears the difference between one who had become a convert, and thus could surrender reason to faith, and one who possessed the faith by tradition, and thus sought to justify it and try to give it a "rational" basis, even though within the limits of the possible.

The period of the Council and the immediate aftermath thus saw a crisis in the relations between Newman and Acton. The word "crisis" may seem too strong, because there was no change in the mutual attitude of respect between the two men, but this uniquely applied to external relations; inwardly, much changed.[170] With their subsequent positions, the two chose quite different camps. Newman, above all with his essay defending the

Conciliar Decrees against Gladstone, joined the ranks of the hierarchy, in considering the outcome of the Council to be the closure of the disputes within the world of English Catholicism. With full dignity, which even his adversaries were afterwards to recognize, Newman wished to show that his conversion was not due to a momentary infatuation, but was the product of a full and mature conviction. It goes without saying that this approach won him the plaudits of Catholics, while Acton's silence only brought him greater isolation and incomprehension.

The adoption of this position by Newman, however, should not be seen as an act of uncritical submission. It seems clear that in taking a stand in favour of the Conciliar Decrees against Gladstone (English public opinion was truly fascinated by the dispute), Newman seemed to be treading two parallel paths: on the one hand defence of the Catholic Church seen from a supernatural prospect, and on the other hand criticism of that Catholic world which, stiffened by its own pride, sometimes failed to discern the worth of its adversaries, and was therefore incapable of drawing closer to them and presenting its own case. In the Preface and Dedication to the Duke of Norfolk in his writings in reply to Gladstone, Newman wrote in the clearest terms: I am deeply convinced that the Catholics must, in many cases, recite the *mea culpa*, and attribute not to others but to themselves the blame for having alienated such a profoundly religious spirit as that of Gladstone.[171]

He also made strenuous efforts in his writings to show how the Catholic Church, perfectly in keeping with its tradition, had almost always sought to distinguish the religious sphere from the political one. Quoting a passage from Ranke, Newman made a specific point which was especially relevant to England at that time. In part of the passage quoted from Ranke we read: In this separation of the Church and the State consists the greatest, most pervading and influential of all the Christian centuries. The spiritual power and the temporal power may march alongside one another but they cannot find themselves perfectly united with each other, except in certain rare moments of conjuncture, and for quite brief periods of time.[172] Their distinction is one of the greatest achievements of history. This consideration was very useful to Newman in showing public opinion that it was possible to be a Catholic and a good English citizen at the same time, and in full right.

When this necessary distinction had been made – and it seemed to Newman to give a meaning to the doctrine of infallibility – one can understand better the choice that he made in considering the Pope, both on the theological and the historical plane, to be identified with the Catholic Church; its representative and guide beyond all measure of doubt.

Papal supremacy was meant to be, and must be, purely spiritual, and it was in this light that infallibility should be understood. On the contrary, though the Pope had played a political role in the past, this should be attributed to historical contingencies. It is curious that in this matter, Newman turned to German religious historiography (and in this too we may be able to spot some influence by Acton). The temporal power of the Popes, the future Cardinal asserted, had been a historical necessity. This is generally recognized today, even by Protestant historians, namely that the concentration of ecclesiastical power in the hands of the Popes was a benefit to the European civilization of that era.[173] But history is made up of contingencies and these not only change but also decay.

In the pages addressed to Gladstone, there is a revelation of a spirit which is capable, as were few in its day, of looking beyond history. For this reason he is able to allow himself to make a valid rebuke to a politician about those who seek to criticize the Church's past without being able to enter into its spirituality. Speaking of the Middle Ages, Newman was able to deduce what only the truly great historians are able to perceive. In the now distant centuries of the supremacy of the Catholic Church, there is something which cannot any longer be confirmed without a truly exceptional miracle, i.e a return to that universal religious sentiment, to that condition of public opinion which prevailed in the Middle Ages. The Pope himself refers to those centuries by the name of the "centuries of faith".[174] This means that it is impossible to make any historico-political observation without taking into account the common spirit which gave life to the civilization of the Middle Ages: a spirit which today we cannot even aspire to imagine.

In the Middle Ages too there was that valid distinction in the moral field, between necessary and contingent realities on which a great part of the doctrine of infallibility rests. The Pope, in fact, speaks in a definitive manner on moral arguments, and what he propounds must refer to things which are in themselves good or evil, and not to things which are accidental, changeable and simply matters of convenience.[175] The latter, just because of their mutability, are almost always matters of discretion, and thus have no part in a principle which aims at the eternal, and seeks to point it out to others as well.

It is simply absurd and out of place to speak of a double allegiance of Catholics. Newman felt the "historical" necessity to state and clarify this contradiction. It should not be forgotten that in England, this sort of accusation was laid against Catholics even before Hobbes justified the religion of the State. There had always been a real misunderstanding about the figure of the Pope, which had evidently originated in historical contingencies, and ended up by forgetting the profound and ancient motives for the mandate to Peter. It was on that very mandate that Catholicism was based. Newman was well aware of this, and did not hesitate to remind Englishmen who, through Gladstone, made it clear that they had forgotten it. For this reason they considered the conciliar principle with regard to infallibility as an abuse or a sentimental return to the past.

To affirm and accept the conciliar decree was certainly not, for Newman, to obey blindly every statement that the Pope made. Moreover, in England, the conflicts with the Crown had shown that total submission could not even be made to the sovereign. Obedience is always played out and decided on the plane of conscience, and it was the latter, for Newman, which guaranteed to the Catholic the possibility of being faithful to his religion while being at the same time, a good subject of the Queen.

Over and above what is mentioned above, another element was constantly present in the high-minded dispute between Newman and Gladstone, and indirectly between the former and all those who viewed the Catholic world with suspicion. English liberalism accused the Catholic Church, after the Syllabus, of having taken a dangerous step backwards, taking on board in the fullest sense the ideals of the 1815 Restoration. Newman, rather than directly refuting this impression, directed a similar criticism to Gladstone and his numerous followers. Here the tone is clear and firm, like that of the early Fathers of the Church: When Mr Gladstone thinks he is in the right to say that the laws of England and the people of England condemn those who uphold the freedom of conscience, of the press, *in toto*, then and not before can he also say that the Encyclical does the same thing, making use of those words which have for him such a terrible significance.[176] There is an implicit call here to examine the very difficult conditions in which the Catholic minority had lived for centuries, and the no less difficult conditions in which the Irish emigrants lived, the working masses, some of their organizations and especially the incomprehension and obstacles that certain Catholic initiatives met with before the hyper-critical Protestant world. Newman's taking up of a position was as specific as ever: the document should be criticized for the facts and not the words; where is the government which is ready in practice to make itself the guarantor of all liberties pertaining to the individual or to a people? Why, Newman exclaimed, directing his words without half measures to Gladstone, in Ireland have we stifled the press, deeming it seditious? Why is the British Constitution not applied in its entirety to India?[177] How could the British government criticize a papal document if, in practice, it did even worse? As well as having an apologetic intent, Newman's statements show the same attachment to the rights of the weakest, and in general of minorities, that was so dear to the English Catholics, and in particular to Acton.

It may seem like a contradiction, but at the very time when the influence of Newman was increasing in British public opinion, the dispute with Acton was gradually getting sharper for apparently inexplicable reasons: there were never polemical tones between the two men, but the fact remains that after a letter of January 1877, there was not even an exchange of letters. The most plausible reason is that after Newman had taken up his position, he appeared to Acton to be a perfect ultramontane, and the English historian always felt a profound aversion to the ultramontanes because in them Catholicism seemed to have the struggle against liberalism as its main aim. This was, as far as Acton was concerned, the greatest of contradictions. He was, in fact, "a sincere Catholic and a sincere Liberal; he renounced everything in Catholicism incompatible with Liberty, and everything in Liberalism incompatible with Catholicism. Liberalism he identified with morality".[178] For this reason Acton was able to assert that a great evil had penetrated subcutaneously into the Church, revealing itself particularly in some members of the hierarchy, and in certain moments, the spirit of intolerance which, although it was present in other confessions and in various political systems, did not, even so, justify the Church's fear when confronted with freedom. And when, for various reasons, the Papacy had espoused, and even earlier encouraged, the ultramontane cause, the aversion to freedom had become even more evident. It can now be seen why Acton, although never leaving the Church, never wished to support papal infallibility, and we can also understand why, even though he had been so close a friend of Newman's, he became critical of him after Leo XIII made him a cardinal. This appointment meant for Acton a confirmation and a recognition on the part of Rome of the ultramontanism of the new Cardinal. It was in these circumstances that Acton became polemical beyond measure at one point.[179] Newman was emphatically and exclusively an ultramontane. He had never made any profession of liberalism, but had in fact several times taken a stand in favour of absurd institutions like that of the Inquisition.

In reality these conclusions were forced on Acton by the fact that Newman too, who had become a part of the Catholic hierarchy, became a distant friend, a "compromised" friend who had made a clear choice, a friend who, having let him down, increased his solitude.

This is the only explanation that can be found for the often gratuitous criticism which Acton made of Newman in these years. As MacDougall has pointed out, it would be difficult for the most liberal of liberals to find even a minimum trace of intolerance in Newman's dealings with non-Catholics. Perhaps in those days, no one was more sensitive than Newman to the problems of conscience, and more contrary to any form of inculcation of a religious creed, especially on those who showed the possibility of conversion.[180] Certainly all this made Newman anything but an ultramontane, and Leo XIII knew this very well when, in a moment of great difficulty for the Church, he sought cardinals who would be above all suspicion and not compromised.

Certainly Newman lacked many of Acton's possibilities, for example, direct knowledge of German theology, but in compensation he had a natural predilection for dialogue. He felt the need to criticize his adversaries not in order to drive them away, but to clarify and to build bridges. All this was very clear to Acton, and it is likely that he was reminded of it when in the last fifteen years of his life, with so many situations now changed even on the international level, he sought open reconciliation with the decrees of the Council (with which he had never sensed a real interior break).[181]

In the nineties there was a new reason which brought Acton closer to Newman's position of twenty years earlier: age. By now an elderly man, the historian was viewing the events in the Church's history in a different light, and he acquired that sense of detachment which permits real understanding of the questions of faith. With regard to faith and its integrity, Acton probably understood that this was exactly one of the motives that had induced Newman to accept infallibility, and that without prevarication. This definition (and he repeated this several times in the *Apologia*), served to assure the faith of the Apostles full development in strict continuity, and served above all to identify the Catholic Church with the orthodoxy of Scripture and with the teaching of the Fathers. Without authority, who could assure authenticity? This question went far beyond the limits of history, but carried numerous moral and theological implications. Newman saw everything in a dimension which we could call "vertical", and which passed beyond historical-sociological schemes of analysis, and thus kept well away from the temptation, typical of many currents of thought in the eighteenth and nineteenth centuries, to believe that history under all circumstances assured development and progress. "Newman saw development operating in all fields involving mental activity. But in fields outside the doctrinal, he saw no certain protection against false developments, i.e. corruptions. His pessimistic view of fallen man led him to reject the possibility of a Church's permanently avoiding corruptions without a divine *assistentia*".[182] The historical continuity (in orthodoxy) of the Church of Rome was for him the greatest proof of the divine assistance to the successor of Peter.

In Newman's historical sense, there is the firm conviction of the decayed state of nature which thus staves off facile optimisms and enthusiasms. There is no doubt that we must search for development and progress, but it is also true that the doctrine of original sin must put us on our guard against those analyses of German historicism which too hastily, in the name of "becoming" or of the dialectical method, subjugate moral principles and justify everything in terms of the success of an idea, or of a class or a State. This could well have been another reason for conflict between Acton and Newman. For the former, in fact, even in respect of metaphysical and theological considerations on human nature which have always inspired Catholicism, there is a *lex continui* which reveals itself in history and which marks the path of humankind, however painstakingly, towards an ever greater manifestation of its morality.

This optimistic vision, as we shall see more clearly in the next chapter, with its evident Leibnitzean overtones, made Acton more prone to consider all novelties of history as a competition for the growth of liberty and thus of morality. Such a conception reveals once more, and more notably, the influence exerted on Acton by German culture. A simultaneous development of rationality, freedom and morality which, through Fichte, had become the heritage of so many European intellectuals in the nineteenth century.

Newman, on the other hand, had a less secular view of history. For him, as for Acton, the *lex continui* was guaranteed only within Catholicism, which for the Cardinal was, however, taken in its relation with the ecclesiastical structure, and not in the broader, cultural sense, as Benedetto Croce understood it in the twentieth century. For Newman the Church of Rome was, despite certain difficulties and contradictory moments, the guarantee of the *lex continui* operating in history. For Acton, on the other hand, the latter was guaranteed by all those contributions from ideas which, although they did not arise from the fount of Catholicism, nevertheless showed that they were not opposed to it. This same interpretation has been given in the twentieth century by certain circles and individuals of French Catholicism, and even by the Roman hierarchy. But at that time it forced Acton into greater isolation and incomprehension. In his case, however, the latter also derived from his over-hasty and at times inopportune behaviour during the Council.[183] Many of his adversaries, especially the ultramontanes, were never to forgive him for his friendships and the positions he took up during the Roman period of Vatican I. It should also be added that Acton, even when he put forward ideas and conclusions that were too bold, was always sharp and stimulating, and this, because of the envy it provoked, led to new problems and criticisms.

By now, Acton's reflections, once his relations with Newman had cooled, were entrusted only to his notes (following an occasional other article), many of which are only to be found in his much later published works. In this period the English historian was in fact deepening his basic notions about history. There is no political concept which can appeal to Divine Providence and which at the same time stands in the way of progress. If God works in history, his operation cannot do other than reveal a path, a movement, a surpassing – and certainly not a static state. In a letter of 22 September 1882, to Döllinger, Acton clearly expressed how, according to him, there subsisted in history a great unity of ideas, of conscience and morality.[184] This was, to his way of seeing things, the great mystery of becoming, which justified the encounter between the ways of man and the ways of God.

In expressing this notion of his, Acton should not appear as a Romantic dreamer devoid of all concrete reference to reality. On the contrary, it is in fact the latter which confirms the validity of his affirmation. It is possible to read certain passages of the *Essays on Freedom and Power* (which will also be quoted later) in order to see how the famous project of the *History of Liberty* had constantly stimulated and fascinated Acton's intelligence. There were so many signs which, in the course of time, indicated the validity of the pattern traced by the Catholic historian. Representative government, the progressive elimination of slavery, the freedom of conscience, respect for opinions, the safeguarding of weaker groups, and so on – all this meant that God, in the person of Christ[185] was genuinely operating in history. Perhaps the ultramontanes were wholly closed to the spirit of their own times, but surely Acton, motivated and animated by the convictions mentioned above, was completely soaked in that faith in progress which animated the greater part of European culture in his times. It often seems as if (and this was Newman's fear) he undervalues the range of evil in history – a scope which according to the Cardinal, contributed to bestowing a sense of realism on those who examined it.

Newman made various critical comments on Acton's historical interpretation. He showed a deep scepticism with regard to those who supposed that they found in "becoming" a justification of the ways of God, or who actually supposed that they could trace the signs of his providence in history. For him, this was not only a task of cyclopic dimensions, but it was also meaningless. It was only possible to approach the mysteries of God with faith.[186] Starting from this presupposition, Newman came to a serious point of contrast with Acton. He knew and admitted, like every man of culture, that great progress had been made on the plane of knowledge, and on that of science; but he did not delude himself that such conclusions could be drawn on the moral plane. As far as this aspect was concerned, it seemed to him that humankind was still living in its infancy,[187] but above all on the historical plane, and because of the implications of history for morality, he can be said to be a solitary thinker[188] in the enormous proliferation of philosophers of the nineteenth century. Against what most of the latter maintained, Newman put forward many reservations, and above all he did not believe that it could be taken for granted that there would soon be a period of social stability, as did quite a few theorists of the perfectionism dear above all to historians of the socialist school.

Perhaps more clearly than Acton, Newman held that the great contribution made by Christianity to historicism was the sense of moral responsibility of the individual. And it was specifically the latter which, despite the development of science and technology, still appeared ineffective. To understand what Newman really meant by historical development, it is necessary to bear in mind the following conclusions: "He did not transfix history, reducing it to an already established process, of which the intelligence could only gain knowledge of the laws: nor did he make of man the demiurge of history, exalted and anguished at the same time by this power which is in his possession; he does not admit the existence in man of the power to create values ... he holds that the plan of truth is transcendent in relation to the plan of becoming and of the essences present in history: consequently history cannot be a norm or a judge of itself, but supposes a transcendent judgement".[189] This explains why the Cardinal should have viewed Acton's sympathies towards German historicism with a certain scepticism, for that school claimed to consider history almost as if it were an ultimate criterion of truth. In this case, however, the anxieties seem to me to be unfounded, in view of the judgements pronounced by Acton on the Hegelian dialectical method (we shall return to this subject in the next chapter).

It should also be borne in mind that both Acton and Newman had a genuinely pluralistic vision of history as of politics, and thus could not in any way tolerate visions such as that of Hegel, which made the historical process of becoming a rigidly unitary one, which gathers all into itself and justifies everything according to an intrinsic logic of a Machiavellian kind, seeing reason as always siding with the victor. All this, especially in Newman's thought, is confounded by the actual existence of the Church, which inserts itself into, but is at the same time distanced from "political" history (understood in the broad sense). As can easily be seen, this is a typically Augustinian vision, which ultimately calls into question all forms of rigidly deterministic and immanentist historicism: those, in other words, which claim to sum up human existence in the present.

Here too, in order to understand Newman's historicist vision and its differences from Acton's, we need to remember that the former was a convert. "He had been tormented by doubts about the true Church, and it is this that explains his journey and his conversion".[190] Landfall in Catholicism was to him the arrival at truth, and thus he could not conceive of historical interpretations which might speak of momentary truths, products of time, and subject to revision. Moreover, when speaking of the "development of truth", it is essential to recall that the latter is not subject solely to a process of a rational type, since comprehension of the truth does not uniquely imply reason, but also faith, which offers a substantially different yardstick for judgement.

It has been supposed that the difference between Acton and Newman with regard to German historicism may have been due to the fact that the former may have experienced the fascination of German culture partly because of his familiarity, including linguistic familiarity, with that world, while the latter, who did not even know German at all, remained completely alienated from the world of idealism and the consequences which it generated in Germany. In reality, though, this supposition seems somewhat superficial. The real difference is to be met with in the different "nature" of the two scholars before the central problems of the faith: dogma, authority, and so on. Indeed, to be more specific, given that their ultimate conclusions on these problems were identical, the difference is shown in the suitability or otherwise of insisting on such points with "those afar off", or those belonging to other religious confessions. Acton, who had grown up and lived in a liberal environment, had a less decisive position than his distinguished friend who, while not being able to consider himself illiberal, was more thirsting for certainties, for himself and for others, which would indicate sure paths. In Acton, the preferred way seems to be that of caution. "Newman, on the other hand, strongly affirmed the dogmatic principle; i.e. the existence of an objective revealed truth, which would come to be known progressively".[191] This explains why the future Cardinal was prepared to accept the conclusions of the first Vatican Council.

To follow in the wake of the Church gave Newman that security which otherwise proved impossible to find. Unlike Acton, he did not have the certainty of the future achievement of "a liberal kingdom of freedom", even in the far distant future. In fact he had many doubts on the subject, while he was certain that in the Church even Acton's dreams would prove to be possible. But what most typified Newman was another characteristic conviction, apart from that of the great converts, that of the great apostles of the faith of Christ. "In Newman's mind, the primary work of the Church was not the reformation of society, but the salvation of individual souls".[192] This explains why history seen in a horizontal, "flat" perspective (which was the way of the majority of German historical theorists) did not satisfy him at all. It was necessary to safeguard the rights of transcendence, without which every notion about salvation proved to be devoid of meaning. Only the Church, even by scandalizing the most advanced circles and currents of thought, could provide a discourse of this kind. Its presence in the world constituted the seed of transcendence and the warning not to ignore it.

Mention has been made of Newman having a greater realism than the liberal Catholics of his time. This is undoubtedly just. In fact, despite his undeniable attachment to the problems of freedom, Newman never fully espoused liberalism because in this theory, the doctrine of fulfilment and of salvation was transferred, in its more radical version, completely to the temporal plane. Such an interpretation completely repudiated the sense of expectation, and hence the hope in the second and final coming of Christ. This liberalism, of which German idealism was one expression, condemned the doctrine of papal infallibility which was expressed on a spiritual plane, but then claimed itself to speak *ex cathedra* when it proclaimed the infallibility of historical judgement, to which were attributed characteristics of undeniable and incontrovertible truth. From this measuring-stick, there then followed the claim to judge not only history but also the spiritual dimension of humankind, because even moral criteria were to be subjected to historical judgement. The final point of arrival of all this was that immanence claimed to exhaust transcendence in itself. In short, Newman acknowledged the great importance of history and historical method, but he was not willing to recognize Christianity as a mere historical religion. Although being closely tied to history, Christianity was also above it, and in certain senses, it took precedence over it, since it was capable of giving it a meaning, a significance and a perspective. Acton was less drastic in this matter: as a liberal and Catholic historian, he recognized in the various moments of history, different contributions to the path of liberty which, explicitly, did not derive from Catholicism, but which even so were not in contradiction to it, and were thus destined to become integrated with it.

To make matters simpler, we might say that the difference concerning historical reflection between Acton and Newman lies in the fact that the departure point for the former consists in searching in history for the possibility of giving concrete expression to an ideal. The latter, in contrast, was resigned to the impossibility of realizing a dream of this kind, but strove to seek, in individual existences, the opportunity to realize to some degree the divine perfection. It follows that for Newman politics could not be the daring intention of realizing illusory ideals, but the effort of sinful man to find, little by little, solutions to concrete problems.[193] This does not mean, certainly, that Newman had a Manichaean conception of politics, or of history or religion. Perhaps his thinking risks being trivialized if we do not bear in mind that the Cardinal, perhaps more than other Catholics of his time, and certainly more than the liberal Catholics, was aware of the danger of losing the sense of sin, and once again as a convert, he did everything he could to renew it, not as a pessimist but in order to overcome facile optimism.

At this point Newman may seem to be a mediaevalist – and perhaps Acton too came to form a similar judgement – one who revived the Augustinian doctrine of the City of God contrasted with the earthly city. However, over and beyond that, one thing is certain: only the Church is able to take action against the sense of sin. Only from the Church emerges the distinction between *amor dei* and *amor sui*, to use Augustinian terminology again. Only from the Church echoes a cry of accusation against that egoism and individualism which other theories have erected into a principle of a system of life, and of choice of values. Only the Church is able to present values which are not the product of time and space, in short of contingency. Only the Church, therefore, is able to place itself above time (and here we are returning to the basic theme and point of departure), and to overcome the simple concept of utility which derives from it.

If the Church did not exist, mankind would never have lifted itself up from the mud. For Newman, this is a certainty of such importance that it leads him to reject the idea that politics is an all-embracing sphere for humankind. "Religion is higher than politics. Politics were of the earth, and earth could never lead one to heaven"[194]. Total and genuine salvation of humankind does not, therefore, belong to politics, which conceives the human being only in corporeal terms, or even worse, in material terms. Even though Acton was of the same opinion, it should be said that for him, political reality, if it were identified with the "realm of freedom", contributed equally with religion to the moral and spiritual growth of humankind. This conviction was at the basis of his liberal Catholicism, and also derived from his rigorous historical analysis through which he believed that he had identified the guiding thread of what humanity was becoming in the growth of freedom. It is probably on this point that Acton and Newman split, and ended by being considered a liberal Catholic in one case and an ultramontane in the other.

Acton was deeply convinced that politics inspired by the Christian religion would have reconciled the *Civitas Dei* with the *Civitas terrena*, and would have made easier the understanding of the meta-historical mystery of salvation. But he also knew that the rivalry and dualism of the powers could have contributed to safeguarding the powers themselves from dangerous involutions, even if, inevitably it could not have eliminated recurring conflicts. Acton, in short, was convinced that it was the destiny of mankind to live under the "two counterposed realms", but with the capacity to contribute to the progress of morality and freedom. Newman may have had the same conviction, but he was less optimistic because in the persistence of the conflicts he often saw the differing positions get worse and worse, and not infrequently increase misunderstandings.[195] Because of this, he finally decided to support one party rather than the other.

Even if we seek to discuss Newman's liberalism, we have to bear in mind that for him, given that the human being is a

106

creature contaminated by sin, the best kind of state is the one which leaves the Church free to carry on its mission, which is above all to reconcile man with God. Indeed, a state based on Christian principles should almost be compelled to help the Church in this task. It should be said, however, that Newman realised that a political system of this kind would end by damaging the Church rather than aiding it. For him it was one thing to theorize about the best solution, or to dream of it, and quite another to realize it. For this reason he was little disposed to follow Acton in his political notions. What interested him was not so much social schemes or political systems, but souls for sanctification, and this shows that Newman, at base, had the soul of a mystic rather than that of a scholar (even though he was a man of outstanding cultural gifts). In the seventies and even after, Acton, with his scheme for a universal history which would follow the goal of full liberty, must have seemed to him more of a utopian than a historian. If he were to be considered as a historian, he must be regarded as a follower of nineteenth century historicism which, having hidden transcendence in the human process of becoming, had given the latter a completely earthly goal, and an immanentist meaning.[196] But to look at Acton in this extreme way seems to me a little too bold, as I shall seek to show in the next chapter.

Varied and contradictory judgements have been formulated about Acton. But the fact remains that very few loved liberty as greatly as he did, or sought in all ways to reconcile it with Catholicism at a historical moment when such a task could certainly not be considered a simple one. This probably explains the difficulty Acton met with in concluding the *History of Freedom*, a work which was only sketched out, but to which the author devoted much of his energy. In the choice between freedom and Catholicism, in my opinion, he loved the second more, so that it is true that he was unwilling for any reason in the world to leave the Catholic Church, and preferred isolation and incomprehension as long as he could remain within it.

9) The University project

Newman's reflections on university education do not come within the field of this study; only those elements which were to find Acton himself in favour of the project will be taken briefly into account here. From the actual moment that the future Cardinal set to work to found the Catholic University of Dublin, Acton formed the idea of creating a new circle in that setting similar to those he had frequented in Munich. The fact that Newman had lived for a long time in Oxford led him to suppose that now, in the role of Rector (a post which he held from 1852 to 1858), he could give a new impulse to those Catholic groups who were seeking the way to dialogue with the culture of the nineteenth century, as was already happening in Germany. The hopes of the young Acton seemed to be confirmed by the request by Newman that the young scholar's name should be included in the "University Books".[197]

Even after Newman left the Rector's post and returned to England, there was a constant exchange of views on educational problems between the future Cardinal and Acton. So much so that the young nobleman even thought of founding a Catholic university in England, a project which met with some favour, but which was supplanted by an even greater dream – that of founding an English university in Rome.

The problem of the university was strongly felt in England because young Catholics had no way of frequenting the Protestant universities (and anyway the Catholic hierarchy was against their doing so). They were thus deprived of a modern scientific education, and remained at the margins of civil society as well. Newman and Acton, but above all the former, knew that to organize a university or college of higher education for Catholics, apart from good intentions, would require a great deal of time. Thus they devised the idea of letting Catholics frequent Protestant cultural institutions, but organizing qualified groups of experienced and capable Catholic theologians, as "missionaries", to shape the faith of Catholics, safeguarding them from the "errors" of the reformed religions:[198] missions like those which in the past the Jesuits had organized to protect the integrity of Catholicism, and to allow them to penetrate into the Anglican world. The request, put forward several times by Newman, shows the importance which the converts above all attached to the university and cultural world in general, because they knew the enormous weight that this world could exercise on public opinion, and on political activity.

This aspect interested Newman and Acton for some time, and because of the motives described above, they undertook, after the experience of the University of Dublin, to found higher-grade institutions in England. The idea also came from a substantial group of converts who still trusted in the leadership of Newman – who always seemed to be the most suited to realizing a project of this kind. To Acton, who supported the initiative with great enthusiasm, it seemed that the necessity to found schools of this kind would in the future determine and facilitate the aim of founding a Catholic university in England, this prospect being the dream of liberal Catholics in those years. To understand the meaning of this project, we must remember that, as Acton wrote in a letter to Döllinger, seeking to support the opening of small Catholic public schools would eventually lead to the need to reform the whole Catholic educational system, to bring it more up to date with the times.[199]

This renewal was considered decisive by the liberal Catholics above all in terms of their rivalry with the ultramontanes; a rivalry that because of the intrinsic weakness of the former, could only be resolved in their favour in a long-term perspective, where there was an excellent opportunity for confrontation in the cultural dimension. The ultramontanes, for their part, understood the intention of their rivals, and because of this, put obstacles in the way of "cultural reform" for a long time.

In this area too, as in that of the magazines, the English Catholic hierarchy probably deluded itself into thinking that it could calm the disputes between the two parties by calling on Newman to take on the role of mediator. The opportunity was offered by the difficulties encountered by the *Rambler* in 1859 and 1860 (difficulties which had come to the fore even earlier). But the real motive can be described in terms of "cultural politics" since it was really a matter of reconciling two contrasting wings of English Catholicism, and more specifically, a matter of re-establishing a balance between freedom of scientific research, and faith and respect for religious authority.[200] These problems lay behind the pedagogical problems of the institutes, colleges and universities, as they underlay in general the whole Catholic press. This may also possibly explain why, rather than expose himself directly, Newman at first sought to adopt the path of anonymity in journalistic terms, so as not to irritate the more conservative forces which counted on him to bring the liberal Catholics back on to the "path of reason".

As we have mentioned, Newman's position was not easy, because on the one hand he was faithful to the hierarchy, but on the other he recognized the great merits of the theories of the liberal tradition, and the commitment of the laity. "I think certainly", he stated clearly in that context, "that the *Ecclesia docens* is more happy when she has such enthusiastic partisans about her ... than when she cuts off the faithful from the study of her divine doctrines ... and requires from them a *fides implicita* in her word, which in the educated classes will terminate in indifference, and in the poorer in superstition".[201] Despite the delicacy of the problem, then, the question of education was of maximum importance because on the one hand it would purify Catholicism of the pointless superstitions of the poorer classes, and on the other it would put the Catholics in a position to dialogue with the Anglican world, preparing itself in this way to undertake in civil society those roles which had once been reserved exclusively for the adherents of the State religion.

From what has been said, it is easy to understand that the role of the Catholic laity in civil society and within the Church was closely linked to the problem of education. The church authorities understood that the two problems were indissolubly linked. The immaturity of the times, however, led to the exaggeration of the disputes, and this explains the central motif which perhaps determined the failure of Catholic educational projects. The Holy See itself intervened in the matter;[202] through Cardinal Barnabò, who dealt with questions concerning the English Church, Rome asked Cardinal Wiseman to explain, and since he himself was perplexed by what had happened, he invited Newman to give due explanation. The future Cardinal replied with great ability, and in an outstanding spirit of obedience he gave a new dimension to the problem both of the laity and of Catholic education. This factor may be considered one of the many *coups de gràce* inflicted on liberal Catholicism, since from then onwards Newman became more cautious in his proposals, seeking to march in step with the intentions of the hierarchy. It was exactly at the moment when Cardinal Barnabò seemed about to open the enquiry that Newman began to think about writing his famous *Apologia.*

It would seem, however, that even this event is based on a doubt. Newman's educational project, which can be seen quite clearly in his ideas of a university, fits perfectly with the Catholic tradition, even though in its various disciplines it pays notable attention to the novelties of contemporary culture, and especially science. Newman wished to recover, while bringing up to date, the unitary motive of knowledge, the *ratio studiorum*, from which different forms of speculation depart. "This *ratio* consists in philosophy, or in liberal education, the basis of which is the conviction that knowledge is an organic whole, and that its various branches are partial aspects ... An order which should condition students to follow a purely scientific or purely literary course would dispose them towards a partial vision, and distortion of reality".[203] All wisdom descends in the end from unitary principles which constitute the *raison d'être* not only of science but of all existence.

Such an interpretation could not have found easy and happy acceptance in a world where, especially in the Anglo-Saxon cultural tradition, everything was directed towards the search for and realization of the criterion of utility. From many sides, Newman was accused of drawing up educational projects incapable of preparing students for their future professions, but he defended himself by "demonstrating that the immediate aim of the university is not professional competence but the total formation of the intelligence; in fact knowledge communicated in ordered, and almost hierarchical, form, sharpens and perfects the intellect … the education of the mind and the perfection of the intellect … such perfection is precisely what is called liberal education".[204] Education of this kind shows us yet again how all Newman's intentions were aimed at the discovery, and hence the pursuit, of the ultimate purpose of existence, without which, even in the illusions provided by the principle of utility which rules liberal society, one is wrecked on the rocks of time and loses the sense of transcendence, and hence of salvation.

It must also be said that "while professional ability does not constitute the immediate aim of the university, it is nonetheless true that the individual disciplines are not excluded from having their own role in the plan of studies, which must include the three great sectors of knowledge: theology, literature and physical sciences. The study of these disciplines certainly does not provide a *useful* preparation for the different professions … The student who is educated for his future tasks according to the liberal vision is, in parity of circumstances, much better prepared to undertake them that the one who is devoid of such preparation".[205] And this is because philosophy, which animates a type of study understood in this way, is in a position to realize a different development of the young student, by constructing a genuine spiritual habit. With this habit, the student can apply himself to all the various fields of knowledge with a sensitivity which the environment in which one studies, too, is capable of forming.

Newman knew (as indeed did Acton, who had experienced it in the first person) that apart from the Church and the family, the colleges were acquiring greater and greater weight as formative instruments. All possible attention and efforts must be concentrated on them, because while the cultural training came from the individual disciplines, it was from the environment in which they lived that the moral shaping which really distinguishes one human being from another derived. This "complete" education frees the young person "from degrading inclinations and vices and vulgar habits".[206] The characteristics which are the foundation of a true education – not only Catholic but typical, for different reasons, of a gentleman – are acquired in this way. There is no contradiction between education understood in the broad sense and education in a more strictly Catholic sense. The latter embraces the former, and indeed perfects and refines it still further.

"Newman is convinced that not only science, but also the conscience, is indispensable to the formation of humankind, and they must always be joined; the Catholic University, giving itself a truly Enlightened character, is meant to bring these two aspects into relation with each other".[207] Moreover (and Acton too was of this opinion) any Catholic educational institution must be concerned, over and above the technical preparation of the students, with their religious sensibilities or at least with the right degree of liberty, and in general with moral behaviour. Both Acton and Newman seem to anticipate some themes of personalism in our own recent century, for when speaking of pedagogical problems, they go well beyond the purely utilitarian sphere, and show the moment of responsibility which accompanies, and then follows, any serious cultural training. It would seem, however, that such a conviction, apart from anticipating some of the conclusions of twentieth-century Catholicism, is well-integrated into the Catholic tradition because it tends to lead one to become aware of the individual elements of one's own personality, and above all it tends to care in a special way for the ultimate aims of life, which are the point of witness and incitement held out to the weak and the doubtful. This personal encounter between different students, and between the latter and their teachers, must be seen as an aspect which characterizes Catholic education, because the efforts to create an alternative to that of the state collapsed completely.

Catholic education must be seen as a real *iter* of training for truth; a path to be undertaken in the refining of character and the development of the intellect. This teaching is still fundamental even today for those Catholic cultural bodies which, losing sight of their roots, are often merely a poor copy of state institutions.

10) Readings and reference points

Acton's readings and points of reference were very varied. Thanks to his long continental experience, he seemed to some to neglect English authors. Such critics, perhaps because of his prolonged stay in Germany, accused Acton of being too tied up with the Germanic cultural tradition, where "words like religion, faith, morals, ethics, phenomena, forces, are used in a strange sense".[208] If we add to this the weight of the historical studies then flourishing in Germany, we can see why Acton would have been regarded with suspicion. German historical analysis had given numerous ideas to Protestant circles, and even, by reflection, to some Catholic scholars. The Church authorities were therefore alarmed and, in Acton's case, the alarm was justified more by his relations with the Germanic environment than by his own particular statements. His cultural inheritance had indeed been enriched by the content of the various countries where he had lived, and the environments in which he had studied and the people he had met in various states. His political and philosophical thinking rested more, in reality, on firmly established reference points which ranged from France to North America and England to Italy. It should not be forgotten that he was born in Italy, and that he returned often to that country, especially during the 1860s.

Italy was for Acton the land which, with its wars at the time of the Renaissance, had seen the birth of the modern state,[209] and which, thanks to the thought of Machiavelli, had put the relations between the State and the Church in a new way. It was also in Italy, according to Acton, that the modern man, completely dedicated to creating for himself an independent conscience and judgement, had been born.[210] It was in Italy that the analysis of power was begun with Machiavelli. This analysis may at times have been negative because it eliminated morality from political life, extolling the political system, sometimes in obscure fashion[211] – and yet it was always analysis which confronted real humanity with those defects which a benevolent vision is not enough to cancel. For Acton, with this vision of power there began what could be defined as "the age of Machiavelli",[212] in which politics is seen above all as an observation of facts.

The birth of the modern notion of the management of society, to which the other great exponent of Italian historicism (Guicciardini) contributed considerably, is due to Machiavelli, who, for the first time, examined politics as a science of relations of strength,[213] and as a cause of change. The study of these relations of strength made politics intelligible, and analysable, and hence set it on its way towards models of participation unthinkable when it was wrapped in a metaphysical aura.

Politics, understood in the new way by Machiavelli, not only influenced the whole of European thought (take Hobbes, for example), but engaged the interest of every historical thinker in its process of development. Paradoxically it seems almost as if, for Acton, Machiavelli only apparently denied morality. In fact politics, being closely linked to the historical process reveals a species of "secular" morality in its stages of progress – a morality which is manifested in the progress of humankind. Machiavelli certainly did not think of a result of this kind, but the thinkers who "rehabilitated" him in the Romantic age were of this opinion. In thinking of such a hypothesis, Acton had in mind authors such as Fichte, for whom history, an expression of the relations of strength, is indivisible from a moral development of humankind.

To return to the Renaissance, we should remember that Acton, in stressing the need for historical and political sciences in Italy, seems almost to claim that in his opinion Catholicism has permeated Italian culture to such a point that the best products of the Renaissance are a natural consequence of it. The idea of historical progress belongs to the historical patrimony of the Church in a way no one can deny. "To refuse to the Church this character of progress is to deny the divinity of her Founder; and if we seek it anywhere else than in the order of truth which is subject to the immediate guidance of the Holy Ghost, we are contradicted alike by the holiness of the early ages, and by the most memorable lessons of later religious history".[214] The idea of progress is endemic in the actual eschatology of Christianity, and all historicist theories are indebted to it.

It is interesting that Acton, in this context, reached certain conclusions which Rosmini had reached some years earlier. For the Englishman too, the idea of progress was a launching-pad towards an unreachable target. Perfection appears, rather than a historical and verifiable end, as a path to be undertaken, and that path leads into a meta-historical perspective. The idea of progress, however, cannot be eliminated at any cost. "Progress is a necessity of her (the Church's) existence, and a law of her nature. She does not positively undergo it, but actively imposes it upon society. Whilst she continually and continuously develops her doctrines, and evolves truth from the inexhaustible tradition of the teaching of Our Lord, her action is the ever-present impulse, pattern and guide of society in the formation of law and in the advancement of learning".[215] The novelty of Christianity, from the historical point of view, is specifically this impulse, always present because God, who reveals himself through history, never completely satisfies humankind which always has in itself a sort of discontent which drives it to go on and on in the search of a perfection which history will never show as completed.

The progress of the human spirit shows, among other things, that the historical path clarifies certain truths, but at the same time broadens them so as to render them virtually inexhaustible. Every branch of learning, sooner or later, must face up to a religious problem. For this reason, the Church must follow the findings of modern science with care and attention. In fact, "all science may become tributary to religion".[216] There is in Acton the conviction that contemporary culture, despite the current incomprehensions, will reconcile itself with religion because the final intent for both is the search for truth. "A science", wrote Acton, "that for the sake of protecting faith, wavers and dissembles, in the pursuit of Knowledge (is an) instrument at least as well adapted to serve the cause of falsehood as to combat it".[217] Before the evidence of the truth we must surrender, and religion has everything to gain from this attempt.

We can now understand why Acton judges St Augustine to be the person who has exercised "the deepest influence of one mind in the Church".[218] It was the Bishop of Hippo, in fact, who first elaborated a philosophy of history. To him belongs the idea of a path towards the final return of Christ. This idea was little by little enriched; a basic contribution was made to it by St Thomas Aquinas. It is to his works and those of his contemporaries that we owe a new achievement: "The doctrine that prevailed was the divine right of the people to raise up and bring down princes".[219] With this possibility of resistance to a tyrant, the bases are laid for the theory of the conscience, which was to lighten up modern history with its ideas of liberty. This is why, in Acton's opinion, St Thomas "devised Whiggism to prop religious absolutism".[220] The discovery of conscience is in fact the presupposition of every manifestation of freedom, and as a consequence, the full revelation of the dignity of humankind which is founded and realized on the basis of freedom of conscience.

We can now very easily understand why history, when it shows real progress in the human spirit, which means for Acton a greater and greater awareness of conscience by the individual, is virtually a religious story, and the authors who examine it "are profoundly religious and are agreed that states lacking the secure foundation of a religious belief are doomed to destruction".[221] For Acton, one of these thinkers is Alexis de Tocqueville.

De Tocqueville not only warned against the dangers of the "omnipotence of a majority", but, like Burke, seems to have maintained that "liberty, too, must be limited in order to be possessed".[222] When the limits to liberty fail, liberty itself fails too, because when it becomes absolute, it is at an end. What must be done therefore is to establish a liberty within the law, without which arbitrariness rules. Another great merit of De Tocqueville

120

is "to detect that tendency towards absolutism inherent in a search for political equality".[223] This conviction was of the greatest importance for an aristocrat like Acton, who did not understand how liberty and equality could work together without one abdicating in favour of the other. The despotism of the majority, the ultimate goal of a search for equality driven to its extreme consequences, can also emerge thanks to the plebiscitary electoral system. The outcome of a popular vote can at times lead to the opposite result to what was expected by the people. One may cite, for example, the outcome of the presidential elections in France in 1848 which led to the victory of Napoleon III.[224]

It seems clear at this point that the presence of an aristocracy in political life becomes almost a natural and unalterable factor. "Society is not in process of modification, but of transformation":[225] a process of modification which may also lead to the substitution of certain aristocracies, but never to their elimination. De Tocqueville understood, according to Acton, not only the greatness – and one may also say the fragility – of freedom, but he saw the precautions which it implies, and the limits which it must meet with. Freedom and the individual cannot depend on the capricious will of the majority, because they come before all forms of politics, just as religion cannot be regulated by the state because it stands above it. And this is another motive which drove Acton to remain a Catholic, just because the universality of this religion placed it clearly above state religions such as Anglicanism.[226]

Apart from having spoken about what we might call the correctives to majority despotism (of which we shall have more to say when dealing with federalism, the truly great achievement of the American Revolution), De Tocqueville is also essential to Acton because he was "a Liberal of the purest breed, a liberal and nothing else, deeply suspicious of democracy, equality, centralization, utilitarianism":[227] a liberal who had caused further steps to be taken in the freedom of mankind. For him, as for Acton, "freedom of conscience is the root of self-government, individually and collectively, for both depend on moral responsibility. The cause of liberty is the cause of morality, of duty and rights, for its meaning is freedom of conscience".[228] It goes without saying that for Acton, *self-government* requires a moral growth which every other political manifestation ignores.

What Acton admired in De Tocqueville, apart from his actual thought, was his existential experience: the meeting between the European tradition and the attempt to order society according to new criteria linked to a breadth of territory and immensity of resources never before available. It is from this that Acton derives the special teachings of the French thinker. "Three of Tocqueville's ideas specially interested Acton: (1) the need to reconcile democracy and religion; (2) democracy leads to centralisation; (3) the idea, which Tocqueville made a corner stone, that nations that lack the self-governing force of religion are unfit for freedom".[229] Probably this last point is also due to Italian historicism which from Machiavelli onwards had stressed, even when at times it did not agree with it, the importance of religion as a brake on the degeneration of liberty. Religion, in fact, could put forward a series of "limiting ideas" within which human life should be regulated.

Alongside Tocqueville (and in addition to other French writers, among them Montesquieu who, according to Acton, "defined the theory of Constitutionalism",[230]) another central figure in the cultural shaping of Lord Acton was Edmund Burke. The latter was numbered among his teachers, along with Döllinger and Leibniz, because together with De Tocqueville, he was reputed to be a profoundly religious spirit who examined history in the concrete without losing himself in the abstractions of certain typical methodologies, for example German idealism. The religious belief and the concrete element that Acton encountered in Burke allowed him to take his distance from Hegelian historicism, for which he never had very much sympathy. "Hegel remained, in his eyes, the strongest of all enemies of religion; the guide of Tübingen in its aberrations, the reasoner whose abstract dialectics made a generation of clever men incapable of facing facts".[231] Convinced Catholic as he was, Acton could never accept that Hegel should reduce religion too within the sterile rigour of the dialectical method – removing from history any possible metaphysical perspective, which would have ended by creating in humankind an emptiness and pessimism with no way of escape. Because of this, Acton was, on the other hand, in favour of Leibniz whose optimism was not exclusively the product of a thought which succeeded in elaborating a theory about the best of possible worlds, but derived from his drawing close to the Catholic perspective on history. This actual approach allowed Leibniz to avoid falling into those errors towards which Protestantism (from which Leibniz himself emerged) was heading: "rationalism, pantheism, materialism, atheism"[232] – errors on which the German thought of the nineteenth century was to be based.

Finding a certain element of religious belief in the thought of Burke does not mean that Burke is in line with the Catholic way of seeing history, peculiar to Acton; quite the reverse, because the latter does not understand ethics as *expediency*, as Burke implies it to be.[233] This helps to explain why Burke was viewed in various ways by Acton during the course of the years,[234] passing from enthusiastic judgements to precise and detailed comments on his historical analysis. (We may mention, for instance, the interpretation given by Burke of the 1688 Revolution,[235] which Acton did not agree with).

In Acton's eyes, Burke had the undeniable merit of having found the genuine voice of the English tradition. This latter aspect was of considerable importance, because in Burke the tradition is quite closely linked to the "theory of continuity", which in turn comes from Leibniz. This is why Burke rejected what we call today the "theory of leaps" – i.e. revolutions. It also serves to explain the different opinions he held concerning the English and French Revolutions.[236] In England, in fact, the institutions survived and were reinforced by the Revolution, which only modified them and adapted them to their times. In France, on the other hand, the monarchy ended up destroyed, and from the democratic illusion the country passed to a real and genuine involution. Belief in tradition led Burke to theorize that constitutionalism too had its own genuine history, the roots of which lay in the mythical legislators of Greece, and then above all in the practical sense of Roman law, and from there slowly on to the juridical speculations of the modern world.[237] Among the latter, Burke, in Acton's opinion, was reminiscent of the ideas of Montesquieu who (and it was no coincidence), took as his main reference point the juridical experience of Rome, and English constitutionalism.

As well as stimulating Acton, Burke also posed several problems to him. One was that of harmonizing the idea of continuity with that of revolution, which Burke had not resolved in a satisfactory way. The same thing can be said of the principle of sovereignty and nation, which (even though Acton changes his stand from that of Burke), he re-elaborates in a personal way, closer to his needs as a liberal Catholic.

At the beginning of this section, I sought to show that the "Germanism" with which Acton was reproached, is partly irrelevant. A further proof of this can be drawn from the interest that Acton shows towards the thought of Leibniz, surely the most open of German thinkers towards problems raised outside Germany, and for this reason, perhaps the least Germanic. "The *lex continui* was a central idea"[238] of the thought of Leibniz, an idea which was well-adapted to the historical notions of Acton. "From Leibniz Acton also took the idea that history is the true demonstration of religion, that is, that slow but sure progress in the direction of liberty is the justification of God to man".[239] In Leibniz, Acton found the confirmation of one of his profound convictions - i.e. that the wisdom of God is manifested little by little in the progress of history, always in more complete fashion, but never in its entirety and definitive form. History, therefore, is in many ways the true demonstration of God and religion.

The "notion of continuity" so effectively expounded by Leibniz, led inevitably not only to an optimistic vision of history (and it could hardly be otherwise), but also to opposition to all atheistic visions of history itself.[240] As we can see, Acton, in terms of the philosophy of history, summarized the most serious elements from a theological standpoint that had come down to him from St Augustine to his own times.

In this context, it will suffice simply to mention a problem which was later to become central to Italian Catholic speculation in the twentieth century (in the work of Capograssi, for instance); a problem which Acton was to deal with more than once, though never tackling it specifically. The difference between authoritarianism and authority, or to be more precise, the value of the latter. "Authority is essentially an ethical term, but when separated from liberty it is nothing but force".[241] If we pause for a moment to consider the importance of that "when separated from liberty it is nothing", we can understand clearly how authority, deprived of that progressive improvement and ethical development, is nothing more than a mere imposition, which ignores every historical tradition and all its laws.

Returning to the "law of continuity" as expressed by Leibniz, it should be stressed that in the Western tradition, if Christian thought be excepted, right through the Enlightenment "we encounter a few dispersed and unsupported passages, suggesting advance towards perfection".[242] Leibniz is thus an exception, and even more so because he does not come from a Catholic tradition and environment. And yet the thought of Leibniz possessed an important novelty for modern man, i.e. that of harmonizing religious expectations with emerging scientific ideals. This novelty became a necessity for Acton, and he expressed it more and more clearly. "To us, in an age of science, it has become difficult to imagine Christianity without the attribute of development and the faculty of improving society as well as soul".[243] This idea would see great efforts made to render it acceptable, and very slowly it became part of the thinking of even the most conservative churchmen.

The theory of continuity places Leibniz in that same current of thought in which many other more or less liberal thinkers found themselves, among whom Burke can be numbered. The path towards perfection in fact implied an ever-increasing openness and comprehension towards the demands of freedom of the individual, and the rejection of any dangerous petrification of history. According to Acton, Leibniz anticipated the best of Hegel and Darwin,[244] since he did not see history only in terms of a sterile development of ideas which follow abstract and predetermined patterns, but neither did he see history as a cold and mechanical process of becoming which only depends on existing fact and knows no specific design. In order to be a real advance towards perfection, what must really be improved and make progress is the conscience of humankind. On this, in fact, liberty is founded when it is not just a "material" prospect (possibility of choice) but an interior dimension which allows the individual to take on board the best in what is traditional and project it into the future. This was the real teaching of Leibniz which genuine liberalism should make its own, if it did not want to risk becoming sclerotic by adopting a historicism which was devoid of meaning.

We have seen that according to Acton the best liberalism develops on the plane of conscience and morality. It will be important to explore this topic in order to see what points of contact and what points of conflict Acton shows with the English tradition. "The Christian notion of conscience imperatively demands a corresponding measure of personal liberty. The feeling of duty and responsibility to God is the only arbiter of a Christian's actions. With this, no human authority can be allowed to interfere. We are bound to extend to the utmost, and to guard from every encroachment, the sphere in which we can act in obedience to the sole voice of conscience, regardless of any other consideration".[245] This rather long but very specific quotation helps us to understand that the relations with English political thought would never succeed in being those of complete harmony. In fact his fellow-countrymen, since the beginning of the nineteenth century, even when they spoke of tolerance, excluded Catholics from its benefits.

It can be understood that for Acton, this point had to be broadened and revised. For him "it was seen that knowledge of good and evil was not the exclusive prerogative of states, nations or majority".[246] The personal belief of the individual must therefore always be safeguarded, whatever his religion might be. In this we can see a complete break with any state religion, or worse, submission to the State, as Hobbes and his followers advocated. Instead there was to be comprehension and closeness to Locke, for whom it could be said, "liberty means security for the rights of conscience".[247] Certainly Locke still did not think of extending tolerance to Catholicism, but in posing the problem he is considered by Acton to be the principal classic exponent of tolerance in a time when, after the success of Hobbes' theories, Machiavellianism reigned unchallenged.[248] The theory of tolerance had great difficulty in making itself accepted, showing that the moral growth of the individual is slow, exhausting and in no way easy.

Although Acton acknowledges that Locke has the merit of being the classical advocate of tolerance, he is not very enthusiastic about his thought in overall terms, judging it to be "always reasonable and sensible, but diluted, pedestrian and poor".[249] This statement, dictated perhaps by the "flat" moral thinking of Locke, clearly shows the difficult position which Acton held within the English cultural tradition. In the latter, Hobbes did not even deserve to be listed in an "intellectual history of the world in a hundred names";[250] Hume was considered the creator of a "philosophy of denial" (which would never enjoy success in religious circles), and Adam Smith and John Stuart Mill were considered "enemies of conscience".[251]

It is quite easy to understand at this point that despite his admiration for liberal ideas, Acton considered himself a stranger in his own land, and this was not because he did not "feel English" (he certainly felt more English than German or Italian or French), but because his education and faith were such as to make him feel a citizen of the world.

PART II

LORD ACTON'S POLITICAL THOUGHT

1) History in ethical perspective

Acton dedicated a great part of his intellectual and moral energy to history. Although he never embraced the deterministic theories and methods which had characterized a large part of the philosophical reflection of the nineteenth century, Acton is to be numbered in that illustrious tradition which runs from St Augustine to Leibniz, and which sees the spirit of salvation and freedom initiated by Christianity at work in the world. The vision is an optimistic one which, despite undeniable difficulties, sees the good seed bearing fruit amid the strangling weeds of discord.

Even in the English intellectual world, Lord Acton's reflections sometimes met with incomprehension, and if this is added to the misunderstandings he met with in the context of the Catholic hierarchy, it goes further to explain the isolation in which this Catholic scholar was forced to live. English historical analysis appeared indeed to Acton to be seriously backward, because it was isolated and thus incapable of taking on board all the novelties which in Italy and Germany especially, had caused historical studies to make notable progress. It was necessary, therefore, to tackle the study of methodologies which, even though they might often be debatable (e.g. Hegel's dialectical historicism) could nevertheless not be ignored, as a certain element in English historicism tended to do.

History, according to Acton, shows a constant: the unlimited exercise of power by the political structure "confuses the intellect" of politicians, and above all causes a progressive exhaustion of the moral sense among individuals, and causes the state to fall into tyrannies of various kinds, the worst of which are those in which the individual is oppressed by the multitude. "It is bad to be oppressed by a minority, but it is worse to be oppressed by a majority".[252] The majority, by virtue of its strength, can only be controlled where it meets up with limits which clearly determine its possibilities of action.

To justify this conviction, Acton did not limit himself only to listing various theories in support of his thesis: he made ample reference to the data of universal history. The crises in Athenian democracy and the Roman Republic[253] showed once and for all that where the power of a few or of a class becomes unlimited, the people are already living in a state of pure demagogy. Limitation is, for Acton, the very essence of a state of law. Where the concept of limitation fails, no guarantee or security remains to the individual, and he finds himself in a condition very close to that described by Hobbes as the "state of nature". Another motive cause of the isolation and incomprehension surrounding Acton may be hidden behind these considerations. In a century in which socialist and democratic theories flourished, Acton perceived the dangers which could arise from their degeneration. Totalitarianism was not just a phantom danger for him, but it was the logical conclusion of a procedure which sought to enable the state to exercise all its powers over the individual without the latter being able to find the possibility of opposing this modern Leviathan in the laws or in any other intermediary body.

We can now understand the importance of a moralistic historiography. For Acton, in fact, progress could never be a mechanical fact, but was the result of humanity's moral effort. Where this internal striving towards true liberty was lacking, it would be ridiculous to speak of progress. Because of this, Acton was intolerant towards all those historicist theories which considered humanity in overall terms or considered the human being as an abstract entity, as something which must be freed from all concrete experience. History cannot be approached with a predetermined scheme, because historical schemes are the greatest offence which can be done to individuality (in Acton we can in fact find a more or less concealed hostility towards all dialectical schemes). It was a matter of rejecting all pre-constituted histories which lead "to consider[ing] man only in the mass, as so much productive machinery".[254] This kind of interpretation was unacceptable in a Catholic view: "In fact, man, as a person, cannot be added to man; soul cannot be mixed with soul; each individual stands apart, or loses his individuality by addition".[255]

Historical schemes are the negation of the human will. Accepting them is equivalent to saying that the latter exists only in relative fashion, and also means rejecting any liberal vision of existence. Accepting them, in fact, means making the totality triumph over individuality; political power over human freedom. It is no chance that in the ideal of the State hypothesized by such historicist methods: "the power tends to expand indefinitely, and will transcend all barriers".[256] As Machiavelli, the theorist of the birth of the modern State, clearly showed, a State of this kind is driven to accept no limits of any kind.

Acton was deeply convinced that a prospect such as this had been reached, where modern scholars had forgotten the sacred element in humankind evidenced at the origins of Christianity. It was specifically this religion which had brought about a notable qualitative leap in the freedom of the ancient world, which, when it reached its highest points, had never succeeded in eliminating a huge number of injustices and distortions. It is the idea that the human soul is more sacred than the State which represents a turning point in the history of humanity,[257] above all because the soul in the Christian perspective is immortal, in contrast to governments and self-interests. "That is the root from which liberty of conscience was developed, and all other liberty needed to confine the sphere of power".[258]

In Western civilization, limits on political power had come above all from Christianity – and from the Church. Because of this "Acton profoundly believed that ... Catholic truth and human liberty did not conflict but were mutually dependent. Without an autonomous and international Church to counterbalance political power, he felt that constitutional liberties could never become genuinely secure".[259] It is probably for this reason that Acton looked forward to the loss of the temporal power on the part of the Popes, in order to make the Church into a supra-national entity capable of defending everywhere, and without arousing suspicions, the rights of the human person. ·

There was probably also a motive of a psychological kind which led Lord Acton to reject an over-rigid historicist vision. In rejecting the tyranny of the majority, he tended not only to defend the rights of the individual, but also and above all those of ethnic and religious minorities. For centuries now such had been the condition of the Catholics in Protestant countries and England. Acton feared that the acceptance of highly state-oriented historicist views would create considerable difficulties for the English Catholics, and would have forced them to feel estranged from their own native country for an even longer period. Because of this Acton rejected all the historicist views of the nineteenth century which saw the political sphere as the *reductio ad unum* of all human activity. For Acton man is not exclusively a political animal; he is something more. "Ethics includes politics".[260] If it were not so, if the individual were determined exclusively by his political behaviour, there would be a great risk of ending up very rapidly in the totalitarian dimension of power, because where the moral dimension is not upheld, only the play of power remains.

Power, in Acton's Christian perspective, also has an ethical dimension. It must in fact be at the service of the individual, who can only call himself truly free when, in his action, he is guaranteed by the power itself. "Liberty is not the power of doing what we like, but the right of being able to do what we ought".[261] The political power must guarantee this possibility. Where it fails, the moral dimension of historical growth also vanishes.

After what has been said, Acton's sympathy for the constitution which had emerged from the American Revolution can be understood; it was judged by him to be "the wisest and most perfect expression of liberal principles yet manifest on earth".[262] This was because the American constitution had succeeded in neutralizing even the possibility of an absolute power. The statement may seem paradoxical, but it suffices to consider the fact that, for Acton, an absolute power does not have to be the result of a monarchy or a tyranny, but can also be the simple expression of a democracy.[263] The latter in fact finds in certain particular mechanisms those limits and that possibility of functioning in the same way as a monarchy when it passes from the absolutist to the constitutional mode. Indeed, one could even say that according to Acton democracy tends more easily than monarchy to go beyond its own limits. What we need to emphasize here is that the merits of the American constitution are in fact those of having established in precise form how to avoid the risks of democratic degeneration.

The principal merit of the Founding Fathers of the USA was that of having saved the freedom of the minority by avoiding any despotic tendency on the part of the majority. The people of the United States have felt it to be a sacred duty to respect all religious convictions. Because of this, Acton openly champions the ideals of federalism, and often shows himself sceptical, or at least equivocal, towards democratic ideals. He often seems to adopt for himself the position of Hamilton, according to whom "the voice of the people may pass for the voice of God, but in reality it is not so. The people are turbulent and capricious: their judgement is very rarely wise".[264] It is no coincidence that Alexander Hamilton proposed to defend the rights of minorities against the oppressive force of majorities. It is this objective which has caused some to maintain that "the Constitution of the USA is essentially a compromise between the necessity of creating a republican government to keep the support of the people, and the desire to arm in advance against demagogy in order to retain the faith of the notables".[265] In this way, the Constitution would be the result of a synthesis between the theoretical element personified by men such as Hamilton, and the practical element emerging from political necessity, personified by individuals such as Jefferson.

In order to show that history is not a mechanical process, and even less an easy progress of the moral aspect, Acton notes that even those happy intuitions which brought the United States into being have experienced decadence, and then failed at the time of the Civil War, opening the way to a dangerous democratic tyranny.[266]

The setting up of a democratic tyranny is, for Acton, a consequence of a wrong theoretical interpretation of the historical problem. History, in fact, in the dialectic and positivist views of the nineteenth century, became a science capable of foreseeing the future of humankind.[267] Out of this arose a quite serious danger for the individual, i.e. that of falling into a deterministic vision of life which among other things leads to the individual with his will or spirituality being crushed by the anonymity of the mass. For Acton, the consequence is an over-summary interpretation of history, which is reduced to a mechanical science devoid of all moral significance. Other aspects of human behaviour, certainly not less important, such as "virtues, vices, and all transitory actions are excluded from his view; of course he has nothing to do with the question of the force on which they depend; hence he is quite right in eliminating free-will from his laws of civilisation".[268]

Anyone who accepts a historical interpretation of this kind thinks "of men not as persons but as machines".[269] There is an almost existentialist concern in Acton's thought, just as Kierkegaard seems to reject the obligations of a rigid necessity in order to make sure that subjectivity is safeguarded. There is the intention of freeing the conscience from deterministic schemes, reminding us, moreover, of a component of human life which cannot be overlooked. God speaks in the conscience of humankind[270] and for this reason, religion is the foundation of liberalism, and more simply of every expression of human freedom. We should remember at this point that even the ecclesiastical hierarchy, in Acton's view, despite having betrayed its mission by some twists in its history, finds its justification in the very fact that it is able to oppose every attempt at absolutism. We have only to think for a moment of how it proved capable of resisting the feudal hierarchy[271] or how it developed the theory of possible resistance to tyranny[272] – a theory on the basis of which modern political thought was developed.

Religion, as a guarantee of liberty and as a manifestation of the human will over and above all deterministic schemes, can only be, in Acton's view, one particular religion, in other words Catholicism. Not that this should be the only religion; indeed, true liberty "is only possible where the co-existence of different religions is admitted",[273] but he sees this faith as having in itself a particular feature which others do not. In fact it has the claim to be distinct from, and where necessary opposed to, the political dimension. In contrast, the Reformed religions, despite the fact that they were created specifically from the need to establish freedom of conscience, subsequently lapsed into that very intolerance of which they accused the Catholic religion. This happened because they were tied to political institutions, to the extent of being identified with them (for example Anglicanism, which ended by making the State the defender and propagator of a single faith).[274] True liberty of conscience and respect for the opinions of others are thus only possible in Catholicism, which by its nature is a more liberal structure. This is demonstrated by the fact that Protestantism, born from the need for liberty of conscience, not only became intolerant towards Catholicism, but even towards the more radical expressions of Protestantism itself.[275] The relations beteen Luther and Münzer testify to this.

The degeneration of the Reformation caused a considerable step backward in the European political systems, several of which actually lapsed into pre-Christian conditions. The sovereigns of the Reformed states raised the institution of monarchy to the level of installing a real theocracy, by means of which the supremacy of politics over religion, and thus over the Reformed Church as against the State, became total.[276] Even recourse to resistance, active or passive, to the sovereign, seemed to be set aside. "In this way, Protestantism became favourable at once to despotism and to revolution"[277] – two alternatives which were to characterize the future history of Europe.

The principle of tolerance was slow to emerge, and it triumphed only when the principle of liberty of conscience was recovered – in defence of which, in the seventeenth century, following the period of the Reformation, the great emigrations to North America began. These emigrants conceived religious freedom as an indispensable condition in founding their colonies, and from this presupposition the first modern constitution was born. One could almost say, perhaps without forcing Acton's hand too much, that *the foundation of the USA constitutes the natural continuation of European Renaissance history*, broken in Europe itself after the Reformation which brought about above all else the defeat of freedom of conscience – a freedom regained and defended, in contrast, by the colonists of North America.[278]

Europe, in contrast, was left with the inheritance of intolerance, which, even when it was defeated on the institutional plane after the birth of liberalism, still shone through very clearly in philosophy. What else, in fact, are the historicist methods devised in the last years of the eighteenth and early years of the nineteenth centuries? They are not only the attempt to lay the foundations of a new historical science – which Acton looked on with great interest – but they are also the claim to extend the concept of necessity from the natural world to the conscience of humankind.[279] This is absolutely pretentious, as well as being ridiculous, because human free will is not rigorously bound to fixed laws, but at times, being guaranteed by divine freedom[280] expresses itself creatively by self-determination, or by proposing new solutions.

This absolutely does not mean that human life is a constant and enduring improvisation, but it does mean that the concept of law and necessity conceived as it is understood in the world of physical nature cannot be applied in the spiritual world of mankind. Anyone who fails to make this distinction initiates a confusion[281] which is highly dangerous for the human species.

The possibility of reducing man to a machine of nature was revealed quite clearly in the theorists of the historical–dialectical method, and even more widely among the positivists – to such an extent that the latter sometimes admit (although clouding over their admission) that "the variations in human conduct are owing to causes of which we are ignorant".[282]

It can be deduced from this that history cannot be a mere list of data (births, deaths, marriages, commercial exchanges, prices, etc.) – though these certainly have their uses – but is something more profound, because man is not a mere exterior being and his history cannot be reduced uniquely to this.[283] It seems almost as if Acton proposed that alongside history, an invisible story should be perceived which nevertheless reveals itself in tangible form, just as human sentiments, even if they are not known to those looking merely at the surface, determine mankind's history to a substantial degree, have an influence on it and re-emerge from it.

2) Lex Continui

Leibniz is one of Acton's favourite authors because more than any other he was able to suggest to Acton himself two fundamental presuppositions, essential to his own reflections: 1) the real significance of toleration with the criterion of ecumenism, and 2) historical optimism, deriving from the faith that God himself accompanies humanity throughout history in its constant progress, which gradually reveals itself as more and more complete even though it can never reach the point of total and definitive fulfilment. The two above points must in fact be kept separate only for methodological reasons, because in Acton's work they are often connected to the point of one becoming the presupposition of the other. For example, when Acton assessed the Piedmontese attack against the Papal States in 1870 in positive terms, he certainly did not do so because he was pleased that the Church should be defeated, but because he thought that historical contingency would force the Pope to flee from Rome. Even in diplomatic circles there were at this time rumours that the Pope wished to take refuge in Germany. This fact was judged as quite positive by Acton, Döllinger and others, because it would have favoured a rapprochement between Catholics and Protestants. On the problem of the temporal power, too, Acton had few illusions: history had bestowed it; history could take it away. That power was not the essence of the Church. For centuries it had served to guarantee the independence and the survival of the Church. It had been necessary; now it no longer was. Historical progress was creating a series of international guarantees which would place the Church in a position to carry out its mission without a State. This, specifically because history does not proceed by leaps but constitutes a slow and toilsome path, had not been possible until the nineteenth century, but now the time was ripe.

In a letter to Simpson written in 1860, Acton had already confessed that he did not believe in the future of the temporal power.[284] This was such a firm conviction that Acton virtually cast himself on to the response of history over it.

It must be added, however, that at times Acton also admitted that the renunciation of the temporal power should take place on the basis of specific guarantees on the part of the State. He wrote quite plainly: "A free Church in a free state may substitute the temporal sovereignty as a guarantee of papal independence *only if the state can sufficiently ensure the freedom of the Church both against the government and against the people*... It may be true that this theory points in the direction which events are taking, but it does not seem practicable in Italy; governed by Piedmontese administrators under the Cavourian Statute".[285] We will have to return later to the judgement made by Acton about Cavour; what should be stressed here is that the freedom of the Church, despite the necessity that it should abandon the temporal power, cannot be defended by simple formulae. A problem of this kind could only be raised by a Catholic who, although a foreigner, knew Italy quite well. In fact, even though, as is logical, "the episcopate is national, the papacy is international, and hence the national guarantees which are sufficient for a bishop cannot be so for a Pope. For example, how could a free church in a free state assure the freedom of the relations of the Pope with catholics in a country that was at war with Italy?"[286] As can be seen, although he was saying that the time was ripe for the end of the temporal power, this did not mean that Acton did not suggest some guarantees capable of assuring the supra-national role which the Church had always played. Here too, as we can see, Acton seems almost to seek to eliminate the twists of history which not only make party differences more bitter, but render the path of human progress more tortuous.

History is seen as an inexorable path, a *lex continui* which presents its inevitable goals specifically because of the moral development of humanity. In this light, what interested Acton a good deal more than the end of the temporal power was that the Catholic religion should be reconciled with some of the already consolidated results of both culture and secular science.

This too was a necessary and unavoidable aim which could be postponed, but certainly not evaded. The essential fact of secular culture which had to be taken on board by the Church was the liberalism that had emerged from the English tradition. But it should be carefully noted that according to Acton, *liberalism too had everything to gain* if it were able to come to terms with the Catholic religion; it would in fact be purified from some of its exaggerations and would give maximal value to its own presuppositions, which have an undeniable religious root.

Acton returned to this argument on a number of occasions. For him it was a fixed point, and he expressed this clearly with statements like the following: "I think that there is a philosophy of politics to be derived from Catholicism on the one hand and from the principles of our constitution oh the other − a system as remote from the absolutism of one set of Catholics as from the doctrinaire constitutionalism of another [the *Correspondant,* etc.] I conceive it possible to appeal at one to the example and interest of the Church and to the true notion of the English constitution. I am not on this account an admirer either of all Catholic governments or of all constitutional governments, but I think that the true notion of a Christian State, and the true latent notion of the constitution coincide and complete each other".[287] This too was a goal which could not be renounced, but here too it was necessary to proceed by degrees, and every use of force would be counter-productive and deviant.

Catholic ideals were to make Acton's liberalism even fuller, though not immediately: he counted on the marriage between Catholic and liberal soon becoming indissoluble. It was only necessary, as Rosmini had already found, to have patience, because history has its own rhythms which should be respected as long as there was no wish to bring about revolutions which Acton rejected because they broke into the *lex continui* which gathers up tradition and projects it into the future. Because of this, I find myself in disagreement with Alatri when he says that the greatest contradiction in Acton lies in the fact that he "was from time to time, according to his individual attitudes, either liberal or Catholic".[288] It goes without saying that there was some difficulty in getting certain ideas across, and this was due, as in Rosmini's case, to historical contingency. But this does not mean, as Alatri holds, that "Catholicism and liberalism cannot find a real point of fusion; they start out in fact from two fundamentally different intuitions about life. Catholicism is by its nature transcendent, and heteronomous; liberalism, on the contrary, is immanentist and historicist".[289]

In principle, I see no objection to the schematic interpretation put forward, but the fact remains that Catholicism too, as it lives out its historical life, has its own kind of immanence, its tradition, its being-in-the-world, its future.

Certainly all this does not cancel out its bondage to the transcendent, its need for transcendence (which remains its particular mark), but this does not preclude Catholicism from welcoming on its earthly terrain the best contributions of human history, while permeating them with its ideal and its tradition. This has happened many times: think for example of the origins of Christianity, the era of the Church Fathers, and then that of the Scholastics – and everything seems to point to the fact that it can happen again. Moreover, all this is fully in line with the *lex continui*, or with that *path of perfection* which constitutes the fundamental structure of many liberal Catholics, such as Rosmini for one example. Patience is needed, because history has its own times, but no one could deny that with the Second Vatican Council and with the contribution of so many other Catholic thinkers of the twentieth century, many goals have been reached. This is the law of history, and it is not only liberalism which is historicist: Catholicism too has its own history which has known many conquests and many contributions to the progress of humanity, including that of civil society.

History, this sure path of humanity, is impregnated for Acton with the history of the Church; liberty itself, because it emerges from the tradition, is impregnated with catholicism. Acton repeats this idea frequently, when he states that "legislation ... must be identified with national character and life. On this depends development and freedom and progress, always in respect of tradition. But where a general or different law is imposed *on the people*... the consequence must be state absolutism... The people cannot administer a law which is not its own. This is the contrary of self-government, which does not derive from a law but from custom; is not learnt from books but from practice; is administered by the people itself, class by class and place by place".[290] How much of Montesquieu and Vico there is in this affirmation is clear, and it is yet another proof that for Acton, Catholicism, liberalism, tradition and progress were all elements which could not be separated out from each other.

3) *Inaugural Lecture on the Study of History*

The contribution made by Acton to historical studies in England was notable. With his cosmopolitan outlook, he was able to bring to history a vision which could be described as neither English nor continental, but universal[291] – universal in the way that he experienced his religion, which inspired him throughout his life. It should be said also that while history itself is the teacher of life, seen in a religious light it could also be for Acton a means of bringing his disciples to Christ.[292]

The influence which Acton exercised on his contemporaries in England was far from negligible. Above all, after he became a lecturer in modern history at Cambridge, his efforts to trace the basic lines of modern history and the attempt to identify their unity were the major contribution which he made to English historiography. To understand the fundamental aims which inspired the plan for the *Cambridge Modern History*, and in general the whole of his historical vision, the *Inaugural Lecture on the study of history* remains a document of crucial importance.[293]

Right from the opening words of this inaugural lecture, it is possible to trace the Leibnizian vision of the *lex continui*, which is one of the cornerstones of Acton's thought. History as a dense web of human fortunes is a fabric without gaps, and the structure of society, like that of nature, is continuous.[294] In the first statements we thus find a repetition of that ideal of progress without leaps and bounds, which had acquired so many adversaries in the Europe of the nineteenth century. In Acton, this conviction is not only dictated by a rejection of revolutionary ideologies, but it derives from his almost religious conviction that in history there are fixed points, constants which characterize it; everything else is extraneous. History constrains us to fixed well-established and constant points of view, and this frees us from everything which is temporary and transient.[295] This seems to mean that in analysing history, we must set aside that passion which indeed may guide us in political events, but which here, before the evidence of facts, is out of place. This is so true that for Acton, if politics and history interweave, they cannot, even so, be identified with one another.[296]

Despite the fact that history presents an undeniable continuity, in certain extraordinary epochs various elements exist which determine a breach with the past, or if we prefer, a quantum leap. To what extent these elements can be judged as valid is yet to be verified completely; however, the fact remains that without them, history would have had quite different rhythms. This is the case with the period of Renaissance humanism, which determined the passage from the mediaeval to the modern eras. The new epoch established a new order of things, under an innovative law, undermining the old realm of continuity. In those days Columbus revolutionized the notion of the world; Machiavelli freed the government of the binding force of law; Erasmus directed the course of pagan classical culture in Christian directions; Luther broke the chain of authority and tradition in its strongest link (elsewhere Acton pointed out how this attempt later produced contrary results); and Copernicus erected an invincible power that established the sign of progress for the future.[297] The same happened in the other fields of culture, and especially in philosophy.

It is important to point out that for Acton it was in fact a greater and more accurate study of history that allowed the quantum leap between the middle ages and the modern era. Not by chance, in the Italian Renaissance especially, the understanding of history as we understand it emerged.[298] It was in fact the historians of the sixteenth century who brought about a real renewal in the field of historical studies. If the past constituted an obstacle and a burden, the knowledge of the past was the surest means of its emancipation; and one of the marks which distinguishes the four centuries of which I am speaking from those before them is the greater seriousness and profundity shown in historiographical activity.[299] It is historical consciousness, the value of the past, which is the genuine sign of novelty in the modern epoch. The past can only appear as a sterile static picture to a distracted eye. The true renewal of ideas took place, according to Acton, above all where there was confrontation and dialogue. Tradition is a very rich instrument of confrontation, which makes us understand the validity and effectiveness of ideas, their strength and their importance. But above all, what counts most is that the study of history obliges us to emerge from a strictly nationalist viewpoint. The study of history leads us to see how ideas acquire the vogour to cross seas and frontiers, making the study of the course of events from a purely nationalist point of view a total impossibility. These ideas compel us to relive the existence of social worlds a good deal wider than our own and to live in company with heroes and saints and genii who cannot be the product of one single country.[300] History, in short, gives a vision of a superior world, more open and more comprehensive; it also makes us more humble.

Acton perhaps found himself unconsciously attracted by history because this discipline, in his view, required a human characteristic of a typically religious type: reflection, so near to the real spirit of meditation and of the examination of conscience. Reflection was not only a methodological datum, but also a human quality which made itself felt in an approach to the great figures of the past. Only the best and greatest spirits, in fact, offer examples worthy of reflection; a man of ordinary proportions or inferior nature does not know how to think beyond the restricted circle of his own ideas; he does not know how to raise himself above the titanic influence of time, of the race, of circumstance.[301] It is precisely contact with the greatest human experiences which shows the true pedagogical value of history, which makes it the teacher of life in that what we must bring out from the facts are the existential choices, the dramas of conscience, the interior turmoils and triumphs. These are the aspects that make history into a reality for us today. Only thus can we understand why it is the story, and almost the expression, of ourselves, the conscience of a life which is our life, of efforts which are still being made, under our very eyes, of problems which still impede humanity's passage and disturb the hearts of humankind.[302] The totality of modern history seems to Acton a "whole", an "all" which is divided up into a diversity of problems, which, however, all in all form the personality of modern man.

From this totality of experiences of modern history, however, two important aspects – surely the most important – emerge: religion and politics. These aspects on the practical level are divided up into the often dramatic relations between Church and State, on which a large part of history is centred. It is from the Protestant experience, which generated a religious despotism much stronger than the one it had sought to overthrow, and in general from all the political struggles which followed upon it, that he reached the conviction, which subsequently became a key element, that every human being demands of his own kind to be left free in the fulfilment of his duty towards God.[303] Religion reserves for itself and claims almost a sphere, within the human conscience, *where no earthly authority can or should enter*. The Reformed churches were incapable of realizing this intention because they descended to compromises, in order to consolidate their position, with the political authorities, but the political struggles against absolutism led, little by little, to the attainment of those results which Protestantism had generally failed to reach. The fact that interior and exterior liberty should have been first theorized and then guaranteed was, for Acton, an almost providential event, which demonstrated once again that there can be no liberty if it is not derived from religion.

If history is the path of liberty, it cannot be a mere exposition of what might be called "factuality". Liberty manifests itself in exterior terms, but it is first and foremost an interior condition. Alongside visible history, there is thus an invisible history in Acton's view, since liberty, like religion, cannot be uniquely reduced to what can be seen. In this light we can understand sayings such as "I hope that even this narrow and disedifying section of history will aid you to see that the action of Christ who is risen on mankind whom he redeemed fails not, but increases; that the wisdom of divine rule appears not in the perfection but in the improvement of the world; and that achieved liberty is the one ethical result that rests on the converging and combined conditions of advancing civilisation. Then you will understand what a famous philosopher said, that History is the true demonstration of Religion".[304] It will be well to remember that this position was not an isolated one in the Catholicism of the nineteenth century. That "perfecting" which is opposed to a "static" perfection is definitive, and is thus near to the theory of perfectibility which animates the whole political and philosophical thought of Rosmini, the determined – and unheeded – adversary of all nineteenth-century utopian theories.

A large number of revolutionary theories can also be described as utopian – not all of them, of course, because the American Revolution, for example, demonstrates some of the central elements for the understanding of the development of liberty. They can be termed utopian because they claim not only to break with history, but actually to repudiate it. But it is historical events themselves which take revenge on revolutionary thought. This is what happened, for instance, after the French Revolution. In Acton's opinion there is a curious paradox revealed there. The triumph of the revolutionaries wipes out the value of the historian. Through its true representatives, Jefferson and Sieyès, the revolution of the nineteenth century repudiated history: its followers renounced history, and were prepared to destroy its documents and sweep away its harmless scholars and teachers. Stranger still, this was not the ruin but the revival of history.[305]

History is thus considered as a discipline capable of updating the methodologies themselves. After the French Revolution, history thus underwent transformations in its methods of analysis and judgement, much as in the Renaissance a no less important transformation took place in the subtle minds of the Italians,[306] and the passage was made from chronicle to genuine history.

Since the Renaissance, however, history, like other disciplines, had been carrying along certain defects with it, which at times had resulted in harm to history itself. The most characteristic of these defects is the personal passion of the historian, which can prejudice the analysis of the facts. But history must avoid the opinions of those who are analysing it as far as possible; it must be based on documentation. By means of the greatest reserve, much self-control, an appropriate and determined impartiality; by means of the maximum caution in pronouncing condemnatory judgments, history could cease to be the subject of discussion and of controversy in order to become a tribunal accepted by all.[307] In order to achieve this intention, Acton realizes that men must be genuinely sincere and endowed with a strict morality – only on the basis of this can they express judgements.

This is certainly one of the most debated – and perhaps one of the most debatable – of Acton's convictions. In his opinion, it seems almost as if history must attain the same rigour as the physical sciences and mathematics, but history is a "humane science", and it is this which makes the aim of turning it into a "tribunal acceptable to all" a pious hope – and it could hardly be otherwise. This does not mean, however, that as a working hypothesis it cannot contribute to "purifying", as far as possible, the mind of the historian who, in the nature of things, carries with him a burden of passions, choices and values which must rightly guide him, and yet not influence his work. Acton, moreover, was convinced that the study of history too can be purified little by little, like all human activity in general. We only have to think of "his dream of a *History of Liberty*, in which he would have sought to explain the whole course of history by showing how progress towards an ever-increasingly established and organized liberty was the result of the religious and political struggles which have continued from the pagan era to the present day".[308] From this viewpoint (which also has a certain air of idealistic vision, thinking in particular of Fichte), along with the moral progress of the whole of humanity, it was perhaps logical for Acton to demand an increasing depersonalization on the part of scientists and scholars in general – and hence also of historians – of their own opinions. It is here that Acton's Catholic persona emerges most strongly, in the conviction that evil will always end by being unmasked.

This new manner of analysing history, even though it may appear utopian, could be facilitated by the fact that the historian is already a scholar who has more and more need of the collaboration of other disciplines. Above all, nineteenth-century historiography was enriched by contributions deriving from areas of research which in the past had always been considered separate from history.[309] Law transformed the simple data of the chronicle into an organic whole.

The economists derived a practical reason for the actions of mankind from the "flow of events". Even scientific discoveries gave a new meaning to the development of civilization. But what interested Acton most was the fact that from about 1820 onward, the theologians too had begun to remodel their doctrine according to that conception of development of which Newman had said much later that the theory of evolution was a confirmation.[310] History, and above all the way of interpreting it, was becoming an organic mosaic which gathered contributions from all the most diverse branches of learning.

History appears to Acton as a complex and multiform discipline, which can only and uniquely have real value if an effort is made to understand it in all its incredible riches, which, it should not be forgotten, are the riches of the human spirit. History, we should perhaps remind ourselves, apart from its exterior aspect (to examine which a large number of disciplines are needed), has its own interior force. It has its "soul", which cannot be set aside, otherwise not only will history not be understood, but it will even be betrayed. It is this concentration on interior motives which makes for the greatness of the historian. Acton is very clear on this point: the lack of a clear comprehension of the succession and significance of events, which would be fatal to a politician, is no less so to a student of history, who is a politician with his gaze directed at the past. Not to see anything but the insignificant superficiality of things, as we generally do, is to play with the study of history. We abandon ourselves in such a case to the curious tendency to pass over, and sometimes forget, what has been certainly noted in the past.[311] To set aside this latter element means making history merely into our own opinion, for what emerges is produced entirely by our own motivations, and not by those which have determined the facts.

The effort to understand the inner motivations of historical facts has only a cognitive value, but for Acton it satisfies the need to formulate historical moral judgements justly. Without such judgements, history would have little value for us, and would be deprived of lessons. In the *Inaugural Lecture* there is a statement which deserves to be stressed: "On such a propitious occasion a lecturer may well be tempted to recall some passed-over truth, some important proposition … I beseech you never to deprave your moral judgement and never to lower the level of your rectitude, to judge others according to the maxim which governs your own existence, and not allow a man or a cause to escape from the immortal punishment that history has the power to inflict on evil. A pretext for excusing the guilty can always be found. At every stage we meet with arguments which are meant to excuse, attenuate, confound virtue with vice, and place the just man and the reprobate on the same level".[312] This long quotation reveals the whole character of Acton. History is indeed a complex and multiform discipline which has a need of other branches of knowledge. But it cannot remain a pure intellectual curiosity or a simple manifestation of vanity. History is the path of civilization, it is our past soul; it must serve to improve us, to correct us. The character of this historiographical analysis may seem debatable, but for Acton it is a true examination of conscience that the historian must apply to the facts. How can one judge the importance of a Crusade, for instance, if one fails to penetrate the fervour of the individuals who left for it taking up the Cross after receiving Communion? Certainly there were other motives behind the Crusades, but they absolutely cannot cancel the crusading spirit which animated a whole epoch and which, if forgotten, leads us to misinterpret the facts. Examples of this kind recur in Acton.

Acton's essential preoccupation as a historian is that of not lowering the level of morality. Because of this, history cannot be judged only on the basis of its triumphs. If no other merit is seen than success, a winning cause cannot be bad, duration legitimizes everything, and all that exists is just and rational.[313] This affirmation appears to Acton to be somewhat too Machiavellian because it deprives historical judgement of moral content, and judges facts solely on the basis of the logic of outcomes, which are clearly positive only for the winners. This too may mean betraying history and only seeing it in one perspective.

A Catholic, or more generally a Christian, cannot in Acton's view refuse to discern a moral judgement on the basis of the values that animate and guide him. If, in our uncertainty, we may often err, it may be better at times to exceed in rigour than in indulgence, because in that way at least we will not be committing a wrong because of lack of principle.[314] This statement may seem excessive, but just as Acton rejects any pessimistic interpretation of history, he also rejects any mindless optimism which never wishes to see evil, or worse still, holds it to be necessary to historical development. "A Christian", Acton maintains, echoing the words of the theologian Morley, is on the contrary bound by his belief to see evil: he cannot renounce it. He sees it where it does not appear to others; his intuition is reinforced by God himself; his eye is penetrated in a supernatural way; he has a spiritual discernment and senses exercised for that end. He professes the doctrine of original sin, which places him naturally on guard against appearances, and upholds his intelligence in perplexity.[315]

This issue of original sin is essential if we wish to understand why this Catholic thinker could not fully accept all the dialectical, historicist and sociological theories of the nineteenth century. In these theories the conviction was met with, more or less clearly, that evil, having solely social roots, would be eliminated when its causes were eliminated by a change of society. In Acton's opinion, as in that of Rosmini before him, this is pure presumption. Evil, in the Christian interpretation, also has metaphysical causes, so that by changing society it may be little by little circumscribed, and perhaps also mitigated, but never completely eliminated. This is the real meaning of perfectibility. If this interpretation is not understood, there is a risk that evil will overtake us and enlarge itself with our more or less explicit consent.

Taking these premises into account, we can understand the last few phrases of the *Inaugural*, even though they may seem too dry and clear-cut. Everything can change, and in fact does change, in history: opinions, customs, even faiths, but the essence of the moral law is written on the tablets of eternity.[316] From this conviction comes his agreement with Burke's statement: My principles, independent of events and characters present or past, give me the possibility of forming historical judgements on men and actions, just as in private life. History teaches prudence, not principles. True political principles are a wide application of moral ones, and I do not admit nor will I admit others.[317] Here we have the adoption of a position which for many today is devoid of meaning. *But to understand it, it is necessary to remember that if evil also has a metaphysical cause, the moral principles which seek to combat it too cannot be derived from the contingent, the changeable, but on the contrary must have a metaphysical presupposition which is based, as Acton maintains, "on the tablets of eternity".*

Only by examining history with this precise intention can we succeed in making it into something living. History touches us in this way, directly; it is such a profound question of life or death that we are bound to find our own way through it and to be ourselves the artificers of our own personality we should look to the past with a critical moral sense, and to the future with a firm hope of better things.[318] This firm hope emanates from the vitality of history itself, and obliges us to be as far as possible impersonal, overcoming our own opinions and basing ourselves on those moral principles which are exclusive to us, and yet belong to the whole of humanity.

To ignore moral principles means for Acton to ignore the true value and the true greatness of history, but it also means to forget what is eternal in *us*. Just as history ends up by being almost an examination of conscience on the past, so the clear perception of moral principles constitutes a motive in us for advance and improvement. *Basically, we end by judging our own personal past by the same yardstick as we judge the past of humanity, and the same should be the case for our present.* If we want to be extremely consequential, then present and past are profoundly linked to each other and consequent upon each other. Here the Leibnizian *lex continui* re-appears, one of the cardinal points of Acton's thought; however, there is also the firm conviction that the Christian must live in the truth and not in duplicity. Let us keep this clearly in mind: if we lower our standard in history, we cannot keep it high in the State or in the Church.[319] These are the consistent words with which Acton ends the *Inaugural Lecture*, words which show us how our yardstick of judgement must also be our yardstick of action, but which show us above all how history is a means for gathering in the wisdom of the past so as to live it in the present "as the firm hope of better things".

4) History from the point of view of eternity

"*Tout est contemporain pour celui qui connait la notion de l'éternité*".[320] This saying of the mystic Saint-Martin was found among Acton's notes, and throws a clear light on what was meant by this English historian when he spoke of "the contemporary". History is our soul, our conscience, but – it has been said – it must be judged on the basis of valid and certain moral principles which do not change with the changing of opinions; indestructible principles, which make it possible to consider history in an objective way. "Morality is neutral in its procedure", says Acton.[321] For him, the stability of these moral principles constitutes the presence of eternity in the flow of time. The way in which certain phenomena appear may change, but the moral criteria inherent in them do not: conquests, mass wars, slavery, oppression of the poor by the rich, criminality, etc. – "all these manifestations of the abuse of man by man stood on the same level when considered from the moral point of view".[322] Anyone who is endowed with a minimum of moral sense can, according to Acton, discern over and above the mutations of time, the constants of an evil, which seem to have ways of appearing different, and yet are opposed to moral principles which are always the same. In Acton's work we find several repeats of a long list of crimes which run from the days of antiquity through the Middle Ages and right up to the modern era – an age which still knew the horrors of slavery in America and the serfdom in Russia. These phenomena, like the massacres of religious minorities, show in Acton's view the same lack of moral principles: respect for humankind is absent. To use the terminology of St Augustine, *amor sui* prevails over *Amor Dei*. Self-interest, egoism and other evils of a metaphysical nature prevail in certain people who end up by subjugating others and denying to these poor souls the most elementary human prerogatives. Liberty and the dignity of certain individuals is denied because the divine presence in every human being is set aside.

Abuses are possible only where certain conditions, or presuppositions, are not observed. Because of this, as has been rightly observed, there exist in Acton's view two species of politics and two species of history: the moral and the immoral, defined by him as "Machiavellian", despite the fact that "Acton was probably fascinated by Machiavelli. He could respect him for his honesty in being dishonest".[323] It is in this honesty in being dishonest that the greatness of Machiavelli resides; Acton also acknowledges his other merits, such as the birth of the national movement which was to give life to the ideas of unity, first in Italy and then in Germany – ideas thanks to which Machiavelli opened a new era.[324] But the most important thing is that after Machiavelli, history too must be considered in the light of Machiavellianism: i.e. considering the presence of a constant immorality which drives men to act by separating political action from moral principles in the public sphere. "This separation was the precondition to the abuse of man".[325] But there is yet more. If we carry Acton's analysis further, we may arrive at the affirmation that this separation leads the individual who puts it into practice to forget the eternal, because he forgets the moral principles which depend on it. The individual thus lapses into the finite, the contingent, the everyday, the temporal.

He ignores his own destiny; he persists in seeking perfection on earth. He eliminates from history all teleological content, all transcendence, and risks ending up either in pure chance or in the pursuit of immediate pleasure and nothing more. In this way we can understand why Acton considers *that the criterion of the contemporaneity of history is inextricably linked to that of progress.* Everything may be contemporary if based on immutable moral principles, but everything concurs in progress because it is all embraced within that perfectibility which will never exhaust its tensions in the dimension of time.

Paradoxically, the latter concept becomes clearer in Acton's work thanks to none other than Machiavelli. It is in fact on the Florentine writer's conception of typical human nature that the English scholar makes clear his concept of "perennial crisis", in which man will always be caught up. "Man is born to be respected; but he is at all times abused. In this contrast is born the crisis, the perennial crisis of man".[326] As Machiavelli had clearly stated, this crisis finds its cause in the very soul of mankind. By nature, this soul wanders in boredom, searching for the pleasing, the useful, the good, only to become weary immediately. In short, a soul which finds no more peace in itself, which can never find repose in actions whose results bring only momentary satisfaction. The analysis of history is to some extent the analysis of this given fact, like the analysis of ourselves, our examination of conscience and the search for the evil that is in us. It could be said at this point that even history, since Machiavelli, has discovered its own original sin. The original sin of man (discontent, selfishness, boredom, etc.) has become the sin of humanity, a sin from which only history which has eternity in its sights is capable of enabling us to emerge, progressively even though never completely.

It is certainly not a coincidence that in Machiavelli's own age there began that idea of the modern state which, with all its merits, nevertheless constitutes the egoistic fragmentation (thinking of *raison d'état)* of the great mediaeval idea which had sustained the *Respublica Christiana.* In terms of modern history, the state had become, for Acton, the main protagonist against the abuses of which it was essential to beware in order to avoid falling into the most absurd despotisms, which claim to remove everything from the individual – even his conscience, if that were possible. In this light, we can understand why Acton was afraid of over-democratic outcomes, which could limit the freedom of the individual with their demagoguery. The past – wars, revolutions, everything – must be judged with this measure in mind. This is why, just as Burke had done, Acton pointed out substantial differences between the English Revolution and that in France. Acton saw in the latter "the salient and fundamental factor in the modern development of Europe and the world, but he shows a particular hostility towards those revolutionary principles in which every threat to liberty is summed up, and every danger of absolutism on the part of the masses".[327] *Almost as if the revolution had reinforced the powers of the state only to go on then to weaken them.* This anxiety animated the whole of Acton's life and led him, often in isolation, to defend a position which appeared to many to be utopian. "In this sense, all his life was a single whole; all his interests were inspired by the determination to ensure, both in the Church and in the State, the recognition of principles over interests, of liberty over tyranny, of truth over all forms, however evasive and equivocal they might be, of falsehood".[328] *As can be seen, the sense of the eternal and the immutable embraces everything that is changeable, and contingent, and gives it a meaning which otherwise it would not have.*

With regard to this issue, what we can describe as the "theory of limitations" (to which we shall return in the next chapter) stands out as having great importance, constituting a genuine guarantee for individual liberties. The first limits are to be placed on the powers of the State, whether it be tyrannical or democratic, because it is in fact from the State that all the worst dangers for the individual come. Because of this, as we shall see, Acton proposed, following in the footsteps of Montesquieu and De Tocqueville, the vital enrichment of all those intermediary forms (often the expression of minorities) which give dynamic character to civil life. For this same reason, he was to show great appreciation of the local autonomies so clearly expressed in the American federal principle.

Acton's fear with regard to the powers of the State is also justified by historical reasons. Without ignoring the merits of the birth of the modern state, it can be shown that it, for example, took away from the Church that autonomy, sometimes also a spiritual autonomy, which is its basic characteristic. Rome at the time of the Renaissance can be said to have become a dependency of the ruling Italian princes (e.g. the Borgias)[329] first of all, and then of the European rulers. While there had first been an attempt by the Church to act as intermediary, and often even to manage political affairs, we now have the converse attempt, not entirely new either, to manage religious affairs with a political hand. The wars which took place in Italy during the whole of the sixteenth century can also be seen in this light.[330] Acton traces the logical consequences with extreme clarity and skill at producing a synthesis: "Italy passed out of general politicism, and was a force in Europe only through Rome. The Conclave, and the creation of Cardinals to compose the Conclave, made it a constant school of negotiation and intrigue for the best diplomacy in the world".[331] This aspect was to endure into our own times, and in Acton's view stood in the way of the spiritual force of the Church, still too closely anchored to an earthly vision; the same vision that characterized the birth of the modern state.

According to Acton, this state is the manifestation of the new state according to the conception put forward by Machiavelli. A state which allows no limitation because, in its search for success, it aims at eliminating every obstacle. Its power tends to expand infinitely, and to surpass every barrier, almost as if it were endowed with supernatural strength. From the Renaissance onward, the whole history of the Western countries can be seen as the strength of the individual exerted to preserve liberty, and to render it more secure and extend it, and above all to make it comprehensible to all in the hope of not allowing it ever to capitulate in the face of any power whatsoever.[332]

Liberty, just because it has transcendental roots, can succeed in limiting the power which may oppress it, and above all, as long as it succeeds in making itself a guarantee of this, it has infinite possibilities for development. The metaphysical riches from which it emerges are in fact inexhaustible, and it is certainly not true that for example in the Renaissance even from the naturalistic and logical standpoints, certain barriers collapsed which had existed since the beginning of civilization. Voyages became intercontinental, spaces widened, new and unknown lands presented themselves and the universe, which no longer had centres and boundaries, expanded prodigiously. Acton reminds his contemporaries, and he seems moved by the thought, of the first adventurous sailors, who left Europe behind them and discovered that the Ocean was no longer a boundary[333] but a world to explore.

Certainly, this conclusion may seem somewhat idyllic. But Acton was under no illusion; he knew perfectly well that even in the discovery of the New World selfishness, as well as nationalism and suppression, played a substantial part. It was, for example, the search for gold and other riches which spurred some of the European crowned heads to send missions to distant lands,[334] but this does not cancel the fact that soon afterwards, adventurous spirits in search of liberty were to head for these lands, and to undertake risky voyages almost as if they were heading for a promised land. From that same land there was to emerge a new spirit of freedom, with religious roots in no way contaminated, and for that reason capable of becoming a model for the whole continent. The American Revolution was to be the best product of this history of the New World.[335] And it was a revolution which came from the logic of things and fitted perfectly into that idea of the *lex continui* which is the guiding thread of Acton's work as a historian.

5) The political lessons of the Middle Ages

In preceding pages we have referred to the enormous importance which contemporary history has for Acton. However, for him it has to be viewed in the light of the Middle Ages, in the context of which it is possible to trace the essential and indispensable lines of modern political thought. The advent of Christianity, according to Acton, had in fact brought about that dualism between Church and State which is an authentic guarantee of freedom; a dualism which is clearly evidenced, and finds its theoretical rationale, in the Middle Ages above all.

More than this, however, as he stresses clearly in a letter dated 1861, society itself must also be distinguished from the state.[336] This means that after the advent of Christianity, the social dimension became something far wider than the ancient political dimension typical of the pagan world. The "political man" who ends up by identifying himself with the state does not completely fulfil the role of the human being who, on the contrary, finds in social life many ways of self-expression, ways which he seeks rightly to safeguard against a political power which can easily become too intrusive. To the mediaeval period, therefore, belongs the undeniable merit of reducing "all political authority within certain defined limits".[337] This idea was completely unknown to the Greek and Roman world.

From this it follows that for Acton, a genuine Christian state must first of all guarantee and ensure the liberty of the individual against any possible abuses of power on the part of the state. This was the main drift of the mediaeval theorists, and to ignore it means to abandon the wisdom of the times and of history – a wisdom on

161

which the genuine growth of the individual and of political institutions is based. Here too, the *lex continui* is also present, without which Acton cannot conceive even the political improvement of the structures of the state. "I cannot conceive a State in which reform should not be a normal condition of progress, that is of existence".[338]

For Acton, the Middle Ages also had another merit, that of producing the theory of the distinction between the two powers, and the distinction deriving from the cultural outcomes of these two powers. In other words, ecclesiastical culture was distinguished from secular culture. The latter certainly had its own autonomy, but this was not a polemical counterposition to the former.

Secular culture, in fact, served the Christian world for the pursuit of certain ends which the Church would not have been able to attain directly. "In politics as in science, the Church need not seek her own ends. She will obtain them if she encourages the pursuit of the ends of science, which are truth, and of the State, which are liberty".[339] The Church is thus again seen as a real guarantee of the liberty of the individual, who can count on it when the State oppresses him, or when science, denying truth, places itself at the service of power.

Even though historical contingency has not always maintained this principle over the centuries, it was always so strikingly clear on the theoretical plane that Acton had no hesitation in describing the political thinking of St Thomas Aquinas or Marsilius of Padua, (whatever their differences) as the true presupposition of liberal thought. "Aquinas was the first Whig. Marsilius founded government on consent".[340] The phenomenon of consent is in fact a logical consequence of the phenomenon of resistance, or dissent as we should put it today, which finds its *raison d'être* only in the Christian view of the world.

But it is also the diverse distinction of the laws, applied in the Middle Ages, which guarantees the individual against power, and creates the conditions to react against every abuse perpetrated by those who hold it. Here too, the great exposition of mediaeval thought culminates in the two great Italian thinkers named above – Thomas Aquinas and Marsilius of Padua. By examining these two writers with great rigour, one can perceive how in the former "all political authority is derived from popular suffrage, and all laws must be made by the people or their representatives". In the latter, "Laws derive their authority from the nation and are invalid without its assent. In obeying laws to which all men have agreed, all men in reality govern themselves".[341] In the best of mediaeval thought, Acton also finds the extremely modern distinction between authority and authoritarianism, a difference deriving from an erroneous way of understanding the law. The latter absolutely cannot be imposed *ex novo* on a people, but is the product of the centuries-long life of the people itself, which only in such circumstances feels that the law is its own, rather than something to be submitted to. This is yet another point which finds many echoes in modern thought, beginning early on with Montesquieu.

The link between law and tradition is of basic importance in Western culture, to such a degree that historicism itself has developed in its footsteps. The latter grew up as a need at the very beginning of the modern era, when the mediaeval world had brought the fruits of its thought to maturity in the Renaissance. There was a whole profusion of historical studies which took up the mediaeval tradition and tested it in the light of new methodologies. One example is that of Lorenzo Valla. He "applied scientific methods to ecclesiastical claims. He is the founder of freedom of speech in history. He is the first in the line of discoverers ... who have made history a science".[342] In fact it is on the idea of scientific knowledge that the new world is born. But it is born into continuity, enriching and giving new value to the best teachings of the Middle Ages, as another great Catholic scholar, Étienne Gilson, was to show, for very different reasons and in other sectors.

6) Liberalism, Catholicism and Democracy
(the notion of limitation)

Acton spent much thought on mediaeval and modern history because he saw emerging from them two aspects which should be reconciled and possibly also revitalized by liberalism. These two aspects were Catholicism and democracy. While he met with no small difficulty in establishing a close link between liberalism and Catholicism, especially in the circles of the ecclesiastical hierarchy, the difficulties encountered in realizing any kind of harmonious marriage between liberalism and democracy were even greater. Here it was not a matter of external difficulties, but of perplexities which Acton's cultural upbringing sometimes made even greater, and which he never succeeded in completely overcoming. For him, there is one unavoidable issue when it comes to politics: how to safeguard the interior being of man in the face of the overweening power of the State which often emerges in a disordered way from the logic of the majority? Hence there is a very basic concern: "how to save an element of freedom, in the new society in which the demands of democracy are so much felt?".[343] This corresponds to another concern: how to defend the principles of liberalism in the face of the new logic of the masses? To respond to this demand, we have to bear in mind that Acton's liberalism is of a historical kind, i.e. one which is founded on tradition and rejects all those revolutionary theories which, by the often illogical action of the masses, tend to cancel out the guarantees of liberty which the individual has so painstakingly acquired over the years. This is probably the reason why Acton appeared to some to be a conservative,[344] but it would certainly be doing him a great wrong to ignore this, his most fundamental concern.

Catholicism itself, in basic terms, has to accept democracy with limitations, if it wishes to safeguard that sphere of interior liberty from which all other liberties derive.[345] Keeping Church and State separate only makes sense if it is sought to safeguard freedom of conscience; otherwise it merely produces a sterile counterposition which becomes an end in itself. Both Church and State are structures which must serve human beings and not reduce them to their service. Their counterposition derives from the fact that neither of the two structures should leave the individual at the mercy of the other. This is the meaning of the expression in the Gospel: "Render unto Caesar the things that are Caesar's, and unto God the things that are God's". Only by keeping the two spheres distinct can absolutisms of every kind be avoided.[346] Distinction is, for Acton, a sense of limitation, and the unsurpassable limit is set where the interior being comes into play; where the human being establishes his or her relationship with God. To abolish this limit is to suppress the individual, and to annul centuries of history. It is to fall back into paganism which saw religion and politics as inextricably connected.

In Acton's thinking, the notion of "limitation" is one of the most essential achievements of Western culture: a "historical" achievement, in the sense that it can neither be imposed nor improvised because, like all real achievements of the human spirit, it needs a long and progressive gestation. Little by little as this limitation finds rational expression, it also becomes customary: law, a fundamental part of the "constitution" of a people. This is why the constitution itself is the product of history – so much so that it is true that "the machine of a free constitution is no simple thing, but as intricate and delicate as it is valuable ... A constitution made up of balanced powers must ever be a critical thing.[347] The constitution has in itself the wisdom of the ages during which a people has shown its worth, its defects, and hence its "limitations".

Mathew has rightly observed that if we begin with this consideration it is easy to understand the curious approach of

Acton towards the most notable French thinkers in the field of political reflection. They are undoubtedly esteemed for the depth of their analysis, but there is equally no doubt that certain over-radical tendencies often seem to irritate those who, like Acton, conceive tradition as a patient and toilsome path of construction and also of moral elevation. The vision of some thinkers – possibly too radical in character – is the true root of the most absurd examples of overbearingness and above all of intolerance. *To cancel tradition, and with it the sense of limitation, brings the collapse of all respect, because anything can then be imposed as long as there is the necessary force to will it.*

The anti-historical mentality is thus not combatted on the cultural plane but above all on the political one. It is in reality that the harms and contradictions of such thinking are seen immediately. It is in this light that, once again, we can understand the firm judgements of Acton about certain interpreters of the French Revolution. Earlier, in his German period, Acton had already learned to suspect those alleged historical tracts which, instead of showing a concern for scientific value, were inspired by the prevailing political logic, and had as their only end the gratification of the political powers that be. "From this it followed that a scholar disliking mythology and hating absolutism, must inevitably discount the body of writing tending to build up Napoleon's legend. To the myth of the Revolution, he was no friendlier. Acton could never tolerate that historical truth should be brought to serve the ends of politics".[348] If rigour and scientific precision is sought, then it is essential to set aside the passions which often explode dramatically in the political terrain, where there is no moral seriousness.

To be carried away by political passions is not only to forget the objectivity of facts, but more serious still, it is to fall into utopianism. Such, it seemed to Acton, were the real manias for equality, unity, nationality or socialism which had affected not a few thinkers of the nineteenth century. Possibly this notion may appear somewhat over-drastic to us today; however, the fact remains that according to Acton, these guiding ideas of the nineteenth century had become more myth than concrete possibililty, and where they were actually put into practice, they always produced results contrary to those expected, setting aside, always and everywhere, the fundamental values of the individual. Democratic ideals themselves, for instance, ended according to Acton in self-contradiction. In this case too, reference to the French Revolution is unavoidable: "The National Assembly did not see that its ecclesiastical policy violated the first principles of the Revolution. Toleration was disregarded".[349] There is here, and surely it should be noted, the same preoccupation that Burke showed in analysing the French Revolution, and in distinguishing it from the English one. The latter was for Acton the expression of a mature liberalism, and subsequent history had demonstrated this fully. On the contrary, the French Revolution had had "over-democratic" pretensions at certain moments, and these had failed above all because they were historically immature.

Here we have the fundamental difference between liberalism and democracy. While the former had a slow growth and development which began with the origins of the Christian era, and which had taken root slowly but profoundly throughout the Middle Ages and the modern era in the consciousness of certain peoples, the latter had a more recent tradition, and thus a more fragile one. Where tradition is weak, no conviction can be serious – not even liberalism which, even though it has such distant roots, has a less than admirable tradition, and thus a sometimes debatable outcome.

Given this consideration, it will not be difficult to understand the criticism which Acton directed at Italian liberalism as expressed by Cavour and his followers. The policy of a "free Church in a free State" seemed to him often to be mere artifice: "The Church has more to fear from political errors than from religious hatred. In a State without freedom, she is almost as much in danger from her friends as from her enemies".[350] In the Italian situation there was very often an incompatibility between the Piedmontese laws and the tradition of the Church, and this probably derived from the fact that the Piedmontese state, which then became the carrying structure of united Italy, did not have a long-standing liberal tradition which might possibly have allowed it to deal with the suppression of the temporal power in a different way.

If there had been some preliminary clarification between the State and the Church in Italy, neither of the two might have had anything to fear. In fact, in a state in which rights are sacred, the independence of the two "orders" is guaranteed, property is secure, the government does not usurp religious and social functions; the episcopate does not meet with obstacles in its religious action. In such a situation the survival of the State and the Church in independent form is possible.[351] But this was not the case with the State under the House of Savoy. "Piedmont was more remote than many foreign countries from the character of freedom. The spirit of her institutions was profoundly hostile to the Church".[352] All this happened because the liberalism of many Piedmontese politicians was "founded on those ideas of 1789 which are in irreconcilable opposition with liberty and with religion".[353]

These ideas are common to the majority of Italian liberals and to Cavour himself. The latter, however, unlike the others, possessed more ability and courage, and also succeeded in freeing himself more easily from passions, and thus attaining results which seemed barred to others. Cavour, however, seemed incapable of understanding the strength of liberty innate to Catholicism, but with a natural moderation which led him to reject extremes[354] he was even able to face the Roman question with an outcome which would be unthinkable for others. The fact remains, however, that the ideological hostility towards the Catholic world that existed in Cavour and in the politicians of his generation and the one that followed it, was to impede the complete acceptance of the united kingdom in the deepest level of many Italians, and would not make any easier an evenly-based distinction between the Church and the State. On the one side and the other there was a lack of trust, and the situation continued to grow sharper. For this reason it could be said that although Cavour "was not intentionally a persecutor, or consciously an enemy of religion",[355] his internal policy was, nevertheless, truly revolutionary as far as the Church was concerned. The Italian state, its liberalism, began life in this way without the consensus of what had been the only historical force of the country: its Catholicism.

What has been said of Italian liberalism could also be said of the French version, though for different reasons. The latter was certainly stronger at theoretical level than its Italian counterpart, but from a practical point of view it had been "polluted" by various democratic ideas, and later even by socialist ones. It was in fact the developments of the French Revolution that ensured that these differing political trends, especially the liberal and "democratic" currents, should become mixed with one another. The genuine character of liberalism had not had time to take root in the consciousness, and this explains many of the failures which took place during the nineteenth century in attempts to achieve a Republic. Too many forces had entered into conflict – forces incapable of finding a catalysing element while they failed to understand that the tyranny of the majority is the greatest of the ills of democracy. The only remedy for this ill, in Acton's view, lay in the representative principle considered as a limitation, the suppression of which causes a degeneracy of democracy.[356] This is why (naturally, as a good Englishman) he defended the monarchy which, justly limited and controlled, is one of the great forces of tradition, capable of guaranteeing liberty. We should note carefully, though – a *limited* monarchy, which finds its tradition in the history of a people; otherwise what is it but an extraneous element which rapidly degenerates? In France this principle had been broken by the Revolution, which had led to a great deal of confusion. The monarchist, liberal, democratic, socialist (etc.) ideals clashed with each other, not being able to find any way of coexistence. The French intellectual who sums them all up and confounds them is in Acton's view, *par excellence* Sieyès – and it is by no means a coincidence that he is one of the most genuinely revolutionary spirits.

Monarchy, as typified by the English experience, is the form of government which has by now made the idea of limits into part of its nature. This idea, according to Acton, indispensable to any form of government, is particularly necessary in democracies[357] where the idea of liberty is practically made absolute. On the contrary, "liberty alone demands for its realization the limitation of the public authority, for liberty is the only object which benefits all alike, and provokes no sincere opposition".[358]

Without seeking to indulge in word-play, given the fact that all are agreed on liberty, it is necessary that it should be limited if we seek to safeguard it: limited among the governed, who must either have a notable sense of responsibility in exercising something like self-government, or must be aided by the laws in protecting their own liberty from its abuses. This is why "it is supremely necessary in a democracy to protect the people against itself".[359] But in addition to being limited among the governed, liberty must also be carefully circumscribed and specified as far as the governing minority is concerned, for otherwise they may abuse it in an even more dangerous way: "Government is limited by reason and ethics. The unwritten law reigns supreme over the municipal law".[360] Perhaps it should be noted that this *unwritten law* (which speaks in the conscience of humankind, and is dictated by those "immutable" principles which then, in the course of history, give rise to tradition) becomes the indispensable precondition from which all positive laws must derive. Wherever this unwritten law is set aside, a revolutionary climate prevails, because the wisdom of tradition is denied. The only possible consequence is produced by absolutism, whether it be tyrannical or democratic – for absolutism it always is.

It is easier to understand now why in Acton's thought, which assumes some suggestions from St Augustine in this context, the form of a legitimate government is of little importance. In order to be legitimate, government must be self-government, based on individual and collective moral responsibility. He stated clearly, in an article that appeared in the *Rambler* in May 1861, that it was not the form of government which mattered so much, because if this is devoid of the legitimacy mentioned above, it can rest in the hands of an individual or of the many. [361]For this reason, it could be said that a legitimate government, which always contains within itself a form of self-government, "requires certain conditions: long and arduous experience, a rampart of tried conviction and accumulated knowledge, a fair level of general morality, education, courage, self-restraint".[362] It is clear that such a government certainly cannot be improvised, and even less can the precise limitations which characterize it and make it vital be improvised.

Wherever these limitations are present and are respected, there is a state and a constitution which are related to the timeless moral principles which animate the life of a people. By this means, all forms of particularism are eliminated – forms which in government are always the product of extemporizing, in the sense that they appear from time to time, according to circumstances. But when these expedients of the moment are given in to, then it means that the moral principles have been set aside. "On the contrary, the object of a constitution is not to confirm the predominance of any interest, but to prevent it".[363] In order to ensure that interests and particularisms are eliminated, there is only one remedy, and that is to divide and limit power.

In the division or even the multiplication of the sources of authority, there is the possibility of founding a sound government.[364] In Acton there is a constant preoccupation with reducing the sphere of influence of the central power. Like De Tocqueville, he considered the development of all those intermediary bodies which make civil society richer and more vital as essential to a "democratic" state. In his work we always find the fear that the individual may be crushed either by the demagogy of the majority or by the anonymous operation of the bureaucracy. It is necessary, therefore, to fragment and weaken all those forces which can bring about a crisis in the free growth of consciences and their realization.

The various forms of autonomy are an instrument capable of allowing for the realization of the finest capacities of the individual: however, there is something more. According to Acton, the autonomous elements, "by multiplying the number of authorities", increase the possibilities of participation in which liberty finds its true concrete realization. The political system which best succeeds in achieving this multiplication of sources of authority is the federal system. It succeeds in attaining the genuine division of powers, something which democracies only achieve with difficulty, if at all. It should not be forgotten that for Acton, "liberty depends on the division of power. Democracy tends to unity of power".[365] In order to understand this statement, we need to bear in mind two considerations. The first is that

Acton had seen the genuine division of power as being theorized by the federalists (more of this in the next section) during and after the American Revolution. The second is that *when Acton speaks of democracy he has in mind above all the type theorized by the revolutionaries, or by the theorists of mass movements*. So when he says that democracy tends towards the unity of power, he is speaking of a particular type of unity, which in Platonic terms we might call 'monolithic', differing from that articulated unity proper to federalism which appeals to the most genuine liberal principles. In other words, Acton seems to foresee those problems which were later to make for rigidity in *what today we refer to as "popular democracies"* : states in which everything which is not strictly political is sacrificed to unity.

The problem, moreover, is not new in the Western world, since it can be traced even in the political thought of the ancients.[366] In this light, we can understand how the federal system may become the most natural form of control of a democracy, one which prevents democracy from becoming a "tyranny of the majority". Put in other terms, the federal system constitutes a limit beyond which a democracy, in Acton's view, may not pass if it wishes to avoid degeneration.

Any other discussion of democracy appears to him devoid of meaning. "Democracy claims to be not only supreme, without authority above, but absolute, without independence below".[367] There is always the concern that behind the screen of democracy, the most acute injustices against the individual may be lurking. Thus it is absolutely not enough simply to distinguish the English liberal-democratic tradition from the French one, but it is necessary to show the elements which not only distinguish them in their historic assumptions (in which Acton agrees, as we have seen, with Burke), but also in their present institutional characteristics. One primary and indispensable element has been provided by the freedom of the press. "The Whig system required that public opinion should control legislation. That could not be done without the liberty of the Press, and the Press was not free while it was forbidden to publish and to discuss the debates of Parliament".[368] This statement, taken from Acton's essay on "The Hanoverian

Settlement", stresses once again that at the basis of any authentic democracy, there must be the most elementary and fundamental premises of liberalism.

There are also other elements to ensure that a system is really democratic. "In a Christian democracy, the guarantees and constituent elements are universal suffrage, popular education, national representation, ministerial responsibility, a second chamber, equality before the Law, freedom of the Press".[369] It may be necessary to stress two aspects, among all these other elements, because they probably seem the least obvious. *Equality before the Law* stresses an equality which is strongly differentiated from all the utopian theories which had made equality into a standard for social planning. It goes without saying that Acton is decidedly against any form of levelling which intimately threatens individual liberty. The second aspect derives from the first: By the term *a Second Chamber* Acton wishes to show how a certain social differentiation must be institutionalized. It is a matter of giving a political system a further element of stability. Two chambers avoid hasty or improvised decisions. They guarantee greater reflection on the decisions that must be taken. In short, they aid the system to change with fewer sudden leaps, and in continuity.

When Acton speaks of *a Christian democracy*, we may understand this as meaning a possible democracy, to distinguish it from those of a utopian stamp. The latter may be admirable in theory, but they have no possibility of a practical realization. Taking up an old saying of Tacitus, Acton is of the opinion that "however admirable in theory, it was difficult to establish and impossible to maintain".[370] We must stress that in Acton's thinking, *the utopian is different from the ideal*; the former teaches perfectionism while the latter teaches perfectibility. "Ideals in politics are never realized, but the pursuit of them determines history".[371] A toilsome path towards an unrealizable ideal, but a safe path because it is based on the moral strength of mankind, which tends towards self-improvement.

Acton saw *Christian democracy* as being opposed by the *democracy of the Caesars:* the kind that had emerged, and not by mere chance, from France because of the varied intentions of its revolution. We should be quite clear that *Acton was not totally critical of the French Revolution*. In his understanding, the latter had had genuine liberal intentions. Its purpose was that of weakening the central authority and decentralizing power itself. But in contrast to its English counterpart, the French Revolution had been "wrecked" during its subsequent developments – when, in fact, the revolution passed from demands relating to liberty to those relating to equality, and from the decentralization and redistribution of power to the idea of redistribution of property; from liberal intentions to democratic ones, with the first faint signs of socialism.[372] In this way the *Grand Peur* had spread, and an unprecedented insecurity followed, which led a substantial majority to accept the Napoleonic outcome, the *"democracy of the Caesars"*, (though in fact in using this terminology, Acton was referring more particularly to the actions of Napoleon III). Behind these notions, we should stress, there lies the fact that while for Acton the problem of limitations is fundamental for any political system, it is above all so for a democracy which, without limitations, is quite unthinkable.

In Acton's view democracy also risks another grave responsibility: that of *tempting the individual to become irresponsible* in a system in which mass ideals, collectivism and anonymity tend to suffocate personal responsibility.[373] This conviction may be described as a constant in Acton's political thought, despite the fact that in his later years he did draw closer to the democratic ideal. In the last twenty years of his existence, democracy had made a number of steps forward, so that it seemed to Acton that democratic theories and conceptions were accumulating the experience of the many errors committed during the course of the century. *In short, democracy was heading towards maturity.*

It should not be forgotten that it was towards the end of the last century that the first revisionist critiques of socialism began to be made by socialists themselves. The over-exaggerated egalitarian criteria came to be regarded as impracticable – even though sometimes only for tactical reasons – by various theorists. But in reality there was another reason that urged Acton to draw closer to democratic ideals: the notable institutional developments which these ideals had undergone in Britain, France and America. Despite all this, and even though democracy itself was viewed more and more favourably by Acton, the fact remains that he believed that *if it were to function properly it could not ignore the importance of personal responsibility.* This was the foundation on which not only the basis of a civil government must be laid, but also the moral conscience of the individual must be formed.

This makes it clear why Acton thought: "democracy means conscience, but to be effective there must be constitutional safeguards to secure the supremacy of those tested convictions which rest on experience and certain knowledge".[374] This reference to the constitutional safeguards is of the greatest importance, because it not only refers us to the certainty of Law, but also to the fact that Law is the product of the conscience of a people in its historical growth. Law understood in this way keeps all demagogical tendencies at a distance. Moreover, Law of this kind also guarantees the organic unity of the state, because the roots which are buried deep in the past are not set aside, nor are the historical wisdom and the will to grow and develop, which have meaning and prospects only if they rest on that same wisdom. Acton has an awareness akin to that of Vico of why, in democracy, law should be seen as the opportunity to rationalize history and make it present and vital. And more: law is to be seen as the supreme guarantee for the growth of a people and the effective bulwark against lapsing into irrationality. Law exemplifies and *codifies the concept of limitations, without which the fragile barrier between the rational and the irrational will be constantly broken down*, with the gravest possible dangers, probably not even reparable, not only for freedom but also for individual security. This is why liberalism is, for Acton, in essence Christian; it is also why, in a somewhat Augustinian perspective, he is led to accept any political system from constitutional monarchy to democracy, as long as there is a concrete respect for the human being.

The political system which seeks to give this concrete respect to the human individual must take account, in everything that it does, or in anything which occurs, not only of the appearance, what is displayed, what can be seen – *the outside* – but also of what is interior – the inside. And it is the latter which must be particularly respected, because it is more fragile, even though it is also more important. Again in an Augustinian perspective, the idea develops through Acton's thought that alongside visible history there is also an invisible history, and the same thing applies to politics. Neither of these two perspectives can be ignored without a profound imbalance. "Since history had this double aspect, it followed that either aspect was incomplete without its contrary to balance it".[375]

It was of the greatest importance to stress this interior aspect of history and politics, because amid the welter of dialectical viewpoints, it was essential to give human activity the possibility of escaping from the rigid determinism into which too many philosophies of history had fallen. "Interiority" here is not in fact the Hegelian idea that one falls into reality and then carries on dialectic with it. "Interiority" in this case is the soul of the individual which struggles, chooses and is often silent; lives in concealment but does not disappear from history for that reason. Invisible crosses, sufferings of all kinds, all concur to make the path of man more human, and to imprint on history rhythms which are barely discernible to those who observe apparent reality but which, sooner or later, will break out visibly before all.

The interior quality of facts has another value for Acton: that of binding together events of history which otherwise of themselves would seem to be nothing but simple accident. It should not be forgotten that apart from dialectical and deterministic interpretations, history was also seen from a positivist standpoint in the second half of the nineteenth century. "History, in the positivist's eyes, is conceived of as a series of isolated facts which exist, in their own right, in a world entirely separate from that of the historian. Mind and nature are two separate entities. The possibility of interaction between them is excluded".[376]

On the contrary, the interaction between the interior and exterior facets is a given fact for Acton, essential if we wish to understand history, and above all if we wish to save the possibility of the moral growth of the individual. In opposition to positivism, the English historian's spirit resumes some of the criticisms that were made of the characteristic thought of the Enlightenment. Both these philosophical positions, though for different reasons, had failed to understand the real value of history.

The romantics, too, although they had ascribed an enormous importance to history and politics, had committed another type of error. They had lowered human action to an "earthly-historical" level, forgetting that all that happens also possesses a "*non-historical level*, without understanding which, the essence of history is missed. "It was precisely on this basis that Acton signified his disagreement with Hegel, the archpriest of *Romantik*. If, with Hegel – he wrote – we considered history as all reason, as the expansion of reason, we should probably be tempted to ignore evil and to deny morality".[377] The law of "all that is rational is real" absolutely did not convince Acton; the interior aspect is not always obvious, but it is no less important and real for that.

Beginning with the interior aspect of man, two poles develop which are always present in any examination of his actions, above all, his political actions: extreme pessimism (typical of the observations made by Machiavelli and his followers), and a weighty optimism (the attitude of those who see political action as not an end in itself). But it is in any case from the interior aspect that one must begin, because in this the individual fights his personal battle which leads him to choose good or evil in all their possible manifestations. It goes without saying that the most admirable person is the one who, having made a moral choice, upholds it even at the price of his own blood.[378] For such a person, human life is "a Sacred Area", and no one will ever have the courage to condemn a human being who goes to the point of death in defending it.

Personal convictions based on an agonizing moral choice *have no equal as a value:* there is nothing that is worth more in the whole of history. For this reason, it could be said that the dissident and the martyr are the highest expressions of the human spirit. They are the individuals most worthy of praise, those who by their example make possible the liberty of all. And once more, for this reason *there is no liberalism which cannot be called 'Christian', because the first and most important liberty is that of conscience, on which all the others are based.*

In addition to all that has been said so far, we have to make a further important distinction. Politics, like history, is to be seen from a liberal perspective and in an ethical dimension. However, anyone who might be tempted to equate this interpretation by Acton with Hegel's "ethical moment", or in general with the ethics of the Romantic perspective, would be making a grave error. Even though Acton acknowledges more than a few merits to the latter, he ends by keeping a substantial distance from it. Acton's ethical principles are – it has been said – written for ever in the conscience of the individual, even if the way they are manifested changes in time. *Their essence lies not in becoming, but in the effort that every individual makes to live by them.* The moral life is thus realized with the attempt by each individual to live up to the moral principles. For this reason we must beware of speaking of morality of a people in which, on the contrary, "anti-moral tendencies could have free play"[379] if there is no effort on the part of all, individually, to live by the moral principles.

The idea of a general morality, of a degree of morality already attained, could conceal the greatest absurdities if examined on a plane of genuine moral rigour.

If care is not taken, democracies too may incur this risk. Their motto of "*vox populi vox dei* was usually regarded by Acton with aversion".[380] What the people suppport is not always just and moral. We should be quite clear: Acton does not demand that government should be against the people. He only demands that majority decisions, an essential principle of all democratic life, should not be declared superior to the conscience of the individual. What is necessary is to choose between a form of democracy which respects minorities and individuals, and another form that oppresses them from a purely demagogic perspective which only possesses the name of democracy.

Liberty should be the supreme aim of every political system, and the first concern of a state must be that of educating individuals to respect it, and of creating instruments which will be designed to make it respected. Only if it chooses this mode can a democracy say that it has chosen the track marked out by liberalism, which in turn has chosen that marked out by Catholicism. Alone neither liberalism nor Catholicism can say that they are true,[381] because they need mutual integration and both must be maintained in a democracy which seeks truly to improve humanity. The explanation of what has been said probably lies in the fact that Acton holds Catholicism to be the custodian of those moral principles written in the conscience for all time, and liberalism to be the instrument capable of defending them against any assault, and spreading them through all cultures. Liberalism must, if it seeks to carry out its task, ensure that the sphere of the moral principles typical of the individual, which is expressed religiously in individuality, are extended into the public and collective sphere; i.e. that they inform and inspire the whole of political life. "Political" is understood here in the broadest sense, as a Christian may understand it.

At this point we may also understand why Acton fears that the future development of democracy may supplant liberal and Catholic ideals. On this path, democracy would, he believed, renegue on itself, and on all the efforts made to build it. Acton takes up a good deal of De Tocqueville's argument on this score, for he shared with him a fear of the dangers of a tyranny of the majority. But he goes further. He fears that in such a perspective, new dictatorships may appear which, supported by a suitably manipulated public opinion, could give birth to great military systems uniquely capable of denying the moral effort of whole generations. *Catholicism and liberalism are thus not, in Acton's thinking, the reactionary dream of a return to antiquity, but the roots of democracy and its limitations. If they are suppressed then there is no longer any democratic vitality left.*

7) Federalism

Another guarantee of democratic life needs separate treatment: another principle which might be judged to be a further limit on the unchecked development of democracy: federalism. "Federalism, in Acton's view, is the necessary safeguard in a democracy, otherwise democracy will be corrupted by its own possession of unlimited power. In practice, the division of power, which is what federalism means, is the supreme political principle".[382] This supreme principle not only guarantees administrative decentralization, and thus a greater participation in the management of power, but it also guarantees that democracy will not degenerate, or create any kind of a totalitarian system.

Federalism brings with it the habit of participation in the management of power; it helps people to feel the political institutions as something of their own; in short it develops the sense of self-government. The federalist idea, always present in Acton's thinking, which was a form of institution capable of defending minorities, developed more and more organically after his journey to the United States. Here, its value could be experienced to the full. "The true natural check on absolute democracy is the federal system, which limits the central government by the powers reserved, and the state governments by the powers they have ceded. It is the immortal tribute of America to political science".[383] Federalism thus appears to Acton as one of the greatest attainments of humanity.

Over and beyond his travels in Europe, his journey to the USA is of fundamental importance if we seek to understand the personality of Acton and the formation of his outlook. Apart from anything else, this journey, as well as enabling him to sample the federalist experience at first hand, was made almost immediately after another journey – the trip to Russia. The latter was also a truly first-hand experience because in Moscow itself Acton had contested that absolutist system for which he had declared himself to have an undying hatred.[384] "It is better, said Acton, to be citizen of a humble republic in the Alps, than a subject of the superb autocracy which overshadows half of Europe and of Asia".[385] The federalist idea, according to Acton, could not in fact come from a continent, such as Asia, which had only been marginally affected by Christianity. As we can deduce, federalism was also one of the most mature products of the Christian tradition, and it is certainly no accident that it was expressed in a land, North America, which had welcomed all the exiles, mostly for religious reasons, from the English revolution.

"Hamilton's *Federalist* is the textbook of Conservative Democracy":[386] by the term "conservative" we have to understand all the basic characteristics which found, and maintain, and "conserve" a democracy. It has rightly been said, with regard to federalism, that "the federal system and the constitution which corresponds to it have as their aim the rule of reason, which must always be guaranteed against all assaults, and against the prevalence of passions and party interests. At certain moments, these may attenuate or even overthrow the good sense of a people who could demand provisions contrary to their own interests and to those of the community as a whole".[387] It would seem, after what has been said, that the concerns of the federalists are those of Acton himself. He remained for the whole of his life, on the psychological plane, basically an English Catholic, which means a representative of a minority which for centuries had been crushed by the law of the majority, the law of numbers. The United States had arisen specifically from that ensemble of minorities which had not found room in Europe for their freedom. This aspect is the soul of the American revolution and constitution, which has as a constant point of reference the respect for the individual on the part of the masses and the multitude.

Like Acton, the federalists have a profoundly religious spirit, because of which they are aware of the sinful condition of humanity and thus do not put their trust in mere good intentions. If men were angels, governments and guarantees of any type would not be needed, but things are not like that. In order to guarantee liberty of conscience, strong and effective instruments are needed, able to overcome the various contingencies. If liberty is, as Montesquieu said, that good which makes us enjoy all other goods, then we must indeed safeguard it because its loss means the loss of everything.

In *The Federalist* we can also find another of Acton's great convictions: "there is the rejection of egalitarian democracy, and the profound conviction that only the republican democracy, which mediates the popular will thanks to a representative system, is capable of guaranteeing civil, religious and political liberty, in terms of the interests of both individuals and the community as a whole".[388] This effort at finding harmony was the principal aim of Acton's political thought. For this reason, it is in all likelihood possible to trace a linking thread in the thinking of the federalists, of De Tocqueville and of Acton; all of them convinced as they were that if minorities and individuals are not guaranteed from the prepotency of the majority and the government, the most absurd kinds of despotism will be the outcome.

However, talk of a representative system says little if we do not add that for Acton this means placing all states on a level of perfect equality,[389] otherwise the less populated states would count for less and less, and the constitutional bodies would represent only the economically, and perhaps ethnically, strongest groups. But it should be remembered that this realization, too, is not enough in itself. The exact interpretation of federalism, apart from a plurality of centres of sovereign power and their possibility of being represented in equal terms in the Union, also implies coordination between the various powers. This means that the federal government, even if it does not assume in itself the totality of powers, must have an uncontested monopoly of those which it does manage (for example, foreign policy and the military). Only thus is it possible to guarantee that princip of organic unity which means respect for minorities and for all the intermediary bodies, and at the same time the solidarity of the state.

For this reason, according to Acton, there is in federalism the intention of copying certain criteria of English "constitutionalism". Convinced that it would be impossible to introduce the monarchical principle in America,[390] the Federalists were nevertheless of the opinion that they should create an institution which would identify the unity and independence of the state. And this is the justification for the direct election of the Head of State. The President is the unitary soul of the USA, because he gathers up in himself powers which allow him to keep the Union alive and avoid its dissolution. On the other hand it is specifically the ensemble of powers which remain within the competence of the individual states which constitute the most effective brake on any abuse of power.

The fact that such powers and their related responsibilities are distributed in a clear and final way is of the greatest importance. Every individual must know, and in fact does know, to what power he is subject when he acts. The two powers, that of the central government and that of the federal government, must be separated and not contradictory. It is also important in Acton's view that this system should bestow security on the individual in his civil life – and not constant crises of conscience. This would be deleterious both for the interior security of the individual, and for the unity of the state. In cases of conflict between the two governmental powers, there must be a neutral authority to arbitrate. This is an aspect of primary importance, and constitutes a notable step forward in the life of contemporary political systems. The independence of the Courts, and of the Supreme Court in particular, is a real enrichment of the principle of independence of the magistrature, which Acton had already praised in the Roman Republic and which was taken up and brought up to date in the USA, in the attempt to revise and control the constitutional correctness of the laws, the operation of the various powers and the honesty of individuals. It seems clear why, in this viewpoint, the realization of rights is the task of the state and its constitutional organs, while "society" exists for the protection of "interests".[391] For Acton it is federalism itself which guarantees the independence, the actuation and the maintenance of interests and rights. Their harmonization must be the primary rule if a state wishes truly to prosper.

How important the safeguarding of the unity of the state was, so that it should be capable of harmonizing the various interests, is shown by the fact that certain burning problems which had threatened to divide the Union irreparably, were set aside to await a more propitious moment. One of these, and surely the most dramatic, was the question of slavery, which did not allow of a unitary solution, and was subsequently resolved in the way we all know.[392] This fact seemed to bring about a crisis in many consciences which considered it an essential task of a free government to achieve the security of religious rights on an equal basis to civil ones. But Acton, who was naturally opposed to slavery, seems almost to say that the abolition of this sad plague of American life had brought about a crisis at the end of the eighteenth century in the whole unitary process. We have already mentioned his conviction that everything must proceed gradually, and that any change needs time. Moreover, to ensure that a state may grow and develop, it is essential that each of its principles is respected and held as sacred. It is useless and damaging to make declarations of principle which are then contradicted in practice.

If an insecure path like this is followed, then great instability will ensue for the institutions, and this is exactly the opposite of what the federalists were proposing. It is worth repeating that the greatest approval which Acton gives to federalism is the creation of a system of balances which clearly attributes powers and responsibilities in unequivocal fashion. The division of the country between states with special and inalienable responsibilities on the one hand, and central government on the other, is a principle of stability and security not only for the Federation, but also for individuals, who thus find themselves guaranteed in all their actions. This is the system of weights and counter weights[393] which constitutes the best contrivance against absolutism.

In analysing the causes of the American Revolution, Acton pointed to a problem which might have merited more space.

While in England, and later in the rest of Europe, the revolution had revealed a conflict between the classes, in America this conflict was manifested territorially between states.[394] The task of federalism was to heal these conflicts which could have attacked the roots of unity in the state to the point of compromising the federal ideal. On the other hand, Acton does not seem to have had any illusions about the possibility of achieving social equality which, as has been mentioned, would also involve an inevitable static condition. In transcribing certain passages from *Elliot's Debates*, Acton makes this clear statement: "The reason is that inequality of condition, while it is a necessary consequence of liberty, is at the same time indispensable to progress".[395] Clearly, as had already become clear in classical philosophy, this *inequality* cannot be carried to extremes, otherwise even the reasons for the existence of the state become invalidated. But if kept within a just measure of control, it acts as the driving force for progress and the recognition of merit. Acton here shows all his liberalism and his ineradicable hostility towards any kind of planning. But he also shows an aspect which derives from the fact that he was himself an aristocrat. Every democracy, in fact, if it wants to avoid sliding into demagogy, must preserve, within itself, a certain "meritocratic" vision: an "aristocracy" which may clearly vary according to times and circumstances, but which even so constitutes the most serious bulwark against any attempt at totalitarian democracy.

While Acton showed his liberal feelings and his aristocratic sensibilities in these considerations, he also showed his Catholic spirit. In the same essay on the causes of the American Revolution he makes the following affirmation with great clarity: "No civil government can exist, none is conceivable, even, where every individual is free to disobey its orders, whenever they do not happen to square with his private convictions of what is the law of God … To appeal from the government to private judgement, is to place private judgement above public authority, the individual above the state".[396] Naturally such a position cannot be taken to extremes either, otherwise it would end up by lauding disobedience and supporting the theories of anarchy. But the fact remains that for Acton, the individual is of greater value than the state, and the conscience must never be forced. This, as Acton rightly stresses, is a declaredly Catholic conviction, because that dualism of powers which is the greatest guarantee against all forms of absolutism is typical of catholicism. For this reason Acton admires federalism, because he sees in it the assertion of a series of *intermediary powers which render the individual secure* from all possible oppressive powers wielded by the central power towards him.

For this reason too Acton's political thought could seem to be inspired by distinctly conservative principles. However, what has already been said about his historical vision should not be forgotten: continuity and tradition are, probably, among the greatest riches of a people, and are premises on which a civilization is built. Certain gains are also the heritage of the whole of humanity, and to ignore them is to deprive history of meaning, and often to precipitate epochs of barbarianism. Among these gains, a place in the front rank is held by freedom of conscience which is advocated by Christianity, and the dualism of powers exercised in the name of Catholicism which, for this reason too, has always been opposed to national churches. This is a further reason why the very fact of being a Catholic leads him to prefer federalism. He sees in the federal ideal the best realization of the principles of constitutionalism. The state of law finds its fullest expression when there is a true and substantial distribution of responsibilities and when it is permitted for everyone to attain self-realization in the social context and, where necessary, in the political one.

In federalism, and also in the electoral system, is shown the best of what Western thought has produced. The proportional system is profoundly democratic and shows the possible degenerations of democracy. Wherever it is really operative, there is no danger of totalitarianism of any type. We may think for example of the English political system where it has proved possible to blunt the edge of all attacks on liberal democracy. It is very important that Acton, *taking up cudgels against Marx, holds that England, because of its tradition and also because of its electoral system, will never succumb to the class struggle.* Acton evolved convictions such as these during the periods when Gladstone was in power.[397]

His attachment to the federal ideal also led him to criticize the unitary policy of the Savoy monarchy,[398] which insisted on taking no account of the federal ideals put forward by several of the great thinkers of the Italian Risorgimento. During the Expedition of the Thousand, Acton hoped that the attempt by Garibaldi and Mazzini to achieve an Italian Republic in the South would be achieved. The premises would have been laid for the construction of a future federal Italy. The Italian State would thus have surely developed in a better way, and the Church itself would have more easily surrendered a temporal power which was already anachronistic, in exchange, however, for a security and an autonomy which the policy of the House of Savoy never managed to guarantee effectively. From this came those frictions between Church and State which would have been avoided by the creation of a federation, permitting the two bodies to participate together, in different and autonomous ways, in the development of Italy.

If these notions are kept in mind, many of the accusations levelled against Acton by some of the intransigent elements are also confuted. The end of the temporal power would not, according to him, then have taken place in the way it did, reducing the Church to a subordinate position. It is no secret to anyone that Acton, while not accepting the temporal supremacy of the Papacy, did not accept either the Roman policy adopted by the Savoy monarchy, of which Cavour was the principal inspirer.

8) Nationality and nationalism

In considering Acton's political thought, it would be a great mistake to overlook what he had to say about the problem of nationality. The English historian dealt with this subject in a truly original way, given the times, and it could be said that he was almost prophetic, since he succeeded in realizing how this problem, in worsening form, would lead to the downfall of the political supremacy of Europe. It is important to add that Acton concerned himself with this problem when he was not yet thirty years old, in an essay which appeared in 1862 in the "Home and Foreign Review".[399] It is very probably Acton's Catholic upbringing which had led him to take a universalist and supranational view, but it is in any case to be noted that "not only did Acton distinguish between nationality and nationalism, but he reached the point of seeing them as contradictory".[400] These ideas seemed at that time over-conservative to many (especially because Acton openly admired the multinational Austrian Empire), but the fact remains that Acton saw quite clearly the danger that a nation-state might degenerate into a nationalistic one. Acton almost always felt a natural revulsion for the latter phenomenon, and this showed itself numerous times, for example against Prussian nationalist policy.[401] Behind it, he believed there lurked a truly alarming drive towards rearmament.

In the first sentences of his essay, Acton restates one of his well-known convictions; the belief that led him to consider the dangers that may attack property, the distribution of power, the aristocracy, the middle class, etc. – all elements which make up the real driving-force of history. The theories which oppose these elements are the egalitarian, communist and nationalist ones. It is notable that although they have very different ideological roots and motives, all three of these in the end compromise those liberal principles on which, in Acton's view, civilized co-existence must be based.

Also at the beginning of this important essay, a very perceptive assumption can be seen, at least reading between the lines. The national sentiment had gradually come to maturity in Europe as a parallel development to the weakening of the unitary Christian spirit of the old continent. *The collapse of the ideal supremacy (and only this interests Acton) of the Church, had brought with it the triumph of particularisms, of dynastic and local interests which had buried the supranational and universalist ideal of Catholicism.* It is no coincidence, in fact, that mention of the state in modern terms is first heard when the universal vision of Catholicism is shattered by the Reformation.

However, the idea of nationality in itself does not only involve negative elements. In fact it emerges in order to correct a series of errors committed, often in absurd fashion, by the great European monarchies. These frequently showed an incredible blindness – for example in the case of Poland: the partition of Poland was an act of cynical violence, committed in open violation not only of popular sentiment but also of public legality. For the first time in modern history, a major state was suppressed, and an entire nation was divided up between its enemies.[402] This grave act, which no absolute power had previously committed, began to give rise to national sentiment seen as a just historical aspiration. If the idea of nationality had succeeded in keeping within these bounds, it would be one of the noblest demands of history.

Together with this Polish episode, the French Revolution and above all the military activity of Napoleon must be considered. The latter, with his warlike undertakings, gave rise to national sentiment in Russia, aroused it in Italy, trod on it in Germany and Spain.[403] The national idea which emerged from France, however, was in Acton's view abstract, and from some points of view even dangerous, because it gave enormously great importance to the ethnic factor, making it the principle of nationality, and then ended up by imposing it through the use of power. It is strange, though, that it was precisely those ideals, carried forward by the freest spirits in the immediate post-revolutionary period (ideals which, again, included the idea of nationhood and national unity) that according to Acton brought about the end of the Napoleonic era. Religion, national independence and political liberty, united in a league of brief duration, animated the great revolt which caused the fall of Napoleon.[404] These are romantic ideals which developed during the Napoleonic wars and which were then to cause the fall of the Emperor himself, as though in a crisis of rejection.

Paradoxically, however, after the fall of Napoleon, these ideals, around which his adversaries had gathered in order to defeat him, were wiped out in the Restoration. The main forces which were brought into play for the stabilization of Europe were unaware that they were pursuing a great illusion. Among liberal spirits, romantic ideals had taken root more and more firmly, and gradually the real principle of nationality, as we know it today, began to form. This effect of the Restoration, too, was contrary to its intentions. While during the early movements of 1820–21 there was no specific national content, their failure led to a change of tactics, and to the creation of a new and more satisfactory theory of nationality, of which Mazzini was the prophet. His theory which is the most recent in time, is what attracts most in our own days, and it is possible to predict that it will have the greatest success in establishing itself.[405] The anti-national policies of Metternich would be in vain. Despite his admiration for Austria, Acton could certainly not ignore the fact that the most genuine patriotic movement had developed specifically in opposition to the Austrian government.

National rights, just because they are based on ineluctible values such as religion, culture, language, and so on, aroused great interest in the intellectuals of the time, who succeeded in various ways in contributing to the struggle for liberation. They were convinced that they were not deluding themselves, and they believed that they had received confirmation from history. One episode seemed to give special value to their theories; it was also a historical event which, in contrast, greatly preoccupied the minds of those most decidedly opposed to national ideals. For

Acton, in fact, the real cause of the strength acquired by the nationalist theory was the triumph of the democratic principle in France, and its recognition by the European powers. The nationalist theory is implicit in the democratic theory of popular sovereignty.[406] After the fall of Napoleon Bonaparte, this is the most important stage of European history in the nineteenth century.

Nationalist theory, as it came to be formulated, has two particular aspects which give it two different possible forms. In the first case, when national unity becomes a necessary state of circumstance and an ideal unity founded on race, and this unity tends to identify itself with a state, it is inevitable that such a state will become absolute. Completely different is the theory which represents nationality as an essential but not supreme element in the determination of the form of the state. It is distinguished from the other because it tends to variety instead of uniformity, to harmony instead of unity: it obeys the laws and the results of history instead of the claims of some future ideal.[407] This second way of conceiving the idea of nationality is perfectly in line with the federal ideal conceived by Acton, which sees in the different nationalities present in a state a mutual enrichment capable of guaranteeing a more pacific development. For this reason, Acton admired the supranational states which, among other things, he saw as closer to his Catholic ideals.

Since variety is universal, Acton argued, it is logical that Christianity "favours the mingling of races". Moreover, the accord of various nations under a single sovereignty produces effects similar to the liberty of the Church within the state. Liberty provokes variety, and this in turn guarantees liberty by providing it with its organizational means: thus the mission of the Church should be that of overcoming national differences.[408] This does not mean that the Church should be insensitive to the defence of national liberties (the Polish example testifies to this) but it does mean that although it bears in mind historical contingency, the Church cannot ignore its universal vocation. If the pontificate of Pius IX were to be viewed in this light, many misunderstandings would probably disappear. On the other hand the Church cannot ignore the rights of minorities, rights which, on the contrary, an obtuse nationalistic policy sets aside by subjecting to its own principles everything which takes place within its boundaries.[409]

But this is not enough in itself; a policy conceived in this way necessarily becomes the rival of every other nationalistic policy which develops inside other boundaries. It almost seems that the final aim of nationalism is expansionism. We have unfortunately experienced the degree to which this teaching of Acton is true in the twentieth century, in which, with the enfeebling of the Christian spirit, the ancient form of paganism returned to fashion, favouring and fostering conflict, and for this reason developing nationalistic absurdities and idolatries. Perhaps there is here a nostalgia for a past era when all western Europe obeyed the same laws and expressed itself in literary terms in the same language,[410] showing a universal spirituality which had been built on Roman political and juridical universality. The "unity-in-articulated-form" motif, as we can see, constantly prevails in Acton's work, and in these passages he clearly illustrates his form of liberal Catholicism.

Another basic point in Acton's theory of nationality is that it tends to be regulated in a state which has moral purposes and broader general interests as its aim. The Swiss example should certainly be mentioned because it allows for political criteria which govern the fate of the national life to shape and temper the various principles of nationality. The nationality shaped by the state is thus the only version they have of political duties. From the ethnic point of view, the Swiss are French, Italian or Germans, but no nationality makes the minimal claim on them other than their exclusively political nationality of Switzerland.[411] It seems even clearer at this point why Acton so admires the multi-nationality of the ancient Austrian state. For him (and here we must quote him in full): "Those in which no mixture of races has occurred are imperfect; and those in which its effects have disappeared are decrepit. A State which is incompetent to satisfy different races condemns itself; a State which labours to neutralise, to absorb, or to expel them, destroys its own vitality; a State which does not include them is destitute of the chief basis of self-government. The theory of nationality, therefore, is a retrograde step in history".[412] Nationalism carried to its extreme consequences, for Acton, was not only utopian, but genuine folly.

Acton is almost prophetic in his opposition to nationalism. He held it to be more arbitrary than socialism. In his opinion nationalism does not tend either to liberty or to prosperity, since it sacrifices both to the necessary categories for making the nation the model and measure of the state. It is impossible to conceive any reformist principle that is more absolute, more subversive or more arbitrary.[413] How just this opinion is has been all too clearly shown by history.

9) *Liberalism, democracy and socialism: liberty and equality.*

The point that we have now made several times, that for Lord Acton history treads the path of liberty, illustrates the position which he took towards historicism. For him, over and above the recounting of facts, it is necessary to keep a vision and an ethical perspective capable of eliminating the temptations of the constantly resurgent Machiavellianism which had been so acutely reinterpreted in the nineteenth century by Hegelian historical dialecticism. To avoid falling into this enormous error, it was essential to return to the solemn principle of the independence of the individual conscience and its direct responsibility before God. This was why he held the ethical dimension to be superior to the political which, in contrast, from Machiavelli onward, had been seen as independent of any moral standpoint. This meant that "by asserting the absolute nature of the good, Acton refused to justify evil dialectically. The good was liberty; evil was any assault on it. Not having any doubts about right, and about the need to measure history against an ethical yardstick, he held that men and events should be judged not by the measure of norms and systems, but by considering whether at that historical moment they had promoted or damaged the delicacy, the integrity and the authority of the conscience".[414]

The fact that he saw liberty as the true good immediately explains the doubts that he felt, along with De Tocqueville, about democracy and still more about socialism. It was not that Acton ignored the strength and the future potential of these two political ideals, many of the positive aspects of which he in fact analysed; but he saw in them an insatiability, an incapacity to remain within quite precise limits, a frenzy for making equality absolute, which would have sorely threatened the attainments of liberalism. And there was a further point: by examining what Acton acutely termed the "pedigree" of ideas[415] in relation to socialism and democracy, one could see how these ideas, although seeking to go beyond liberalism, ended by not being able to maintain its best and most salient results, and even by annihilating them.

Many times when Acton spoke of the enemies of freedom, rather than concerning himself with contrary interests and intentions, he dealt with the false ideas which circulated among these enemies. One of these false ideas is to believe that every political notion which goes beyond liberalism or is derived from it is better than it. Democracy and socialism could often be considered to be at the mercy of these false ideas, capable of cancelling liberty altogether, especially when they went beyond the limits within which they must be contained. Acton was very clear on this issue; for him, (as we noted in section 2 of the last chapter), democracy, like monarchy, is salutary if it is kept within certain limits, and fatal if it goes beyond them; it is the truest friend or the most implacable foe of liberty according to whether it is mixed or unadulterated.[416] The same goes for socialism.

Just as for De Tocqueville, his view is that those who initiate a democracy know that if it seeks to function in the right way, it must immediately establish controls and adapt itself to them. Such controls must not merely be given a juridical expression; they must be embedded in the spirit and will of the people. Their failure makes the whole democratic system vain. These controls must be the expression of the moral life of a people; only in this way can they have the necessary strength to act through the laws. And for this reason, though Acton recognizes the very great importance and historical function of democracy and socialism, he tends to distinguish the things in these theories that can coexist with liberty and those which end by denying it. It could almost be said, without pressing conclusions too far, that in Acton there is the desire to oppose a moderate democracy to an over-broad and totalitarian one, and to recommend what we would today call liberal socialism as against an over-egalitarian version. In short, the most diverse political theories can be accepted as long as they can coexist with the basic principles of liberalism.

The moderate democracy of which Acton was speaking was not a chimera, or a pure theory. As a historian, Acton seeks to give it concrete expression. In politics reality is more interesting to him than illusory pipe-dreams or utopias. The political system of the United States embodies the greatest possible democracy. This justifies his strong conviction, which we have already stressed, that sees in the history of the USA the continuation of the history which was compromised in Europe at the beginning of the modern era. In the new continent that progressive and moderate spirit seemed to survive, that *lex continui* which presents history as a logical but slow progress which knows no leaps. Such leaps, far from representing steps forward, result in compromising the true path. The revolution in America respects these principles; that *lex continui* which binds tradition and innovation together, and indeed presents them to the whole contemporary world in a new and more specific way. American independence was the beginning of a new era, not simply in that it was a revolution, but in that no other revolution was born from such a light cause and was conducted with such moderation: it established a pure democracy of rare perfection, armed and vigilant against aristocracy and monarchy and against its own weaknesses and excesses. It seemed still more worthy of admiration for the safeguards which it established against the power of its own sovereign people.[417] According to Acton, a democracy of wide proportions such as had never been seen was born, but was no less secure for that reason for basic liberties, because it was animated by them.

A democracy understood in this way, a moderate democracy, is certainly acceptable to Acton because right from the outset it cancels all state-planning and totalitarian tendencies. Such an enterprise, undertaken in the USA, had failed, on the other hand, in the aftermath of the French Revolution. During the constitutional debates immediately after the fall of the Bastille, all the attempts of the Moderates ("as we may term the Liberals") who were in the dominant position at the outset, became supplanted, and thus the successful outcome of the revolution was compromised.[418] Democracy proved incapable of self-control, and could not even maintain a unitary programme, so that the various ways of interpreting it ended up by bringing about its collapse. In America, by contrast, the value of tradition and the sense of the lessons of history were never set aside, while in France a leap in the dark was taken. It goes without saying that various aspects of this analysis corresponded to that of Burke, but it is important to point out also that in this overcoming of moderate democracy, Acton gives the impression of perceiving the radicalization of certain socialist theories.

France experienced the shipwreck of its revolution because, in distinction from its American and earlier English counterparts, it speeded up the path of history with the sole result that the initial premises of democracy became more and more untenable, simply because they were gradually made absolute, and thus far from the tradition and mindset of France itself. In the six months from January 1789 to the Fall of the Bastille on 14 July, France took as many progressive steps as England had made in 600 years between the era of the Earl of Leicester (Simon de Montfort's revolt) and that of Lord Beaconsfield.[419] Apart from this unacceptable acceleration of the historical process, in France all the measures which would have guaranteed the establishment of American-style democracy were ignored, and as we have seen, these constituted for Acton the limitations of democracy itself. The new French constitution did not allow privileged orders: the characteristic safeguards of the American government were not introduced: federalism, separation of Church and State, the second chamber, the powers of arbitration of the Supreme Court.[420] Everything that was most democratic was borrowed from the American system, but the end result was that it risked weakening and compromising democracy itself.

At this point, it is clear that the freedom of the individual was compromised, and – within a democracy which no longer proved capable of justifying itself or even of surviving – socialist and other even more radical ideas began making headway. The most profound reason that the French Revolution was so damaging for liberty was its theory of equality. Liberty was the watchword of the middle class; equality that of the lower classes. It was the latter who were to win the battle of the Third Estate,[421] and it could be said that because of this, the liberal–democratic outcome of the Revolution was compromised. It was always the lower classes which made France a Republic and buried the notion of a constitutional monarchy.

The basic error, which compromised everything else, was according to Acton committed by the middle class, which should have taken its inspiration from liberal principles and initiated measures to contain the democratic excesses. The middle class made use of the lower class to bring down the aristocracy, but in doing so they did not believe that they would be encouraging the egalitarian dreams of the people. The latter did not in fact accept that the bourgeoisie should establish a new regime of inequality to its own advantage once the upper classes had been brought down. The lower classes who had backed the bourgeoisie, seeing that their own demands were not satisfied, revolted itself against the latter, which seemed to be set on perpetuating old privileges even in the midst of renewal. Everything degenerated at this point, even the initial revolutionary movements, and a state of total chaos and insecurity was reached.

It is interesting to note at this point how, when the disastrous results of this attempt at democracy are taken into account, Acton restates the conclusions of certain absolutist theorists, even though as a liberal he does not share them. In his view these theorists find a momentary justification and value on the actual plane of historical contingency, even though they are unacceptable on the ideal plane. In some pages of his work we seem to hear echoes of Hobbes, who proposed the imposition of Leviathan in just such moments of great insecurity. These moments can be seen in the Reign of Terror. The state of nature returned, in which every man had the right to whatever he could take. The moment had come for the rich to make way for the poor. With this theory of equality, liberty was stifled in blood, and the French ended by being ready to sacrifice everything else in order to save their life and their goods.[422] For Acton this meant sacrificing liberty for security and "equality". The solution might be valid in certain instances but was certainly unacceptable if seen as definitive and bettering.

As he entertained a series of doubts about a democracy which was unable to control itself, Acton sought the support of certain other liberal thinkers who could undoubtedly not be seen as reactionary. This is the case with De Tocqueville and Mill. These and others, in Acton's opinion, have shown that democracy does not foster respect for the past, if it is concerned with the future, and has no regard for public faith and national honour; it is capricious and arbitrary, jealous of genius and culture, indifferent to justice but servile in the face of public opinion, incapable of organizing itself, impatient of authority, adverse to obedience, hostile to religion and to constituted law.[423] These bitter conclusions were, according to Acton, verifiable on the historical plane. They were the properties of a democracy which sought to make itself absolute, and to ignore all possible moderation.

The degenerations of democracy would end by being far more dangerous than those of monarchy and aristocracy. The centralization which it both proposes and puts into effect, is, according to Acton (*who in fact seems here to foresee the dangers of so-called democratic centralism* – or even more of a centralized socialism) an instrument which tends to become crystallized, and which ends by denying the very essence of democracy. While in the past, absolute monarchy had often found its justification beneath a halo of sacrality, the same temptation risked becoming part of a democracy which could not exercise control over itself. When this point is reached, it means that the democratic ideal exists solely in name, and is emptied of all substance. At this pont, the democratic principle according to which no one should be in a position to exercise his own power over the people is understood in the sense that no one must be in a position to limit or escape its power. The true democratic principle according to which one must not do to a people anything which that people does not wish done, is understood in a sense in which it must not be obliged to tolerate what is not to its taste.[424] In this way an unprecedented tyranny is generated, which suffocates all possible dissent and denies, right from the start, all claim to individual liberty.

If democracy does not both provide for and activate the remedies against its own possible degenerations, even from its very foundations, then it will never succeed in turning back once it has degenerated. To put a democracy which no longer exists back on its feet is a more than difficult task, also because it is very difficult for those who live under a demagogic system to admit that they no longer live in a democracy. To escape from a situation of this kind requires greater force than is needed to bring down a tyranny or an oligarchy. And civil wars, too, find their justification in this way.

10) Marxism

To socialism in general and Marxism in particular, Acton pays special attention at certain specific moments of his life. It should be said at once that despite the fact that he considered socialism dangerous in various ways, much as a democracy which respects no limits, he believed it to be less dangerous than nationalism,[425] and possibly capable, in a distant future, of taking on board some basic points of liberalism. Moreover, even though for various motives he rejected Marxism, he always recognized its value on the historical and political plane, even if this recognition was always mixed with the fear that this "conception of the world" could cause no small damage to individual liberties and in general to the bases of liberalism.

Among the books from his library which he subsequently bequeathed to the University of Cambridge, can be found *Towards a critique of the political economy of Marx,* annotated with great care. Other writings of Marx and Engels are sometimes cited (e.g. *Anti-Dühring)*, even *Das Kapital* itself is immediately recognized as a powerful and determinative work, so much so that Acton advised Gladstone to read it and was surprised when the politician replied that he did not have time to do so.[426]

There is almost a scientific detachment with regard to Marxism: the values which conditioned Acton are, of course, incompatible with the dialectical materialism of Marx, but they did not provoke disinterest on that ground. On the contrary there is a serious need to face up to a theory which was winning a large number of followers. It is curious that in judging Marx, Acton formulated notions not very different from those which the liberal thinker Benedetto Croce was to formulate some decades later. Certainly the latter was to insert his judgement on Marxism into the context of a philosophical system, reducing the category of the economic to the notion of the useful, but if we limit ourselves to the premises, we can say that Marx appeared to both as the bearer of a new message of "liberation", which would above all have a practical value.[427]

Acton seems to have the same yardstick of judgement. After having read *Kapital*, he described it as the *Quran* of the new socialists.[428] A most important definition, because while on the one hand it expresses the strength and novelty of Marxism, on the other hand it makes the underlying dangers clear as well. Acton seems to be saying that here we find ourselves confronted with a disguised religion, where there is no distinction between State and Church, and where the individual, deprived of all guarantees, is crushed by the totality. There is a risk of giving birth to a new "religious" form of intolerance, more dangerous than that of the past , which at least in theory allowed the "dissident" to take refuge in the context of the temporal world, which often maintained its autonomy from the spiritual. With the new claims of totalitarian, Marxist and democracy there was the dangerous tendency to substitute for one religious system another system of religious-style obligations which was equally absolute and dangerous.[429] It is certainly no coincidence that Acton describes the theorists of such political ideas as *Monistic philosophers*.[430] In other words, thinkers incapable of seeing in the dualism between religion and politics, between spiritual and temporal, the true roots of the freedom of humankind. The "Monistic philosophers", all in one way or another more or less orthodox offspring of Hegel, saw in dualism the first cause of that unhappy conscience which had criticized Judaeo-Christian history. This dualism, according to its critics, blocked a possible realization of the perfect society because the peculiar reason of the spiritual "moment" was that of always referring to something beyond history, and thus of perpetuating that sense of unhappiness typical of western man. However, these accusations did not affect Acton at all because that inner discontent was for him the spring of history and the dualism itself was the essence of liberty. Orthodox Marxism thus appeared, like the Moslem religion, to be aimed at founding the most monolithic union of religion and politics, spirituality and temporality. The realization of a communist state found vitality in a spirit the intimate *raison d'être* of which was, in fact, the communist ideology. Thus politics enfolded morality in itself, and everything which was politically useful was considered morally justified. We return to the judgement of Benedetto Croce, which described Marx as following in the footsteps of Machiavelli.

The judgement of Marxism is, as we have seen, precise and severe. But Acton was not willing to deny recognition to Marxism, and in particular to its founding father, for a great historical, and it could even be said, "moral" value. Here we must again refer to Croce.

The Italian philosopher acknowledged that Marx had the merit that in politics as in economics it was no use "to trust in moralistic sermons and in ideologies or enlightened chit-chat. And over and beyond admiration, we also owe Marx our gratitude for having succeeded in rendering us invulnerable to 'Alcinan seductions' (Alcina was the decrepit toothless witch who adopted the likeness of a girl in the flower of her youth) of the goddess Justice and the goddess Humanity".[431] This sense of gratitude, mixed however with the rejection of the Marxist vision of the world, can also be found in Acton. The critique made by Marx and other socialists of the classical economists, especially the English ones, influenced Acton almost as the writings of Keynes were to influence politicians and economists after the Second World War.[432] Acton in fact grants Marxism the merit of having caused the contradictions of classical economics to explode, and above all of having highlighted the unhappy conditions of life of some individuals even within the "liberal democracies". On the view of the future, it is impossible to come to an understanding with Marxism, but its importance is great on the practical and immediate plane because it called many scholars away, as Croce would say, from dreams and idyllic temptations.

The ultimate aims of Marxism could not be other than totalitarian, because its *Weltanschauung* was completely illiberal. There was no thought of correcting the contradictions of liberal–capitalist society; the only aim was to destroy it. Free enterprise, free exchange, private initiative – to use terms which still have currency today – cardinal points of liberalism, were the root of all evil for Marxism. Acton's liberalism, on the contrary, like all English liberalism, rested on the theories of Adam Smith, as well as on individual liberties.[433] In a special way in the nineteenth century, when the Whig party was influenced by other economic, liberal and radical theories, the thought of the author of *The Wealth of Nations* always constituted the cardinal point and basis of the liberal party. The divergence from Marxism was thus not only in the view of the future, but also in the way of considering the instruments and economic structures that make up the fabric of civil society.

We also find in Acton's work the perennial problem of the minorities which he saw as being sacrificed, and devoid of any guarantee or respect, in a Marxist perspective, or more generally in that of totalitarian democracy. Because of this, even though at some points it may seem debatable, Acton fully supported those theories of John Stuart Mill which demanded respect for minorities and the recognition of their rights. And in Mill's work too, in antithesis to Marxism, Acton admired his firm distinction between "public" and "private", and the other no less important distinction between public and private power and initiative. Both were at the basis not only of fundamental civil liberties, but also of that liberty of conscience without which a political system worthy of humankind could not exist.[434]

11) What future for democracy and socialism?

The judgement that he made on Marxism certainly did not prevent Acton from following the evolution of socialism with great attention. It had undergone considerable development in the later years of the nineteenth century, to the extent that in the 1880s Acton began considering the problem of why certain socialists were able to appeal to some of the presuppositions of liberalism.[435] Democracy itself had abandoned the disturbing logic of the tyranny of the majority, not only in some theoretical expressions, but also in the more concrete context of several constitutions. The criterion of proportional representation had been proposed. It is profoundly democratic, in that it increases the influence of the masses which would otherwise have no voice in the government, and brings men closer to a situation of equality by providing that no vote shall be wasted, and that every elector shall contribute to sending to Parliament a member who shares his own opinions.[436] As can be seen, democracy which in its extreme form was a constant source of worry to Acton, had by this time found correctives which cured its dangerous excesses – those that threatened the liberty of the individual. The latter was, for Acton, the cornerstone of a true social system. His most deeply rooted conviction was that in order to judge whether a country were truly free, it was necessary to ascertain in concrete terms what degree of security individuals and minorities were able to enjoy.[437] When this security is non-existent, we are in the grip of pure and simple totalitarianism, even if it be camouflaged with the title of democracy.

The proportional system enjoyed Acton's support because in it there is the only possible balance between equality and freedom, terms which, if carried too far, finally exclude one another. Their harmonization proved possible when the various political theories (democracy, socialism, etc.) gradually become less intransigent, and more ready to make comparisons and accept corrections. It cannot be ruled out that in time, a further correction of certain egalitarian claims will be reached, which still exist in too many socialist theorists. We find in Acton – as we saw in Chapter 2 – the firm conviction that history is a *lex continui*, which does not move by leaps and bounds, and in which (where extremism is successfully contained) sooner or later the claims and political demands are tempered, corrected and harmonized with one another. Where egalitarian and socialist claims succeed in overcoming the freedom of the individual and of minorities, there is a lapse into the most absurd of revolutionary logics, the kind that claims to wipe out history.

The freedom of the individual is in fact the product of a slow development of a society.[438] If it be cancelled, there is a lapse into the most absurd and dangerous abstractism, just as the French revolution lapsed when it degenerated. What we were faced with at that point was no longer France, but an unknown country. Every vestige or removable trace of the national history was carefully suppressed.[439] It was of these claims by democracy, which would basically become those of Marxism, that Acton was afraid.

Marxism or scientific socialism appeared to him a logical consequence in the history of democracy[440] – i.e. of that democracy which does not succeed in controlling and limiting itself. In short, totalitarian socialism was bound to be the outcome of totalitarian democracy. And to this Acton was resolutely opposed. From a *liberal* democracy, on the other hand, a *partial* form of socialism could derive, and towards this he seems to nurture a genuine interest. This *partial socialism* derives directly from certain initial assumptions: "1) private enterprise had failed to solve the problem of distribution; 2) what the poor needed before they could make their political power effective was comfort and security; 3) division of power is the condition of liberty; 4) the right of self-government is inherent in all corporations and associations. For these reasons the State must not control the whole of economic life".[441] At this point it seems natural to suppose that in Acton it is easy to see an inclination towards all those political ideas which make the inalienable gains of liberalism their own. *Socialism itself may one day base itself on liberal presuppositions.* In this, Acton, as Fasnacht rightly maintains, was "a true prophet. He was in favour of as much socialism as is compatible with real freedom, and a sense of economic responsibility. He believed that the diffusion of wealth was one of the ways in which the State could give real, though indirect, help to the individual".[442] He was thus a prophet of the liberal socialism which in various parts of Europe is today seeking a difficult, but certainly not impossible, synthesis.

12) A note on J. S. Mill

We have already mentioned (at the end of the second section of this chapter) that Acton always admired Mill's distinction between the private and public spheres, his respect for minorities and the complementary nature, in economic life, of public and private initiative. In fact, however, the thought of Mill was also present in other ways in Acton's reflections, for he considered the author of *On Liberty* to be one of the greatest exponents and defenders of liberalism. It could hardlly be otherwise, since for Acton the basis of politics lay in economics and ethics, and hence the person who does not restrict liberty and conditions it within the context of politics as strictly understood, must be considered a great defender of liberty.

It could be said that Acton found in certain liberals the greatest expression of man as a social animal, the product of Roman and mediaeval thinking, rather than man as a political animal, expressed in revised and corrected form, by the modern theories of statolatry and the totalitarian vision. Starting from this presupposition, true liberalism, before showing its nature on the political plane, where it finds its exterior expression, must manifest itself on the interior plane (liberalism flourished in the golden age of conscience). This explains why before Mill, the true exponents of liberalism are the philosophers from Kant to Rosmini, whose political reflection has a starting point in meditations of a religious kind.[443] This also explains why genuine liberal spirits should detest the prevarications of the majority, because they consider freedom of the individual conscience, and of minorities, as the greatest good to be safeguarded.

Following on from this, it is easy enough to understand why it could even be stated that "Mill treats political economy as a deductive science".[444] *Deductive science* because it is based on ethical values, which rest on religious presuppositions without which not even liberal economics could survive. It must be remembered that freedom, apart from being the departure point which verifies a whole ethical dimension, is a freedom which aims, to put it in Kantian terms, at a real "kingdom of ends", precisely because it is not directed only at political ends and can never find fulfilment in them.

Certainly a liberal who understands freedom in this way cannot be termed a "utilitarian" liberal. Utilitarianism was for Acton a genuine pseudo-religion, to be viewed with suspicion on a par with centralism and extreme egalitarianism.[445] In Acton's view, Mill has nothing of all this. To define him, Acton would have agreed with the words of Norberto Bobbio: "Mill was a liberal and a democrat: he considered democracy, in particular representative government, which he also called popular government, to be the natural and consequent development of liberal principles... In his last writings, he in fact held that liberalism and socialism were not incompatible"[446]. Both of these views were, as we have seen, shared by Acton in his mature years.

If Mill had been a utilitarian pure and simple, he would have been outside Acton's interest, even in historical terms. The latter was, as Popper rightly maintained[447] contrary to any claim of absolute value for historical analysis, just as he was opposed to dialectical or dialectical-materialistic absolutes, he was equally hostile to all those theories such as utilitarianism which tended to give a sole meaning – and that a deterministic one – to human activity. When Mill spoke of utilitarianism, or defended "extreme" notions, in Acton's view, he did not do so methodically, but as a free-thinker, as many English people like to consider themselves, especially if they are liberals. Moreover, liberalism developed not only because of the rigour and the constant and progressive theoretical development which has its roots in tradition, but also because of the courage of certain thinkers who were always in opposition, and who have paid for their isolation by incomprehension, finding extravagant ideas attributed or referred to them which at times they hardly even touched upon.

In Mill as in Locke, Jefferson, Hamilton and others, Acton also sees the great value of consensus, which even leads them to consider those laws which are imposed without regard to tradition, values, and the whole culture which animates a people as quite invalid. The consensus of which these authors speak is for Acton closely connected to the just sense of authority as the Romans understood it. In fact a law which deserves consensus is one which emerges from history, and acquires its authority and respect from it. A law, in other words, which is not the product of arbitrary judgment, but which arises from the intimate element, the conscience, of a state – from its soul. Thus it is easy to see why for Acton real liberalism had an intrinsic religious element and must always be in agreement with the Christian ideas which have permeated the whole of western civilization.

Like De Tocqueville and others, Mill is among the thinkers who according to Acton understood the real value of freedom and the just balance which is needed to safeguard it. Freedom, like democracy in fact, loses its authenticity if it does not succeed in uniting a respect for the past to a care and concern for the future.[448] Here we find resurfacing the idea of history as the *lex continui* which knows nothing of sudden revolutionary accelerations, but rather a history to whose development peoples owe their birth and the slow and progressive growth of the liberal and moderate democratic ideals (the word moderate, for Acton, meant distinction from totalitarian democracy).

The English historian, more or less in the footsteps of the theorists of mixed constitutions, admired in Mill as in De Tocqueville, all the attempts which aimed at limiting any possibility of power becoming absolute. Free institutions are those in which the central government is limited with regard to minorities, but at the same time succeeds in limiting all possible arbitrary behaviour on the part of those who demand that all power should be in the hands of the dominant ethnic group.[449] Thus it is clear how reflections which rest on a plan of maximum balance, and which Acton finds partly present in Mill, show that the latter cannot be considered by him as a pure utilitarian, on a par with Bentham .

These considerations are basic for anyone who seeks to grasp the thought of Lord Acton. He was always deeply convinced, in the line of thinkers like Montesquieu, that history has its own paths, its own times, and that nothing can be improvised. All this, however, never leads him to assume fatalistic attitudes towards history. The famous *lex continui* about which so much has been said already, is to be safeguarded from all its enemies by a series of principles which we could even term *a priori*. Everything that we have seen to be the foundation of freedom, and in the first place, Christian values, the respect for minorities, and the sense of limitation, cannot be at any time or in any place, set aside, because otherwise not only is freedom and the political power which defends and characterizes it "denatured", but the very *lex continui* itself, which has generated it: a *lex continui* which can only be properly understood within a religious view of progressive perfecting, specifically because religious ideals are its soul.

13) Characteristics of Lord Acton's liberalism

Liberalism is a sort of common denominator of many thinkers of contemporary western history, and it is thus difficult to understand a person who describes himself as a liberal unless we examine attentively all the facets of his/her particular way of being a liberal. This is even more true for a many-sided personality like that of Acton. In him a number of elements converge, such as tradition, the need for a distinction between Church and State, federalism, a particular vision of the French Revolution, and a special sense of modernity which makes it possible to give specific character to his liberalism, and distinguish it from that of others.

a) The value of tradition

Lord Acton's liberalism can be described above all as a *moderate* liberalism. This has already been seen in the analysis of his historical reflection,[450] but it is even more clear if we remember that for Acton liberalism has been "fertilized" by Christianity, which not only conceived it, but as time went on defended it against all the forms of absolutism which have emerged during the course of history. Christianity itself is in turn rooted in the classical tradition, and especially the Roman legal tradition, which provided the basis for the western legal state. "In the height of their power, the Romans became aware of a race of men that had not abdicated freedom in the hands of a monarch".[451] The republic, which has permeated the whole history of freedom, "admits monarchy as an occasional incident".[452]

The barbarian invasions, if they had not encountered the legal tradition of Rome, would have plunged Europe into a dramatic prehistory without any way of escape, because the way the Teutonic hordes conceived power was one that "(offered) no security to individuals".[453] The beginning of the Middle Ages should thus be seen as a slow path of more than seven centuries towards the reaffirmation of individual rights which only began to have a new theoretical reflection and formulation after the beginning of the second millennium.

If the monarchial absolutism of those years had any merit at all, it was that with the conversion of sovereigns, there came the conversion of whole peoples who thus received the vital lymph of Christianity with greater rapidity, and gained much sooner that sense of human dignity which slowly undermined mediaeval absolutism itself. It was thus that in the delicate relations between the State and the Church, the need began to be felt to escape from absolutism – sometimes, royal, sometimes local and feudal, of the nobility or of the Church. It was precisely this situation, encouraged and upheld for various reasons by legal reflection on Roman civilization, and by the value given to the individual in the Christian tradition, that made it possible for Western Europe to avoid falling under a form of immobile absolutism typical of Byzantine or Muscovite despotism.[454] This is a deeply-held conviction on the part of Acton, who precisely for these reasons, judged tradition fundamental for liberalism, since without it there would be a backward leap into the darkness of prehistory, setting aside centuries of hard-won progress. Monarchial absolutism was beaten, and with it *the danger of a perpetual absolutism of an oriental kind,* because in the West it was forced to come up against the religious authority of the Papacy, the Italian and Hanseatic autonomous communes, the rising nobility of France and especially of England, and the emergence of the maritime republics. All these elements of contention were lacking in Asia. Even more, it is just in this period that the first parties of the modern world began to appear: the Guelphs and the Ghibellines are certainly the best known, but not the only examples.

It was in the context of these struggles that talk was first heard of a need for representation, of the need to collect taxes within limits determined by the representatives of the people (the Italian example is conspicuous here), and above all a need to resist the powers that be when they appear as a manifestation of tyrannical despotism. All this finds expression in the political thought of Thomas Aquinas and Marsilius of Padua, without whom, according to Acton, one cannot understand the mature mind of modern liberalism as it can be found in Locke and Montesquieu. Acton's language is very clear on this point: "the earliest exposition of the Whig theory of the revolution is taken from the works of St Thomas Aquinas, of whom Lord Bacon says that he had the largest heart of the School divines".[455]

In Acton's view Marsilius was the most important Ghibelline writer, as he was the first to say that the laws derived their authority from consensus, and that without it they were invalid. Moreover Marsilius seems to be the first to speak of tolerance: "The rights of citizens are independent of the faith they profess, and no man may be punished for his religion".[456] From the teachings of Marsilius of Padua and St Thomas Aquinas comes the best of the attainments of their time, because if the former thought of submitting or in some way limiting the power of the clergy, the latter thought that all governments must be tested on the basis of Christian ideals, without which no liberty was possible.

At the same time, another great contribution to the development of the struggle against despotism comes from the Italian communes. The intelligent struggle for independence by the embryonic modern cities produced the first attempt at statutes and a constitution after the long parenthesis of the Dark Ages. These are documents which, however rough they may seem, present the basic aspects of future European institutions. Representative government, the methods of election, the system of tax-gathering, are all elements which, even though not completely defined, are nevertheless clearly present.

With these achievements of the late Middle Ages, a true quantum leap was made in relation to the past. In ancient times, in fact, if we exclude the juridical experience of Rome in the republican period, in Acton's view we have political systems based on absolute states which find all their strength in slavery. In the mediaeval period, on the other hand, the true sense of authority was progressively returning within the limits of the laws; the representatives of the upper classes and the guilds acquired room for political action that in the past they had not had, and became prepared to defend these gains even by struggling at cost of their lives. The true boast of the era of St Thomas Aquinas is that "the right of insurrection was not only admitted but defined, as a duty sanctioned by religion".[457] It is the religious themes which compose the foundation of the right to resist tyranny, and religion provides all the theoretical and practical elements on which to base liberty.

The great inheritance of the ancient and mediaeval world is brought together and developed in England, and from here it passes to the United States which, as we have mentioned, represented for Acton the natural development of European history. It is in England that one of the cardinal points of mediaeval reflection and the modern constitutional state finds complete realization: i.e *representative government*.[458]

In it, the British monarchy found its salvation, which then had the useful support in its liberal phase of development, of the two-chamber system. We hardly need to point out, and the theme will be resumed later,[459] that for Acton this two-chamber system was the most fortunate result of the English Revolution, a result which the French Revolution did not succeed in producing. The latter revolution failed specifically because it was incapable of creating a "higher chamber", capable of opposing the demands of the Assembly and limiting them.

The Americans made use of the English model in their revolution. On the new continent there was no monarchy or aristocracy, but the English juridical tradition was too strong a heritage to be forgotten. The American revolution is thus entirely aimed at following up the experience of the mother country, but avoiding everything in the older model which had caused their forebears to emigrate. The Americans also knew that English law, like that of Rome, was the product of tradition and of multiple influences, but it was also the product of the balancing of various interests.[460] On all this, a modern notion of authority was based, which allowed England to possess an avant-garde political system.

The political fortune of England, which would then become the fortune of the United States as well, lay perhaps in having been able to keep the best of the institutions of the past from the tradition, and then to synthesize them in response to modern necessity. This synthesis, in other words, gave rise to what could be called a *mixed Constitution*; Acton does not use this term, but it is very clear that he refers to it when he maintains that monarchy, aristocracy and democracy must all have their limits, not only to safeguard them from degradation, but also because freedom can only be guaranteed by a form of mutual control between the various institutions. We recall that Acton is opposed to all forms of degeneration of power, but the kind that he regards as most dangerous is the "absolutization" of democracy. It is permissible to take up a struggle against a sovereign or a minority which degenerates. "History is filled with records of resistance provoked by the abuse of power" – but against the abuse of a people without any further limits, it is difficult to resist: "There is no appeal from the people to itself".[461] The experience of the Terror in the French Revolution is the most dramatic proof of this and was to bring the Revolution to disaster.

The experience of the United States, equally with that of Europe (from which the American system is the natural development) has made more than a few contributions which have helped to enrich the liberal tradition. This tradition, we stress again, is basic to liberalism, because without it every desire for liberty is an empty libertarian frenzy, capable of degenerating into every kind of excess. Among the contributions made by the Americans to the development of the ideal of liberty there is the struggle against the centralization of power. This was possible, not only because of the implementation of the federal system, but because the nascent USA adopted from the outset a social system based on a certain inequality ("a society adopting inequality"). This even involved the absurdity of slavery in the southern states, but it also preserved the political and social system from that mania for perfection typical of revolutionary movements – a mania which always risks compromising a large part of what has been so painstakingly gained. Perhaps it is from this that there comes that typical characteristic of American liberalism, of exalting individual merit and seeing property as a logical consequence of it.[462]

It may appear a little forced to interpret Acton in this way, but in fact if we consider what he said immediately after the Civil War, we find an immediate confirmation. At the end of the battle between North and South, Acton regretted that this event had been consigned to history exclusively because of the slavery issue. The latter was surely one of the reasons which lay at the origins of the conflict, but behind it there was something quite different: "Different indeed must our judgement be if we examine the value of secession as a phase in the history of political doctrine ... the North has used the doctrines of Democracy to destroy self-government. The South applied the principle of conditional federation to cure the evils and to correct the errors of a false interpretation of Democracy".[463] The fortune, or better the capacity, of the United States has been that of being able to overcome the tragic effects of a civil war (which as a fratricidal struggle always leaves its mark), mitigating both the spirit of revenge and the democratic "absolutes" of the victors. It could almost be said that for the tradition of American liberalism, the Civil War is as important as the Revolution, because the basic founding criteria of the Federal State found new forms of adjustment after it was over. Many excesses (slavery among them) were rejected and liberty made another fundamental step in its painstaking story. Among other things, it is after this very war that there was that economic and financial development which would lead the USA in a few decades to become a world power.

b) Separation between Church and State

Another characteristic of Acton's liberalism is the idea of the separation of Church and State. It is necessary, he argues, because every time it is lacking, the slow and painful journey of liberty is halted. It is no coincidence that the liberal ferments present in the mediaeval tradition became more robust when this separation was strong, and in contrast came to nothing when a religious crisis involved the birth of state religions and the absolutism that followed. The latter developed all over Europe in the age of the

Reformation. On the one hand, this was because there were sovereigns who for various motives welcomed the reformed religions, after having suppressed or rejected the traditional hierarchy, and became the head of the Church themselves. On the other hand, it was also because, owing to reaction or self-defence, in some states the Catholic hierarchy supported the sovereigns who had remained faithful. Everywhere, including many Catholic circles, there was a dangerous involution. "The clergy, who had in so many ways served the cause of freedom during the prolonged strife against feudalism and slavery, were associated now with the interest of royalty".[464] The very thing which had been the stimulus of liberty was thus amputated. Everywhere, from France to Spain, from Central Europe to England, absolutism reigned supreme.

It is a paradox that in the Renaissance, with the rise of the modern age when it seems that human dignity is at the centre of all attention, all the best political reflection is in favour of absolutism. It would be superfluous to list names, but what needs to be pointed out is that Acton makes certain observations about the political thought of the Reformation which in the twentieth century were made by Ernst Bloch. For both writers the Reformation meant, in political terms, "the end of dreams": zeal for liberty and justice drowned in blood. But what was really grave for Acton was the collapse of the separation between temporal and spiritual, and hence the birth of the Leviathan State.[465] The real religious sense was becoming feebler and feebler, in favour of the exclusive political interest in the light of which everything was justified. "Atrocious deeds were done, in which passion was often the instrument, but policy was the motive".[466] The teaching of the past had no effect in a moment of general folly in which very few kept the necessary lucidity. Acton records, as an example, the case of certain French magistrates who refused to obey the extravagant demands of the mob. But such cases unfortunately remained isolated.

When the last Reformers disappeared, religion everywhere justified the most senseless crimes of absolutism, as if all the "men of faith" had forgotten that religion was supposed to be the precondition for the emancipation of humankind, rather than a tool for bringing it to submission. But all this was nothing less than the logical consequence of the confusion and "commixture" between politics and religious faith; by confusing these, the most absurd degree of intolerance is reached. Tradition seemed all of a sudden cancelled, and with it were wrecked all those efforts and achievements which had attempted to limit power, and subject obedience to legitimate demands. In this period, toleration, resistance to tyrants, separation between religion and politics – aspects on which the whole of mediaeval thought had speculated – seemed to have disappeared. There was no one among the great geniuses of the time who considered these things in adequate fashion. From Machiavelli to Bossuet (advocate of passive obedience to kings), and passing through Luther and Calvin, the search was only to justify absolutism, demonstrating its merits, efficiency and possible success, in the same way as for centuries previously there had been an attempt to limit it.

The gravest fact, in Acton's opinion, is that absolutism, and hence intolerance, also becomes a criterion for moral evaluation. The powers that be, and only they, know how to distinguish between good and evil, between truth and falsehood.[467] If we think of it, it could hardly be otherwise, given that the sovereign, guarantor and custodian of faith, becomes the final judge of all controversies. We are far from the days when Thomas Aquinas maintained that all legislation must be subjected to the laws of nature, because it is through them that, under the form of universal reason, God speaks to the conscience of mankind.[468] To hear such discussions again, we have to wait for the isolated voice of Grotius. Moreover, no one seemed to remember specifically the best teachings of the Middle Ages, and their efforts to distinguish the fields of action of the State and the Church. "Even Spinoza, who was a republican and a Jew, assigned to the State the absolute control of religion".[469]

It is interesting to note that according to Acton, absolutism also constitutes a cultural error, a historical forgetfulness. It does not in fact represent a novelty in western history. It was already present, a thousand years earlier in some of the kingdoms of the Romano-barbarians. "At a time when Arianism was extinct in the empire, it assumed the character of a national religion among the Teutonic tribes, and added a theological incitement to their animosity against the Romans".[470] The Catholic Church with its sense of universality, inherited in part from the Roman tradition, had to make great efforts to conquer the resistance of state churches which in order to distinguish themselves, put their faith in heresies, but also ended up by rendering religion the instrument of power. The evidence for all this can, in Acton's view, be found in the study of political thought. For centuries it developed and was protected within the context of the Church. Absolute power has never tolerated anyone who sought to limit its abuses. Moreover this is the true reason, in Acton's view, why European civilization, in contrast to that of China or Islam, has been able to guarantee real civil progress and development. And the latter, even while it risked being compromised in Europe, was transferred to the "savage tribes – as the natives of California and Paraguay – were converted to a religion which first initiated them in civilization and government".[471] It is not too bold to state that for Acton, without an adequate conversion to Christianity it is impossible to suppose civil political conditions. Beause of this, the Christian religion is, wherever it maintains the distinction between Church and State, the basis on which real liberalism rests.

The Church, as long as it does not become confused with the State, is the first guarantor against absolutism, because in its genuine nature, it cannot tolerate any form of government which offends against liberty and the rights of conscience. Because of this, it sets itself up as an "irreconcilable enemy" of any despotism, whoever exercises it. The words of Acton, in which it is easy to hear echoes of certain convictions which Rosmini had already expressed, leave us in no doubt at all, so clearly stated are they: "The Christian notion of conscience imperatively demands a corresponding measure of personal liberty. The feeling of duty and responsibility to God is the only arbiter of a Christian's actions. With this no human authority can be permitted to interfere … the Church cannot tolerate any species of government in which this right is not recognized. She is the irreconcilable enemy of the despotism of the state".[472] Despite certain historical contingencies, this was the road that the Church had taken.

Acton's liberalism *thus defends not only the distinction and separation between State and Church, but also the centuries-old history of that distinction.* Because of this, it should be made clear that there is in the thinking of the English writer a certain type of *criticism towards the kind of abstract liberalism* which characterized those who, uncritically and with some references to the teachings of the enlightenment, claimed to speak of liberty while ignoring the past. "Real freedom has been known in no state that did not pass through her mediaeval action. The history of the Middle Ages is the history of the gradual emancipation of man from every species of servitude".[473] As we can see, this is an enormous revaluation of a whole historical era too often analysed superficially and hastily judged to have been obscurantist. And yet for Acton there are no doubts that "in proportion to the influence of religion", one may speak of a real development of liberalism. To Christianity alone belongs the merit of having destroyed the authoritarianism of ancient times (Acton claims this to be a special merit of the Church of Rome), and only in the countries where the dualism between Church and state was put into effect, or where there was a struggle over this issue, has modern liberalism become possible.

In politics, one must always look at the substance of things. Thus Acton, taking up a happy intuition of Augustine's, holds that the Church above all holds dear its autonomy in relation to the State, and is little concerned with the political system of the State itself. Monarchy, aristocracy, democracy may depend on times and places. "Christianity could neither produce nor abolish them. They are all compatible with liberty and religion, and are liable to diverge into tyranny by the exclusive exaggeration of their principle. It is this exaggeration that has ever been the greatest danger to religion and liberty, and the object of constant resistance, the source of constant suffering for the Church".[474] What counts, therefore, is the nature of the governments: they may be monarchies, like that of England, surely more liberal than a republic based on the totalizing principle of the general will. We should not allow ourselves, he stresses, to be led astray by empty formulae.

The best political systems cannot be allowed to lose themselves in dreams. Where religion and politics become confused – as for example in the Jewish theocratic system, and in general in all the religions of the ancient states, including those of Greece – liberty is lacking. This begins in Rome, when under the guarantees of law, the indelible and inescapable criterion of giving to God what is God's and to Caesar what is Caesar's is installed. This principle not only opens the new path to liberty, but during the confusion of the great invasions, it prevented a return to the chaos of prehistory. This explains the origins and mediaeval solutions of the problem of the relation between Church and State. The former certainly possessed a temporal power contrary to its nature, but it was instrumental, at a certain moment, in slowing down the irrationality of the barbarians (initially) and the pretensions of the sovereigns (later). The struggle was not easy, and as in all struggles, exaggerations were not lacking.

State absolutism was always the enemy of the Church, even in those circumstances in which, for example during the Counter-Reformation, it seemed to be necessary. In the light of this concept, the most absurd actions in Spain and France and Germany were justified, but these actions, when examined closely, are far more of an adaption of Catholicism to historical contingency rather than a manifestation of its integrity. That all this was contrary to the real spirit of the Church is confirmed by the fact that, specifically in Catholic countries, the Church was subjected and insulted, and it seems almost as if, to defend its integrity, it wished to go into hiding until better times appeared. A paradoxical conclusion which finds its justification if we remember that it was necessary to wait a long time before the idea of tolerance became common again in Europe ... It is certainly no accident that in England, where the rights of minorities were strongly felt. the necessity of limiting the power which was also the expression of the state church emanated from a reborn sense of religious enquiry, for that Church had long ignored the distinction between religion and politics. What counted, according to Acton, is that those non-Catholic countries which gave rise to the path to liberty did so because after the period of crisis due to the Reformation, they resumed, better than the Catholic states, the teaching of the tradition.[475] They tempered the demands of the radicals, and as in England, in a slow and continuous fashion they permitted the revival of liberalism and its development.

Catholic thinkers continued in their message far from Europe, and to the advantage of the peoples of the "New World". Acton did not in fact underestimate the teachings of the School of Salamanca, and the Spanish theorists in general. To them belongs the merit, in the Catholic camp, of having defended the right of peoples against the arrogance of absolutism. How can we overlook the fact that "Las Casas asserted the duties of Christians and the rights of savages"?[476] In the name of the Church, although they were Spanish, they opposed the claims of the conquistadores, who, forgetting the dualism between Church and State, made religion an important shield of their interests.

c) Modernity and Religion: the problem of autonomy

With the period of the Reformation, the possibility of a serious dualism between Church and State had, unfortunately, to be temporarily set aside. Since politics and religion were confused almost everywhere, other forces were needed which, recovering the precepts of Christian liberty laid down by tradition, would be capable of resisting the absurd demands and exigiencies of power. The historical credit for this undertaking belongs to England, but it should immediately be made clear that it was possible because, according to Acton, the English were capable of struggling on the basis of demands motivated by religious intentions, such as for example freedom of conscience.

Freedom of conscience was the dream of great Christian spirits of whom there were many before the age of Milton, Taylor, Baxter and Locke. "The idea that religious liberty is the generating principle of civil, and that civil liberty is the necessary condition of religious, was a discovery reserved for the seventeenth century".[477] To defend this liberty seemed to the English an act of justice and charity. It constituted the soul of progress, almost a form of consecration to God. In order to enjoy this liberty, it was thought that the best thing was to guarantee one's own physical safety and that of one's own goods.

Since the Church was no longer present in England to contest the power of the state, the English were able to find in the future political parties that dualism capable of guaranteeing freedom of conscience. The conflict between Whigs and Tories, once the civil war was over, allowed the English to resume the path of liberty. Not liberty for all, of course, in the sense that quite large numbers remained excluded from it and many chose the path to the colonies. These people did not in fact leave England in search of easy riches, but because they could not bear to live where many English were, on the contrary, by now happy to live.[478] For Acton, choosing the path to the colonies was a little like continuing the "gamble" with liberty.

One principle was immediately clear to the American colonists: "a nation can never abandon its fate to an authority it cannot control".[479] As long as the authority of England was present but did not interfere too much, all went well enough, but later, the situation changed. At the time of the American Revolution, the British government was already claiming powers that could not be enforced, and to the Americans this began to seem absurd. This was a new historical factor, as Acton saw it.

The traditional causes of discontent (poverty, ignorance, contrasts between rich and poor, religious struggles, public debt, states of war) were completely absent in America. The sole problem was that the colonists could not decide their own future, to say nothing of their present. Despite dreams of liberty, they had returned to a state of *de facto* absolutism. And this is the light in which the policy later adopted by Monroe should be seen; he not only believed that the American continent should be left to the self-determination of the individual peoples, but in fact by acting on this belief he defied the Holy Alliance, the final manifestation of absolutism.

The most modern outcome of the English and American Revolutions was the separation of powers which, for Acton, was realized because, since the authority of the popes had been annihilated in the states of the Reformed faith, another solution to limit the central power needed to be found. The Protestant states had literally usurped the functions of the Church by assuming total

227

control.[480] The revolutions thus responded to that need of autonomy from the central power which had, for example, characterized the struggles of the Communes. It is no surprise that in considering these revolutions, Acton should be of the opinion that the conservative forces of the Tory party are more hostile to the Catholic religion, because they consider that Church to be contrary to pre-established stability and an enemy of all "conservatism". The Catholic Church still appears (justly) in their eyes as the most tenacious adversary of the central power.[481] The actual structure of the Church could appear to people who were highly conservative as too "revolutionary". Baptism, in fact, renders all human beings equal in the Church, and by reflection in society. It escaped these critics of Catholicism, however, in Acton's opinion, that there is also an "element of aristocracy" in the Church, which apart from the monarchical authority of the Popes, permits Catholicism to have, in similarity to the Roman republic, a mixed Constitution.

For Acton, the Catholic Church has a perennial teaching which tends towards liberalism. Only from the Church, in fact, can that constant zeal for perfection come, which turns the quest for liberty into an endless process. From the dogmatic point of view, the Church has a perpetually defined teaching, but it nevertheless senses need that is valid for all times, from which an endless task descends on its shoulders; "It was necessary not only to restore the image of God in man, but to establish the divine order in the world. Religion had to transform the public as well as the private life of nations".[482] This is an endless task which reduces to ashes all those utopias which claim to realize the perfect society once and for all. *Liberalism* is presented as a process which, although being reassumed by modern times, must be *constantly revivified by a religious spirit*, without which no criterion of freedom can be defended.

Another element which liberalism cannot find fulfilled in modernity alone, if it seeks not to become sterile, is patriotism, which can easily turn into nationalism.[483] Catholicism, by its very universal nature, is contrary not only to state churches, but also to every extremist concept of nationhood. Now liberalism, having been sown and grown in Catholicism, cannot be crushed into the narrow limits of nationalism if it does not want to betray its own nature. The earliest Christians struggled against it when they emerged from the Judaeo-Christian framework and turned to the Gentiles, but also when, with the disintegration of the Roman state, they turned to the barbarians and introduced them to the paths of civilization. It hardly needs to be mentioned that keeping in mind the way Europe was managed, what most concerned Acton was not the just search for national unity but the failure to recognize the rights of minorities without which it is not possible to speak of liberalism.

The defence of minorities and their autonomy is, as we have seen, another aspect of Acton's liberalism, and explains the reason that in England, in his view, Catholicism had not been favourably viewed for a long time. Unfortunately, during the second half of the seventeenth century, Catholicism was a form of intermediary for French monarchical absolutism in England. It stood, therefore, for a policy of prevarication by a great foreign power in a land where the political parties were already taking their first steps.[484] Catholicism thus passed through one of those phases in which, in France as in Spain, instead of being the counterpoise of power, it became its greatest sustainer, ending at times by ignoring its own tradition and damaging all those elements of autonomy which expected its support. This justified the promulgation of the Test Act, which excluded Catholics from political participation. However, while this Act might have its historical rationale, it seemed completely unjustified to Acton that the Test Act should have had such long-lasting consequences, which came to offend the very principles of the English Revolution and its achievements. It should also be said that for Acton the Test Act lasted so long because in England power was influenced more by the royalist party of the Tories than by the Liberals.

The Tories were a force fearful of radical change (such as might have derived from the abolition of the Test Act), because "they had a passion for order ... and they believed that it would not be secured if the supreme authority was called in question".[485] Acton reminds us that this party of order is also the party of the Reformation. It is thus the party which speaks of an order that excludes no small number of minorities from public affairs. It is the party of the close union between the Church and the State, thus it cannot in fact be called the party of continuity and of the path of liberty, which sees order in the dynamic sense, because it demands a constant adaption. It can be said to be the party of perfectionism, to which is opposed – once again using a Rosminian term – to the party of perfectibility, which is in fact the Whig party. This party too speaks of order and security, but it "desired security against justice and oppression".[486] In this, the Whig party may be called the more modern party, even though this modernity is built on the recovery of the best tradition.

The greatest merit of the Whigs in Acton's eyes was precisely that of understanding that the forces of the past, such as the monarchy and the aristocracy, were not to be destroyed but rendered innocuous, "adjusted, limited and preserved".[487] The liberalism of the Whig party, for this reason, may be called realist, historical and contrary to all forms of abstractism, which, in contrast, often characterize more radical forms of liberalism. This Whig realism is moreover a consequence of the English situation. Those who defend liberalism have concrete interests in English society. They are all elements devoted to commerce, productive activity, banks, etc. A matter therefore, of people engaged in private activity, who wish for safeguards against the central power because they consider such activities perfectly in harmony with the aims of the state itself.

Acton believed that what has been said in the foregoing found confirmation in the fact that "a hundred years passed before Whiggism assumed the universal and scientific character".[488] At first, rather than an acknowledged political doctrine, it was a way of thinking; a combination of concrete principles based on a few presumptions which could not be renounced, such as, for example, the limitation of the (central) power, the defence of property, the security of the individual person, and a certain freedom in work and trade. These principles were only theorized later, and in this case too, thanks to the American experience. This explains why even Burke felt obliged to praise the colonists and their just demands.

The English Revolution, the basic premise for the future American Revolution, was based on distinctly concrete demands which had been put forward for some time, and at times put into practice. This is demonstrated by the fact that in Acton's opinion, some had claimed that "the Revolution of 1688 was not revolutionary but conservative; that it was little more than a rectification of recent error, and a return to ancient principles".[489] Among these, "conditional obedience and the right of resistance became the law. Authority was limited and controlled".[490] All these elements are not, however, the product of mere improvisation. They took shape after centuries of gestation. They became law, indeed fundamental laws, such as the right to resistance, after experience had shown them to be valid. Free trade itself, the public nature of debates, religious freedom were slowly asserting themselves in Europe *before* they found confirmation in the English system. "Modernity" thus rests on history, and cannot do without it. Everything that the English liberal middle class obtained from the Revolution had been long in preparation, for instance, by the conduct of the Italian merchants since the era of the Communes, but what was practised there, in England as in North America, found recognition in the political sphere in specific legislative provisions. In other words, in England and in the United States, an abundant harvest was made of what the greater part of Europe had sown for much of the mediaeval period. It should not be forgotten that, while in the Middle Ages agriculture was the basic economic activity, "the agrarian interest still largely predominated"[491] in the English Revolution. Thus it is true that the most radical expression of the English Revolution found in the world of the agricultural workers the most decisive and intransigent spirits – those, in other words, who when constrained by events, decided to leave their native soil.

Understood in this way, the best liberal spirit belongs to the English and to the Americans, as to the best spirits of the European tradition (and it should not be forgotten that for Acton, St Thomas Aquinas was one of these). One could therefore speak, with reference to the spirit of modernity and liberalism, of a "system of an international, extra-territorial, universal Whig",[492] which *transcends the individual liberal systems*, even though, in some cases, it takes a different concrete form. The fact remains that, for Acton, liberalism can be described as a *universal category of the whole of western civilization*. Even the democratic and egalitarian demands present among the American colonists (for example, the Quakers), derived from the hope of the English country people, who in turn derived their dreams and illusions from their continental ancestors. We may mention, as Acton does, the atrocious represssions carried out during the Reformation against those, and they were many, who demanded real agrarian justice. Even when the problem arose later in America of "not raising taxes on the property of the people without the consent of the people or their deputies",[493] it was no more than bringing to a logical conclusion an analysis of the problem of consent which had been taken up and debated by many. All this began when the mother country demanded exorbitant and unjust taxes from the colonists, in contradiction of its own history and revolution.

Why did the French not succeed in the same intention as the English and American revolutionaries? Because they claimed to be taking a historical leap. Unlike Burke, Acton is not critical of everything about the French Revolution. He believed that in France, there was a moment at which an irremediable error had been committed, which had invalidated the whole revolution. At the time of the "Tennis Court Oath", an important constitutional debate was going on, in which it was the moderates above all who were involved with the democrats, and it is the former group whom Acton terms "liberals". The former "desired to control the Representatives in three ways: by a second chamber, by the royal veto, and the right of dissolution".[494] The democrats, in contrast, did not want to hold out against popular demand, and thus refused the best achievements of the previous revolutions. These achievements had enabled the English and Americans to save tradition and novelty, by vitalizing modernity with the best achievements of the past. In France this was not possible, and thus the French democrats began to sail into the seas of abstraction. With the abdication to the will of the people, the rights of minorities collapsed, and those of the opposition, which often could not even find the courage to express themselves because with the failure of the three principles of control of power, there was also a failure in security itself, and it was shipwrecked in the Terror, in which every kind of freedom was drowned.

In this saddening experience, everything that was best in the European tradition had been thrown overboard. It was claimed that everything was being rebuilt from the beginning, but no account had been taken of a leap into the dark of prehistory, reviving the most ancient political systems such as military dictatorships. Democracy yielded to the mob, and despite the union of all the opposing forces, it was not possible to avoid the rebirth of a new kind of absolutism. Liberty taken to its extreme was reduced to dust at the hands of the revolutionaries, and disappeared into the void. Liberalism, the highest expression of the modern spirit, had not succeeded in defending itself because of the weakness of a government which had not proved capable of imposing limits which would protect certain basic acquired rights.[495] It was thought that the criterion of equality meant the rejection of any kind of authority, and this was confused with the absurd demands of the most tyrannical superiors. Even the criterion of representation, one of the cornerstones of Western political life, was considered to be a real betrayal of democracy.

Thus the point of maximum irrationality was reached, from which it was impossible to turn back. Not only the revolution, but the spirit of modernity itself, understood as the finest fruit of history, had been betrayed. Thus the revolutionaries became blind. "Political science imperatively demands that powers shall be regulated by multiplication and division. The Assembly preferred ideas of unity and simplicity".[496] Simplicity, indeed, of those who sought to ignore the complexity of the problems which, for a solution to be found, had troubled minds over centuries of ingenuity and conflict. In this case, it could be said that simplicity stands outside history.

The *opposite of the spirit of modernity*, in Acton's view, is the *lack of security and stability*, which are among the most difficult achievements of humanity. In moments of crisis, such as those when it is thought possible to remove everything at once, everything becomes temporary, and even the laws are subjected to constant revision.[497] The insecurity that results is not only physical. Indeed, this is an insecurity which derives from a far graver one: the lack of certainty in the law itself. It could be said that for Acton, by ignoring history one not only betrays the true sense of modernity but one ends up in the most total legal uncertainty. The need constantly to change every disposition, and to review every law is something which pertains to those who have no roots, either because they have rejected them or because they are ignorant of them. This is the way to end up in the most precarious forms of life of which insecurity, and ultimately terror, are the most acute symptoms.

To these moments of extreme insecurity, the response is the need for order. It was always thus, not only after the French Revolution, but also after the crises provoked by the Reformation. These authoritarian shifts were supported, too, by many Catholics, who, however, were more concerned about contingencies, and forgot the great teachings of their own tradition. France, with its post-revolutionary experience, is a witness to this. Many Catholics rediscovered Gallicanism, and carried it to extremes because they saw in religion the most effective way of defending absolutism. Others chose the road of ultramontanism. Fortunately, French Catholicism was not completely summed up in these movements, but also found expression in the liberal Catholic movement which pursued the slow and toilsome path of freedom.[498] This was certainly not easy, partly because it met with difficulties from the "intransigent" Catholics, and suspicion on the part of the anti-clericals. The liberal Catholics learned to their cost how necessary respect for minorities really was.

This experience, the lesson of American history and the great attempt of the free communes of the Middle Ages, suggested to Liberal Catholicism of the nineteenth century a revival of the federal ideal. It is important to realize that for Acton many liberal Catholics of his century were federalists precisely because, in contrast even to many innovators, they had been able to read European history in the right way: something which others had not been able to do – Rousseau, for example. He came from Switzerland, which owed all its stability and safety to the federal system. The multiplication of the communities founded on the basis of self-government rendered all minorities secure.[499] And yet "Rousseau's most advanced point was the doctrine that the people are infallible".[500] Because of this, Rousseau, despite all his undeniable merits, is one of those "abstract" thinkers who appear during the revolutionary period and compromise the revolution itself.

But the federalist principle could not be accepted in France. In fact it is based on the fundamental criterion of respect for the conscience and for minorities, which can be understood only by viewing politics from a religious perspective. In France at a certain period this became impossible. Thought was turned more to the totality, to the people as a whole, to the nation, than to the individual and his rights, or to the minorities. Thus a point was reached where power could be without limits, and a new Leviathan was spawned which instead of being conceived in an authoritarian version, was seen in a collective one. The idea of limitations, a true contribution to political science in American history,[501] was completely unknown in Europe, despite the fact that it had been very much alive in Europe's past. How this could have happened we may perhaps deduce from Acton's perceptiveness. A culture which had seen its religious spirit so weakened had become insensitive to certain problems unless it rediscovered them by perceiving their validity and necessity in the dramatic unfolding of events.

To reject respect for minorities and for the rights of the individual was certainly not in Acton's view in line with modernity, also because it stood in the way of the development of another element which should distinguish modern society: the parties. Federalism, local autonomies, the freedom of conscience, minorities, the diversity of interests and opinions, all favoured the development and growth of this element while, in contrast, all forms of unitary experience tended to stultify it. Parties cannot in fact survive where there is a tendency to uniformity of the will and denial of conscience. For Acton this was the great peril of modern history: Europe seemed, in certain contexts, to have undergone a dangerous involution which could lead it to catastrophic consequences. In order to avoid this gloomy future, which the history of the twentieth century sadly often confirmed, it is necessary to be consistent with our own roots. This means returning, often, to far-distant roots, which the Europeans seemed to have lost the art of doing, but which had fortunately been fully achieved by the Americans. They had taken up from the ancient Romans one of the greatest of all preconditions for a guarantee of liberty: i.e. the division of powers.

The Romans, in Acton's view, understood that power, once divided, always became more innocuous.[502] While in Europe this discovery had been set aside, on the other side of the Atlantic – where, as we have mentioned several times, Acton believed the best of European civilization was to be found – it had been put into effect with great success. Federalism is at one and the same time a premise and a consequence of the division of powers, and it is no coincidence that it was already present in the Roman Republic.

At a certain moment, the French Revolution too seemed to be heading towards federalism. Mirabeau, who specifically referred his ideas to Montesquieu, considered it a basic condition for liberty. He was absolutely convinced that there was no other way towards real liberty for a country like France.[503] But even the fact that Mirabeau referred to Montesquieu shows the reason for his failure. His political thought is based on facts deriving from history – a history which the more abstract and radical revolutionaries rejected, believing that they could build their own future "Realm of Liberty" on the basis of a *tabula rasa*.

During the French Revolution, the federal principle was never voted on. The Girondins considered the notion of adopting it absurd,[504] specifically because it came from an experience in their opinion different from that of France. Their way of understanding liberty was radically different. They did not in fact consider that it should be limited, but that it should be the expression of the entire nation. The idea of continuous assembly did not comprehend the value of federalism, and unfortunately did not comprehend either that in failing to do so, it would kill the revolution.

Federalism was immediately and fully understood, on the other hand, by the Americans, who saw in it not only a means of guaranteeing liberty, but also an instrument capable of assuring well-being and progress. All this was because federalism "produced a community more powerful, more prosperous, more intelligent and more free than any other which the world has seen".[505] Local autonomies, the guarantees against the intrusions of central power, endowed the colonists with that tranquillity and security necessary for all economic development. This security had been partly obfuscated in Europe by certain abstract thinkers of the Enlightenment, who were too drawn towards a concept of liberty which they believed could be based only on principles rather than on concrete facts.[506] But it was on the latter that the Americans based their constitution, aware of not being understood in wide sections of the mother country. These sections had supported the Reformation, and were thus certainly unable to grasp what had been developed within the framework of the Church in the Middle Ages. This is the reason why the Crown, the Anglican ecclesiastical structure and the aristocracy, which had also supported the Reformation, and tolerated quite a few aspects of the English Revolution, were firmly opposed to the American Revolution which seemed in their eyes to be too innovative. And yet it should also be remembered, that the American Revolution is the normal continuation of European history, and this is shown by the fact that hostility to the Americans was only shown in Europe by the most reactionary forces.[507] In England, however, the real enemy of the revolutionary cause was the House of Commons.[508] The nation thought in fact that the revolution could be a cause of disturbances capable of bringing about a crisis in a balance which had been so easily reached.

14) A note on Burke: concerning the French Revolution

The French Revolution was one of the events which provided the greatest stimulus to Acton's thinking about history and politics. It was on this very theme that he differed sharply from a thinker, Burke, whom in other respects he greatly admired. In Acton's opinion, in fact, the French Revolution in its initial actions had all the preconditions for a substantial success: it could be said that it had proved incapable, once it got under way, of managing its own development because certain basic components were not at the level of the tasks they faced, and disappointed expectations.

Acton held above all that in France there were original and important precursors which had combatted absolutism, proposing ideas which would in fact have limited its powers. Apart from figures who are universally known, such as Montesquieu, it was possible also to mention other names, such as Fénélon. Although the latter thinker reserved a major role for the monarchy and the aristocracy, he held that in order to limit absolutism it was necessary to transfer certain responsibilities of the government to local institutions, and to establish a complete freedom of trade and a kind of compulsory education system, almost for the purpose of bringing home the meaning of the state to everyone.[509] Others such as Voltaire, who were later to find their confirmation in Montesquieu[510] maintained that the English model should be imitated, as its superiority was expressed not only by the division of powers but also by the possibility of political dissent, which was the real secret of Britain's prosperity. Furthermore, among the "heralds" of the revolution, it was Montesquieu who had had the greatest perception, when he

239

understood that the greatness of the British political system came from the aristocracy which had been capable of handling the changes and incorporating them into British continuity and tradition. It had, in short, succeeded in the by no means easy task of *modernizing the monarchy and its responsibilities.*

At the beginning the French Revolutionaries, or rather their leaders, had clearly in mind the objectives of the revolution. They rightly thought that combatting absolutism belonged to the natural order of things, and Acton considered this completely justified. "Society is founded, not on the will of man, but on the nature of man, the will of God ... Relief of those who suffer is the duty of all men, and the affair of all".[511] This being "of all" witnesses that at its beginning (in contrast to what Burke maintained) the revolution was on the right road to success. The National Assembly made itself the spokesman of these intentions, which were later lost on the way, for reasons which will be examined shortly. Many of the members of the Assembly, moreover, were favourable, like Burke, almost to "canonizing" the American Revolution and the British Constitution,[512] since they were convinced that to combat absolutism, this was the road to be followed.

Probably an early error of the revolutionaries can be seen in the fact that many of them, who belonged to the aristocracy, had fought in the American Revolution (perhaps because they had been stirred in their national pride which had been humiliated by the British in the Seven Years' War, as a result of which France lost both Canada and India). Their fighting alongside the colonists was probably derived from a desire to cut British power down to size. Once the British were defeated, many of them returned to their native country, but lost one of the historic moments of the history of the United States, that of the "arrangement" of the problem of government. "What the French took from the Americans was their theory of government – their cutting not their sewing. Many French nobles served in the war, and came home republicans and even democrats by conviction. It was America that converted the aristocracy to the reforming policy, and gave leaders to the Revolution".[513] The nobles who remained in the home country were, as we shall see shortly, incapable of putting themselves forward as an alternative force, and thus in France the occasion was lost to create an upper chamber, on the model of the English House of Lords, and hence a two-chamber system which would have been able to avoid the excesses and the degeneration of the Revolution.

As far as political power in the strict sense is concerned, the fact that it derives from those over whom it is exercised and that it depends on their will; the fact that no authority is justified if it does not find consensus, and finally the fact that the past constitutes a necessary warning, all add up to saying that these are characteristics common to all revolutions[514] which, however, run aground at a certain point in the French Revolution. If this revolution failed, it is also due to the fact that another basic element of its tradition, i.e. the monarchy, found one of the sovereigns least able to handle a great event like the revolution, and in all Europe no sovereign was found capable of bringing about a historical turn such as that in the model of the English path followed by William of Orange. The weakness of the sovereign partly influenced and partly arose from the weakness of the aristocracy, which should have been, once formed into a party on the Tory model, the natural interlocutor of the revolutionaries.

Acton thus criticized the French Revolution over what it became, certainly not, unlike Burke, over its premises. In the American Revolution too, the factor that preserved its own initial intentions was that of the adjustments which it made gradually, wholly lacking in the French Revolution. In America "some of the restrictions on the governing power were not fully established at first. The most important of these is the action of the Supreme Court in annulling unconstitutional laws".[515] In France, all of this was impossible, and this is another element which brought about the failure of the revolution.

Thus it was not the abstract character of the preconceptions of the Enlightenment, as Burke maintained, that brought everything to ruin, but the lack of flexibility of certain leaders and aristocrats. It should also be said that according to Acton, even among the men of the Enlightenment (e.g. Fénelon, Montesquieu, Voltaire himself and others, the historical arguments which contradict abstractism and defend tradition can be found). It should be added that for Acton, the French thinkers, at the level of political reflection, are mostly followers of English and American theorists, and for this reason the French Revolution, in its initial demands, cannot be said to be all that different from the two others which had preceded it. What differentiates it from the American Revolution in its premises, rather than in its political thinking, is the social component, and thus the stratification of the two populations. But this can certainly not be described as an abstract element, since it is the most concrete of all, deriving from the history of the two different polities.[516] While privileges existed in France, they were the result of a long and complex history. The error was to lump all these privileges together, like all the hay in a bundle, and it was not realised that by saving some of them, the outcome of the revolution might also be saved.

Among those most responsible for this radical turn of events in the French Revolution was Sieyès. In his hands the democratic upsurge cancelled all possibility of saving a role for the aristocracy, and as a consequence, for the king. One person in France, remembering the experience of England, had made an intelligent observation: "Perish the monarch", cried Cazalès, "but not the monarchy".[517] But this real quantum leap was impossible because there was no force in France to resist the urging of democratic claims which were only held at bay, eventually, by force of arms. For the moment, on the other hand, of the former three orders, the revolution ended by placing all the power in the hands of one which ends by justifying every kind of crime, as always occurs when it meets with no limitations to its activity. The masses believed that they could permit everything, and forced the hand of the Assembly itself, so that it found itself constrained to take certain decisions. Everything was concealed behind its "majestic hypocrisy"[518] against which no one dared to react.

While in the early stages the masses influenced the Assembly, later the process degenerated even more. "From that moment onward, the real needs determined the course of the revolution, with the result, as Lord Acton rightly observed, that power passed from the latter to the disciplined population of Paris, and beyond them and their leaders, to the men who manoeuvred the masses".[519] The mass of the people, in fact, as soon as they discovered that the Constituent Assembly was not capable of resolving all the problems of poverty, rebelled against it, and judged it by the same yardstick as the monarchy. The needs of the masses, as was later to be shown in the Paris Commune, became the cutting edge of the revolution which, in Acton's view, no one was able to resist.[520]

It was the nobles who first realized with dismay the uncontrolled spread of mass power. As we have already mentioned, they had not succeeded in organizing a "Tory" party similar to that in England. In their eyes, the age-old distinction between the three orders had always been a source of stability, and there was thus no reason for it to perish. This blindness on their part is truly surprising when we remember that for some of them, the whole debate about power in a revolutionary era was seen as something passing.[521] This inability to read the signs of the times seems yet more astonishing if we recall that a strong and well-organized middle class was growing up before their very eyes; one that was capable of "protecting liberty against the Crown and property against the poor".[522]

Equally surprising is the fact that the Crown was unable to suggest to the nobles that they should all combine to save their own institutions, even at the cost of reforming them. In fact, both the Crown and the aristocracy seemed to show a certain disapproval even towards the term "party".

The monarchy did not even succeed in having that traditional role of arbitrator which in the past had often conferred honour and dignity on it. The state was thus left to its fate, free to distintegrate. In the provinces there was a clear conflict between the nobles who were rich, and their dependents who were extremely poor. All the wealth was on one side, while on the other was all the rage of those who possess nothing and want to seize something for themselves. This clash, which was to culminate in the Terror, took place without anyone being in a position to intervene, since the monarchy existed only in name, and was first incapable of taking, and then not allowed to take, any decision.[523]

The incapacity of the Crown is another cause of the failure of the revolution. Even when it was thought in several quarters that the monarchy should save itself and be recognized by the Constitution, the *Orleans party* was unable to suggest any substitute, any candidate who could possess a minimum degree of credibility. As a result there was a period which was extremely hard to manage, in which some of those who drew up the Constitution were seeking to restore a role and dignity to a monarch who had not the least idea how to merit it. It was thought that the Crown could have played a certain role in the executive, but not even this attempt succeeded, and the point was reached at which even those few who defended the king no longer knew how to resolve the issue. "The king, ceasing to be a danger, became an embarrassment".[524] This doubt about the king also reveals the increasingly confused state of mind of the nobility. It has been said that they were anything but pessimistic about the future outcome. If they were fatalistic, the fatalism was surely an optimistic one. For Acton, even the aristocrats who were most loyal to the king never succeeded in realizing that the monarchy was near to disaster. For the supporters of the Crown, the Sovereign had only changed residence in this latest stage of his life, but his weight and importance had remained intact.[525] Despite the fact that he was a prisoner, there was the conviction that sooner or later he would recover his role in all its fullness, but no one moved a finger to ensure that this happened.

It should perhaps be pointed out that while Burke in his *Reflections* had spoken of the Enlightenment-style abstraction of the revolutionaries, Acton seems to stress the abstraction of the aristocracy, closed in their prejudices and incapable of reading the signs of the times – as their English counterparts, in contrast, had proved capable of doing. This was once again the confirmation in Acton's view that the French Revolution did not set out from wrong premises, but had been "deflected from its path" during its development.

The blindness of the aristocracy, according to Acton, is also shown in the fact that because they drove their dependents to extremes of poverty, they never succeeded in winning them as allies against the bourgeoisie. They did not understand that with a few concessions they could have organized a great force, capable of challenging the bourgeois class.[526] This ultimate failure rendered them even weaker and more isolated.

Conclusion

We have several times referred in these pages to the importance that Acton gave to the Leibnitzian *lex continui*, and it is precisely in this light that the greatest theme dealt with by him in political terms should be seen. This is the resolution of the ancient problem between stability and change, by finding a balance between the authority of tradition, and progress. When this balance is damaged, the end is a lapse into the most contradictory of demagogueries or into the most dangerous of tyrannies, because tradition crystallizes everything of itself, and progress carried to an absolute value knows no limits of law or morality.

The subject of limitations is one of the major ones in Lord Acton's political thought. Defining boundaries for every type of action and creating bulwarks against any encroachment of the powers that be is the main interest of the true democratic liberal. Because of this Acton, basing himself on the tradition of the great liberal thinkers, is led to defend the right of property which constitutes the primary element of liberty. Western civilization, in Greece and better still in Rome with its system of law, grew up and developed in that very search for limitations, and protection of the individual and of the small group, and the environments in which they express their own personalities.

The crisis of a civilization, in Acton's view, is always due to the destruction of its limits, from which come the monstrous excesses of all instincts. This is the instance in which political life is dominated by paradox; the needs of the moment consume all energies and liberty and even the most elementary justice ends up by being sacrificed to contingency.

It is precisely to strengthen the sense of limitations that Acton advocates federalism. To deprive the central government of any political prerogatives and entrust them to local authorities means strengthening those intermediary bodies which all enemies of totalitarian democracy see as the greatest guarantees for the defence of the individual. Echoing John Stuart Mill, Acton insisted on the fact that it was necessary to be forearmed against the strong and growing inclination which tends (and never more than in the contemporary world) to extend the power of the state over the individual in extreme form, both by means of the force of manipulated opinion and by means of legislation. The power of society was growing to the detriment of that of the individual, provoking a decline which affected the simplest tastes and the most important moral principles. If individuals of high moral fibre were not found, society would soon reach total levelling, which would be followed by a crisis of intelligence.

In defending individual liberty we find in Acton a referral to the teaching of history from which it clearly emerges that when the liberty of the individual is defended, the benefit deriving from it affects the whole of society, which finds the way to renew itself and make progress in the creativity of the individual. From a historical point of view this appears as a glaring truth, and it is in fact paradoxical that the West itself, which invented liberalism, has reached the point where it no longer understands the causes and the very nature of its development. To use the language of Ortega, there is a "mutual incomprehension" between the various historical concepts which have dominated Europe over the last century. This is due to the fact that many of them have forgotten the metaphysical roots of humankind, and the purpose, as well as the nature, of its intelligence.

Like De Tocqueville, Acton was convinced that a genuinely liberal and democratic society could not leave aside religious considerations. These do not only concern the conscience of the individual, but constitute the real defence against all totalitarian claims. Only religious freedom and its consistent expression can force the political power to remain bound within its limits and never to become absolute.

Freedom of conscience and of religion also implies respect for the opinion of others, and is the cause of that need for pluralism which, far from being a natural characteristic of mankind, is one of its most hard-won conquests, through slow evolution and improvement. This pluralism, once acquired, can never be set aside, but on the contrary should be defended with firmness from all those who accept it in word but reject it in action. Acton particularly feared those who proposed leaps in the dark, those who suffered from the fascination of revolutions and who, carried away by over-hasty novelties, compromise in a short time conquests which had cost enormous efforts and which only serious historians could recognize. To forget the teaching of history and accept the logic of revolution leads to wiping out the dignity of the person, revealed by Christianity and confirmed by liberalism, as many revolutionary episodes of the twentieth century have sadly shown.

Appendix 1

Judgements on Lord Acton formed in Italy
in the second half of the nineteenth century

In the 1860s and 70s Lord Acton was quite a well-known figure in Italy, both because of his journeys and because of his family, which had lived in the country for many years. For the most part, however, this acquaintance was superficial. The few writings of Acton published in English reviews had not found much direct response in Italy, but only a few indirect echoes deriving from his "dangerous" friendships (Döllinger, for instance, from whom, as we mentioned, he later distanced himself) rather than from his actual historical and political reflections.

Confirmation of this can be found in an interesting work by the future Cardinal Capecelatro, published in Florence in 1875, under the title *Gli effetti de' decreti Vaticani. Considerazioni.* The prelate was an expert on the English scene, and in this essay he examined the dispute between Gladstone and Newman, examined in the first chapter of this book.[527] We may return briefly to the question in order to see how, even to an astute observer such as Capecelatro, the real personality of Acton went unnoticed; he was confused with those German Catholics who went on to create a schism, and from whom the English historian rapidly took his distance.

Certainly the entire work is dominated by the figure of Newman who, because of the high reputation he already enjoyed (and in England in non-Catholic circles also), had calmed and clarified every dispute by his interventions. "Sufficient to say" writes Capecelatro, "that the Pall Mall Gazette, a quite highly regarded Protestant magazine, writes that the quarrel between the Catholics and Protestants is ended, now that Newman in his book has in effect crushed and conquered his adversary".[528] However, the future Cardinal considers other authors behind the figure of Newman, when he deals with an apologetic question which had a universal value for him. These authors came into the issue because, although they could have intervened, they did not. Among these Acton is mentioned, though many extenuating factors are attributed to him, such as the close friendship which bound him to both the contenders (Newman and Gladstone) and the isolation in which he had found himself in the context of English Catholicism, as well as the prudent distance which he had decided to keep after the defeat of the liberal Catholics, and the subsequent silence of public utterance which he had imposed on himself after the crisis of his reviews, especially after the outcome of the First Vatican Council. After the latter, we are forced to the conclusion that in his heart Acton was reviewing his whole relationship with the German world, and especially with Döllinger.

Capecelatro in his essay shows that he understood quite well the terms of the polemic which had broken out in England at the beginning of the 1870s, so that he is able to focus on the essential point: "That no one can be converted to the *Credo* of the Roman Church without renouncing his own moral and intellectual liberty, and without placing his loyalty and civil duty at the disposal of another (the Pope)".[529] To this problem, which had arisen as a result of the declaration of Papal Infallibility, there was added another slightly earlier one which had aroused a great deal of contention in the Protestant world: the definition of the Immaculate Conception. Newman had dedicated all his intellectual and moral resources to both these problems, and even won the esteem of his adversaries. Among the latter, however, there were nevertheless a few denigrators who took it upon themselves to publish a private letter of Newman in which the convert speculated on the appropriateness of "defining" papal infallibility.

The Italian author clearly reveals the mean-spiritedness of certain interlocutors who made use of a letter from a period well before the Council which showed a characteristically English anxiety about the problem. This anxiety, moreover, was set aside after the Conciliar Definition, which Newman publicly and also through some of his writings, accepted immediately, in contrast to other more timid spirits, Capecelatro stresses. In these "others" it is very easy to recognize Acton and the group around him, and justly so. If there is a difference in these post-Conciliar years between Newman and Acton, this difference is not about the dogmatic definition but about its consequences. Both of them were doubtful about the efficacy of such a definition, certainly not for religious reasons, but rather because both considered that it would make dialogue between Catholics and Protestants more difficult. When the definition was proclaimed anyway, the two found themselves in radically different positions. Newman, faithful to the ancient principle *Roma locuta, causa finita est*, accepted the dogmatic definition and defended it, convinced that the time for discussion was now over. Acton's position was less clearly defined, and we may add, more prudent, and it led him to be silent about an issue on which, nevertheless, he was completely in agreement on the interior plane. All this, as we have seen, helped to isolate Acton and led to incomprehension by many people.

On the other hand, we should remember that the situation was certainly a very delicate one, especially considering the accusation that Gladstone had made against Catholics. Apart from Newman's defence, a firm stand by the group of liberal Catholics was expected and awaited by many people. Capecelatro rightly said "The accusation is very grave indeed: it is one of these which most severely wound anyone who has a mind and heart. On the one hand, therefore, because I am faithful to the Roman *Credo*, or because I am a Catholic, I am a rebel against the civil power: on the other hand I have lost all freedom of mind and will!".[530] Given the problem, a position of support for the dogma by the liberal Catholic wing was almost demanded by many. They waited in vain, however, and suspicions increased.

At this point Capecelatro's words become more specific, and this heartfelt statement follows: "Let Gladstone know that we do not despair of Döllinger and his devoted disciples as long as they are alive … To Döllinger, to Acton in particular, and to the other men of heart and mind who tear our hearts by offending the unity of our Church – which is at the same time theirs – I put before their eyes the example of the highest genius and the most subtle dialectic that the church possesses, that of St Augustine".[531] This saint, right at the end of his life, in his famous *Retractions* sought to correct such of what he had written in the past as was not fully in conformity with Catholic doctrine. It was to this "admirable example" that Capecelatro referred Acton and his followers, hoping that he could galvanize them because when there are periods of persecution, it is an obligation to define one's position. The English bishops were also aiming at this, fearing that if they did not take firm measures against the doubts and hesitations, they would engender confusion; they called on Rome to demand the maximum clarity from everyone. In Rome, however, it was caution that prevailed at this period.

It is odd that Capecelatro, in wishing to recall Döllinger and Acton to greater orthodoxy, sought to challenge them on the historical plane,[532] showing, however, that he was unaware that Acton could not at this point be associated with his former master because for him, on the religious and doctrinal level, the Council should certainly not be brought into dispute. For Acton the problem concerned the appropriateness or otherwise of giving official sanction to a principle which no Catholic would ever have dreamed of disputing, let alone denying. It should also be said, however, that the Italian author, by carrying his polemic on to the historical plane, is also aiming to show the ignorance of Gladstone about ecclesiastical history, to stress the lack of foundation for his accusations.[533]

Appendix II

The building of Catholic churches in the mid nineteenth century

After the restoration of the Roman Catholic hierarchy in England, a great problem arose about the building of churches. To us today the problem may seem quite banal, but then even the question of architecture was approached in a way which could be called "doctrinal". It was thought, in fact, that one style more than any other was more compatible with the Catholic liturgy, and moreover was capable of reminding the faithful of the restored links with Rome. This aspect was of primary importance both for English Catholics and for the numerous Irish workers who had emigrated to England.

In Italy in the last century, Capecelatro once again deals with the problem closely linked to the English Catholic renaissance. How delicate the question was can be seen from the numerous difficulties met with by the restored religious orders in fitting in once more to the great inhabited centres. "From the birth of the Reformation in England, Catholics had never been allowed to have chapels in the poor workhouses, and nor were Catholic priests allowed to preach there freely or hear confessions".[534] The first Order to obtain the possibility of having a stable point from which to carry out their pastoral activities were the Oratorians in Birmingham. The explanation is simple: the adhesion of Newman to the Order of St Philip Neri involved all the followers of the future Cardinal, who became convinced that the institution of oratories in England would be the most suitable solution for the English Catholic revival.

The Oratorians aimed at letting the facts speak eloquently for themselves rather than at discussion with Anglicans and Protestants.

They immediately dedicated themselves to those who today would be described as the outcast, the forgotten. One of the primary subjects of attention were elderly workers, worn out with fatigue and reduced to shame by their poverty and solitude, and now incapable of carrying out any work in the industrial environment of the great cities. It was here rather than in the countryside that the Oratorians preferred to work.

After the early approaches it was realized that for greater stability and continuity in their missionary work, simple buildings also adapted for liturgical use were just not enough; proper parishes were needed which could carry on every type of direct activity towards the faithful of all ages and conditions. The first to set an example was the Oratorian Hutchinson, who "having been converted to Catholicism spent almost all his fortune on building a small and very attractive church in the Gothic style, which later was given by the Oratorian Order to the Passionists".[535] It may seem paradoxical, but specifically as a result of this building, a discussion began which in a broad sense involved the whole of English culture.

The discussion proved fertile, since it had an influence on the building of the Oratories in Birmingham and London which, because of the specific wishes of the Oratorians, sought to imitate in everything the finest churches of Italy. To make such a religious aim possible, the English religious procured drawings and projects of some of the churches of the Italian Renaissance and Baroque, and even invited builders and architects to undertake visits to Italy. In the style of the churches, therefore, there was also the aim of stressing fidelity to and dependence on Rome and on the Pope. In this, Newman's followers showed themselves to be the most zealous. "But Faber more than anyone else proved to be very heated in this judgement; and when he came into conflict with Pugin produced among other things the testimony of St Philip Neri himself which (according to him) had especially recommended the classical forms. But as far as I know, that great apostle never entered into disputes about the style of Christian architecture, and was only concerned that in building churches in Rome and Naples there should be an end to those defects which because of the corruption of the times it was customary to graft on to the Roman style".[536]

It is curious that Capecelatro makes a special point of stressing that St Philip Neri had no intention of concerning himself with architectural matters, and did not even prefer one style to another. It should not be forgotten that Capecelatro was an Oratorian himself, and also a historian, so that he was quite expert in the events of his own order. It is still odd that, to give greater authority to their own position, the English Oratorians did make reference to their founding father. The fact remains however that the architectural issue should be considered as purely instrumental. The real motive was surely another: "Faber and other Oratorians, judging that the salvation of England lay in very close union with Rome, laboured to procure this by building certain imitations of its sacred monuments ... who will deny that the temple should remind everyone of Rome".[537] This is not just a rhetorical statement, if we remember that Newman and his followers had made the choice of their life in Rome, also choosing their religious order and their model of apostolate.

There were those who sought to induce the Oratorians to doubt, saying that if the Gothic style was to be set aside because it was too closely linked to the Reformation world, an alternative choice existed in the Byzantine style which, even in Rome, had found its admirers. It was replied that the oriental style had met with approval before the schism and not after, and that thus the "schismatic" churches of the east could not, on a par with those of the West, act as models. "That indeed Byzantium and London suffered the fate common to cities and realms, which because of too great a greed for lordship, fall into slavery. Having thrown off the salutary yoke of Rome, the Byzantine patriarchs, who called themselves Ecumenical, and refused even to be subject to the Roman See, became instead disgracefully subservient to the weak emperors of the East, while the British clergy and people, in matters of religion, obeyed the King, the parliament and the régime".[538] Statements of this kind show clearly in what difficulty and what suspicion Acton and his friends were forced to act, and how easy it was to look with suspicion on all those who had a more conciliatory attitude towards their adversaries.

In this instance too, Newman's personality proved decisive. The future Cardinal never became immersed in such disputes, but being a member of the Oratory, he in fact tipped the balance even in this dispute over architecture, in favour of those who sought to imitate Rome in everything and for everything. A visit to the London Oratory is more convincing than any discussion. The statues of the apostles in the Berninian style, carved in Carrara marble, the copy of the bronze statue of St Peter attributed to Arnolfo di Cambio, the painting of St Philip Neri by Guido Reni, the statues of the saints, the pulpit, the choir, the dome, are just a few of the countless examples which recall the style of the Roman Renaissance, together with the columns, pillars and ceiling. It was from that Renaissance that the Reformation came, and it was from that Reformation that, by referring back to that period, it was necessary to distinguish themselves.

Notes

[1] H. Butterfield: *Lord Acton: Le conferenze dell'Università cattolica,* Milan 1962, pp. 18-19.

[2] See, for example, the heading "Liberalismo" in N. Bobbio – N. Matteucci: *Dizionario di Politica*, UTET, Turin 1976.

[3] Ibid. p. 529.

[4] Cf. ibid. p. 529.

[5] G. De Ruggiero: *Storia del liberalismo europeo*, Milan 1971, pp. 118-119.

[6] Cf. ibid. pp. 113 ff.

[7] E. Passerin D'Entrèves, *Preface* to various: *I cattolici liberali nell'ottocento*, Turin 1976, p. 6.

[8] Cf. ibid. p. 9.

[9] Cf. among the many affirmations, under the heading *Liberals, Catholic,* in *The Catholic Concise Encyclopedia*, New York 1957.

[10] E. Passerin D'Entrèves: *Preface,* op. cit., p. 9.

[11] On this subject cf. the first three paragraphs of the second part of this book.

[12] V .Conzemius: *I focolai internazionali del cattolicesimo liberale fuori della Francia nel XIX secolo: sommario di una geografia storica,* in various: *I cattolici liberali nell'ottocento*, op. cit., p. 16. The statement is taken from a letter from Acton to Döllinger dated 14 April 1870, *Döllingerbriefwechsel* (ed. Conzemius), t. 11, Munich 1965, p. 314.

[13] Cf. ibid. p. 37.

[14] Cf. ibid. pp. 50 ff.

[15] B. Aspinwall: *Orestes A. Brownson e l'Europa,* in : *I cattolici liberali nell'ottocento,* op. cit., p. 142.

[16] Cf. R. Remond: *Relazione conclusiva,* in various: *I cattolici liberali nell'ottocento,* op. cit., p. 403.

[17] Cf. I. Ker: *John Henry Newman, a Biography,* Oxford 1990, p. 498.

[18] Cf. M. Niveau: *Storia dei fatti economici contemporanei,* Milan 1976, pp. 116 ff.

[19] De Ruggiero: *Storia del liberalismo europeo*, op. cit., p. 95.

[20] Ibid. p. 96.

[21] Ibid. p. 99.

[22] Ibid. p. 115.

[23] Cf. the central part of the 7th paragraph of the first part.

[24] Cf. the most complete study of Gladstone, that of his friend J. Morley: *Life of Gladstone* 3 volumes, London 1903.

[25] Cf. ibid. Vol. I, p. 384.

[26] Cf. again paragraph 7 of the first part.

[27] G. De Ruggiero: *Storia del liberalismo europeo*, op. cit., p. 131.

[28] Cf. various: *Liberalismo ed integralismo. Tra Stati nazionali e diffusione missionaria*, in *Storia della Chiesa*, directed by H. Jedin, Vol. VIII/2, Milan 1977, pp. 80 ff.

[29] Cf. ibid. pp. 240 ff.

[30] Various: *La Chiesa negli Stati moderni e i movimenti sociali, 1878-1914*, in *Storia della Chiesa*, directed by H. Jedin, Vol. IX, Milan 1979, p. 15.

[31] Cf. on this subject see also D. Mathew: *Catholicism in England: the Portrait of a Minority, 1835-1935*, London 1948 (p. 269 of the Italian translation).

[32] Cf. ibid. p. 261.

[33] Cf. G. Himmelfarb: *Introduction* to J. E. E. D. Acton: *Essays on Freedom and Power*, New York 1955, p. 9.

[34] Cf. ibid. p. 9.

[35] Ibid. p. 9.

[36] Cf. D. Mathew: *Acton, the formative years*, London 1946, p. 35.

[37] Cf. M. Belardinelli: *Döllinger e l'Italia: per una storia del dibattito sulla libertà nella Chiesa nell'ottocento*, in *Rivista di storia della Chiesa in Italia*, XXXVI-2, p. 397.

[38] Ibid. pp. 396-397.

[39] *Storia della Chiesa*, Vol. XXI/1: *Il Pontificato di Pio IX*, edited by R. Aubert, 2nd Italian edition based on the 2nd French edition edited by G. Martina, Turin 1976, p. 325. This is the encyclopaedia initiated by Augustin Fliche and Victor Martin.

[40] Cf. D. Mathew: *Acton, the Formative Years*, op. cit., pp. 72-73.

[41] Cf. ibid. p. 74. Cf. also on the problem of the spread of Döllinger's ideas in England, J. E. E. D. Acton: *Döllinger's historical work* in EHR 1 (1890), pp. 700-744.

[42] Cf. D. Mathew: *Lord Acton and his times*, London 1968, p. 164.

[43] Cf. ibid. p. 165.

[44] Cf. ibid. p. 174.

[45] Ibid. p. 185.

[46] Cf. ibid. p. 194.

[47] Ibid. p. 190.

[48] Cf. ibid. p. 191.

[49] Cf. ibid. pp. 202-203.

[50] Cf. D. Woodruff: *Introduction* to Lord Acton: *Essays on Church and State*, London 1952, p. 11.

[51] Ibid. p. 25. The quotation is taken from a letter addressed to Newman.

[52] Cf. ibid. p. 28.

[53] Ibid. p. 33.

[54] Cf. D. Mathew: *Lord Acton and his times*, op. cit., p. 277.

[55] *Storia della Chiesa*, Vol. XXI/1, op. cit., p. 113.

[56] On this matter, cf. D. Mathew: *Catholicism in England: the Portrait of a Minority, 1835-1935*, London 1948 (Italian translation Rome 1951); G. A. Beck (editor): *The English Catholics, 1850-1950. A Centenary of Progress. Essays to*

commemorate the restoration of the Hierarchy of England and Wales, London 1950; O. Chadwick: *The Victorian Church*, 2 vols, London 1966-1970; D. Gwynn: *A Hundred years of Catholic Emancipation (1829-1929)*, London 1929; P. Thureau-Dangin: *La Renaissance catholique en Angleterre au XIXème siècle*, 3 vols, Paris 1903-1908; A. D. Toledano: *Histoire de l'Angleterre chrétienne*, Paris 1955; D. Knowles: *The Religious Orders in England*, London 1963. Also important for understanding the transformations which took place within the English ecclesiastical world are: E. Reynolds: *Three Cardinals: Newman, Wiseman and Manning*, London 1958; V. A. McClelland: *Cardinal Manning: His Public Life and Influence, 1865-1892*, London – New York 1962; W. Ward: *The Life and Times of Cardinal Wiseman*, London 1897; W. Ward: *The Life of J. H.Cardinal Newman*, London 1912, and finally the autobiography of W. Ullathorne: *From Cabin-boy to Archbishop*, London 1943.

[57] *Storia della Chiesa*, op. cit., p. 114.

[58] Ibid. p. 111.

[59] Cf. various: *La Chiesa nella Società liberale*, Turin 1977, p. 269.

[60] The reflections of Newman on the problem were later collected in a work entitled *On the Idea of a University*.

[61] *Storia della Chiesa*, Vol. XXI/1, op. cit., pp. 259-260.

[62] Cf. D. Mathew: *Catholicism in England; the Portrait of a Minority, 1835-1935*, op. cit., p. 245.

[63] Cf. ibid. pp. 257-258.

[64] The problem of organizing the religious masses in the great cities was in fact one that affected all the religious confessions, including the Anglican Church in England. On this, see G. I. T. Machin: *Politics and the Churches in Great Britain, 1869-1921*, Oxford 1987. The author (who dealt with the same subject from 1832 to 1868 in a previous volume) effectively reveals the concerns and the initiatives of the state church in a similar dangerous situation.

[65] Cf. D. Mathew: *Catholicism in England...*, op. cit., p. 275.

[66] Cf. Ibid. pp. 275-276.

[67] Cf. ibid. p. 277.

[68] Cf. ibid. p. 285.

[69] On this subject, see the essay of M. McNarncy: *La Vita parrocchiale*, in : *Catholicisme anglais*, Paris 1960 (Italian translation Rome 1963). Also in this collection, note should be taken of the essays by H. J. Carpenter: *Ordini e congregazioni*; R. P. Walsh: *Le organizzazioni cattoliche*, and M. Bevenst: *Cattolici ed eredi della Riforma*.

[70] A. Prandi: *Introduction* to various: *Catholicisme anglais*, op. cit., p. XV.

[71] Ibid. p. XVII.

[72] Cf. on this subject: R. Brent: *Liberal Anglican Politics*, Oxford U. P. 1987.

[73] Cf. D. Mathew: *Catholicism in England...*, op. cit., p. 227.

[74] Cf. H. Butterfield: *Lord Acton*, op. cit., p. 6.

[75] Ibid. p. 20.

[76] Cf. M. Belardinelli: *Döllinger e l'Italia: per una storia del dibattito sulla libertà nella Chiesa nell'ottocento*, op. cit., p. 398.

[77] Ibid. pp. 399-400.

[78] Cf. G. Himmelfarb: *Introduzione...*, op. cit., p. 11.

79 Cf. ibid. p. 12.

80 Cf. ibid. p. 16.

81 Cf. ibid. p. 17.

82 H. Butterfield: *Lord Acton,* op. cit., p. 7.

83 Cf. G. Himmelfarb: *Introduction...,* op. cit., p. 17.

84 H. Butterfield: *Lord Acton,* op. cit., p. 17.

85 S. Mastellone: *Storia ideologica d'Europa da Stuart Mill a Lenin,* Florence 1982, p. 174.

86 Cf. : *La Chiesa nella Società liberale,* op. cit., p. 268.

87 Cf. on this individual: D. McElrath: *Richard Simpson (1820-1876): A Study in 19th century English Liberal Catholicism,* Louvain 1972; J. L. Altholtz and D. McElrath: *The Correspondence of Lord Acton and Richard Simpson,* Cambridge 1971; D. McElrath: *Richard Simpson and Count de Montalembert,* in The Downside Review, t. LXXXIV, 1966, pp. 150-170.

88 Cf. D. Woodruff: *Introduction,* to Lord Acton: *Essays on Church and State,* op. cit., p. 10.

89 *Storia della Chiesa,* Vol. XXI/1, op. cit., p. 310.

90 Cf. D. Woodruff: *Introduction ...,* op. cit., p. 31.

91 Ibid. p. 17. On the importance which Döllinger's historical works exercised on Acton, see his essay *Döllinger's Historical Work,* which appeared in the E. H. R. No. 1 (1980).

92 Various: *La Chiesa nella Società liberale,* op. cit., p. 270.

93 See on this issue: J. J. Hughes: *Absolutely Null and Utterly Void: the Papal Condemnation of Anglican Orders,* London 1968.

94 Cf. J. L. Altholtz: *The Liberal Catholic Movement in England,* London 1962, p. 1.

95 Cf. "Rich and Poor" in the *Rambler,* I (22-IV-1848).

96 J. L. Altholtz: *The Liberal Catholic Movement in England,* op. cit., p. 11.

97 Cf. ibid. p. 17.

98 Cf. ibid. p. 15. Anyone seeking an example of this argument between the two styles (Gothic and "Roman") is referred to the *London Oratory,* with which we shall deal briefly in an appendix.

99 Cf. ibid. p. 26.

100 Cf. "Religion and Modern Philosophy", in the *Rambler,* VI (September 1850).

101 Cf. various: *Les catholiques libéreaux au XIX siècle.* Grenoble University Press 1974. (Italian translation, Turin 1976, p. 43).

102 Cf. J. L. Altholz: *The Liberal Catholic Movement in England,* op. cit., pp. 43-44.

103 Cf. A. Gasquet: *Lord Acton and his Circle,* London 1906, p. 4.

104 Cf. J. L. Altholz: *The Liberal Catholic Movement in England,* op. cit., p. 65.

105 Ibid. p. 69.

106 Cf. ibid. pp. 83-84.

107 Cf. ibid. pp. 91-93.

108 Cf. J. E. E. D. Acton: *Essays on Church and State,* London 1952, pp. 86-87.

109 Cf. J. L. Altholz: *The Liberal Catholic Movement in England,* op. cit., pp. 137-138.

110 Ibid. p. 139.

111 Cf. R. Simpson: "Reason and Faith", in the *Rambler*, V, July 1861, p. 182.

112 Cf. R. Simpson: "Reason and Faith", (second article), in the *Rambler*, V, Sept 1861, p. 337.

113 Cf. J. E. E. D. Acton: *Essays on Church and State*, op. cit., p. 282.

114 The essay is to be found in the volume: *The History of Freedom and other Essays*, London 1907.

115 Cf. A. Gasquet: *Lord Acton and his Circle,* op. cit., p. 180.

116 Cf. ibid. p. 191.

117 Cf. J. L. Altholz: *The Liberal Catholic Movement in England,* op. cit., pp. 169-171.

118 Ibid. p. 183.

119 Cf. the letter by Lord Acton *The Danger of Physical Science*, contained in the *Rambler,* VI, May 1862.

120 On the whole affair, see also the *Introduction* by Cardinal Gasquet in *Lord Acton and his Circle,* op. cit..

121 Cf. ibid. p. 289.

122 This was R. Simpson: *Bishop Ullathorne and 'The Rambler'*, London 1862.

123 Cf. H. Butterfield: *Lord Acton*, London 1948, p. 9.

124 Cf. the numbers of *The Home and Foreign Review,* from 1863 to 1864.

125 Cf., e.g., the essay of H. E. Manning: "The Work and the Wants of the Catholic Church in England", in *Dublin Review,* I, July 1863.

126 J. L. Altholz: *The Liberal Catholic Movement in England*, op. cit., p. 221.

127 Cf. ibid. p. 222.

128 Cf. Gasquet: *Lord Acton and his Circle*, op. cit., p. 206.

129 Cf. ibid. p. 318. This refers to a letter written to Simpson three days after the publication of the Papal document.

130 Cf. J. L. Altholz: *The Liberal Catholic Movement in England*, op. cit., pp. 225-227. Acton's article *Conflicts with Rome* was subsequently published in J. E. E. D. Acton: *The History of Freedom and other Essays,* op. cit., pp. 461-491.

131 Cf. ibid. p. 233.

132 H. A. MacDougall: *The Acton–Newman relations; the dilemma of Christian Liberalism,* F. U. P. New York 1962, p.IX.

133 Cf. ibid. pp. 24-25.

134 Cf. ibid. p. 28.

135 Cf. ibid. pp. 38-39.

136 Ibid. p. 42.

137 Cf. J. L. Altholz: *The Liberal Catholic Movement in England,* op. cit., p. 100.

138 Cf. ibid. pp. 103-104.

139 Cf. ibid. p. 109.

140 C. Lovera di Castiglione: *Introduction* to J. H. Newman: *Lettere scelte* p. XXXIX.

141 Cf. ibid. p. 145.

142 Cf. ibid. p. 149.

143 Cf. ibid. p. 153.

144 Cf. T. Kenny: *The Political Thought of J. H. Newman,* London 1974, pp. 153-154.

[145] Cf. C. Lovera di Castiglione: *Introduction,* op. cit., p. lix.

[146] This passage is taken from H. A. MacDougall: *The Acton–Newman Relations...*, op. cit., p. 57.

[147] Cf. The first page of H. E. Manning: *The Temporal Power of the Pope*, London 1880.

[148] Cf. H. A. MacDougall: *The Acton–Newman Relations...*, op. cit., pp. 64-65.

[149] Cf. ibid. pp. 68-69. The text in question contains substantial passages from Acton's article.

[150] Ibid.

[151] Cf. A Gasquet: *Lord Acton and his Circle*, op. cit., p. 172.

[152] Cf. ibid. p. 188.

[153] Cf. ibid. p. 241.

[154] H. A. MacDougall: *The Acton–Newman Relations...*, op. cit., p. 92. The letter concerned dates from 1864.

[155] Cf. Ibid.

[156] Ibid, p. 94. The letter is taken from Gasquet's book (op. cit.) on p. 315.

[157] Cf. ibid. p. 94.

[158] D. Battaini: *Introduction* to J. H. Newman: *Il Papa, il Sillabo e l'infallibilità papale*, Turin 1909, p. xvii.

[159] Ibid. pp. xxi-xxii.

[160] Ibid. p. xxiv.

[161] Ibid. p. xxxv.

[162] Cf. H. A. MacDougall: *The Acton–Newman Relations...*, op. cit., p. 96.

[163] Cf. ibid. p. 98.

[164] On the two articles by Acton see ibid. pp. 111-115.

[165] Cf. ibid. p. 121.

[166] Cf. ibid. p. 127.

[167] Cf. ibid. p. 128.

[168] Cf. ibid. p. 130.

[169] Cf. ibid. pp. 133-135: substantial excerpts from this letter of 4.12.1874 are reproduced here.

[170] Cf. ibid. pp. 138-139.

[171] Cf. J. H. Newman: *Il Papa, il Sillabo e l'infallibilità papale*, Turin 1909, p. viii.

[172] Cf. ibid. pp. 40-41. The quotation is taken from the English edition of Ranke's work *The Popes*.

[173] Cf. ibid. p. 52.

[174] Cf. ibid. pp. 61-62.

[175] Cf. ibid. pp. 80-81.

[176] Cf. ibid. p. 138.

[177] Cf. ibid. p. 141.

[178] H. A. MacDougall: *The Acton–Newman Relations...*, op. cit., p. 143.

[179] Cf. ibid. p. 144.

[180] Cf. ibid. p. 152.

[181] Cf. ibid. p. 157.

[182] Cf. ibid. p. 161.

[183] Cf. D. Mathew: *Catholicism in England...*, op. cit., p. 291.

[184] H. A. MacDougall: *The Acton–Newman Relations...,* op. cit., p. 169.

[185] Cf. Ibid.

[186] Cf. ibid. p. 171.

[187] Cf. Ibid.

[188] Cf. G. Velocci: *Newman, il problema della conoscenza,* Rome 1985, p. 7.

[189] Ibid. p. 140.

[190] Ibid. p. 143.

[191] Ibid. p. 147.

[192] H. A. MacDougall: *The Acton–Newman Relations...,* op. cit., p. 173.

[193] Cf. ibid. pp. 178-179.

[194] Cf. ibid. pp. 181-182.

[195] Cf. ibid. p. 182. With regard to the reflections provided by Lord Acton on St. Augustine, see the numerous passages contained in *A History of Freedom and Other Essays,* op. cit.

[196] Cf. ibid. p. 183.

[197] Cf. ibid. p. 12.

[198] Cf. ibid. p. 23.

[199] Cf. J. L. Altholz: *The Liberal Catholic Movement in England*, op. cit., p. 60.

[200] Cf. ibid. p. 98.

[201] J. H. Newman: "On consulting the Faithful in Matters of Doctrine", in the *Rambler,* I, July 1859, p. 230.

[202] Cf. C. Butler: *The Life and Times of Bishop Ullathorne, 1806-1889,* 2 volumes, London 1926, Vol I, pp. 319-320.

[203] G. Velocci: *Newman, il problema della conoscenza,* op. cit., p. 152.

[204] Ibid. p. 152.

[205] Ibid. p. 154.

[206] Ibid. p. 155.

[207] Ibid. p. 156.

[208] D. Woodruff: *Introduction...,* op. cit., p. 29.

[209] Cf. G. E. Fasnacht: *Acton's Political Philosophy,* London 1952, p. 168.

[210] Cf. ibid. p. 168. Cf. also on this issue: J. E. E. D. Acton: *A History of Freedom and Other Essays,* London 1907.

[211] Cf. J. E. E. D. Acton: *A History of Freedom and Other Essays,* op. cit., p. 219.

[212] Ibid. p. 225.

[213] Cf. ibid. p. 231.

[214] J. E. E. D. Acton: "Ultramontanism", in *Essays on Church and State,* London 1952, p. 37.

[215] Ibid. p. 38.

[216] Ibid. p. 38.

[217] D. Mathew: *Lord Acton and his Times,* op. cit., p. 130.

[218] G. E. Fasnacht: *Acton's Political Philosophy,* op. cit., p. 144.

[219] Ibid. p. 166.

[220] Ibid. p. 144.

[221] D. Mathew: *Acton, the formative years,* op. cit., p. 93.

[222] Ibid. p. 93.

[223] Ibid. p. 95.

[224] Cf. ibid. p. 97.

[225] Ibid. p. 94.

226 Cf. J. E. E. D. Acton: "The Political State of the Popes", in *Essays on Church and State*, op. cit., p. 158.

227 G. E. Fasnacht: *Acton's Political Philosophy,* op. cit., pp. 161-162.

228 Ibid. p. 24.

229 Ibid. p. 197.

230 Ibid. p. 145.

231 J. E. E. D. Acton: *Doellinger's Historical Work,* op. cit. The quotation is repeated in D. Mathew: *Lord Acton and his times*, op. cit., p. 42.

232 Ibid. p. 200.

233 Cf. G. E. Fasnacht: *Acton's Political Philosophy,* op. cit., p. 20.

234 Cf. ibid. pp. 7-8.

235 Cf. Ibid.

236 Cf. ibid. p. 63.

237 Cf. ibid. p. 61.

238 J. E. E. D. Acton: *Historical Essays and Studies*, London 1907, p. 361.

239 G. E. Fasnacht: *Acton's Political Philosophy,* op. cit., pp. 28. With regard to Acton's considerations on Leibniz, cf. *Historical Essays and Studies*, op. cit., p. 361, and *The History of Freedom and Other Essays*, op. cit., pp. 381-393.

240 Cf. ibid. p. 20.

241 Ibid. p. 20.

242 J. E. E. D. Acton: "The Heralds of the Revolution", in *Essays in the Liberal Interpretation of History*, Chicago 1967, p. 398.

243 Ibid. p. 368.

244 Cf. G. E. Fasnacht: *Acton's Political Philosophy*, op. cit., p. 196.

245 J. E. E. D. Acton: *The History of Freedom and Other Essays*, London 1907, op. cit., p. 203.

246 G. E. Fasnacht: *Acton's Political Philosophy,* op. cit., p. 35.

247 Ibid. p. 40.

248 In this context there is a curious lapidary statement in which Fasnacht sums up Acton as he describes the world of the sixteenth and seventeenth centuries: "Calvin preached and Bellarmine lectured, but Machiavelli reigned." (Ibid. p. 169).

249 Ibid. p. 196.

250 Ibid. p. 143.

251 Ibid. p. 38.

252 J. E. E. D. Acton: "The History of Freedom in Antiquity", in *Essays on Freedom and Power,* New York 1955, p. 63.

253 Cf. ibid. pp. 65 ff.

254 J. E. E. D. Acton: "Mr Buckle's thesis and method", in Lord Acton: *Essays in the Liberal Interpretation of History,* Chicago 1967, p. 17.

255 Ibid. p. 17.

256 J. E. E. D. Acton: "The Beginning of the Modern State", in Lord Acton: *Essays in the Liberal Interpretation of History,* op. cit., p. 419.

257 Cf. ibid. p. 401.

258 Ibid. p. 401.

259 W. H. McNeill: *Editor's Introduction* to Lord Acton: *Essays in the Liberal Interpretation of History*, op. cit., p. xi.

260 G. E. Fasnacht: *Acton's Political Philosophy,* op. cit., p. 19.

261 Ibid. p. 19. The quotation is taken from the *Rambler*, January 1860, p. 146.

262 W. H. McNeill: *Editor's Introduction* to Lord Acton: *Essays ...* op. cit., p. xv.

263 Cf. J. E. E. D. Acton: "Political causes of the American Revolution", in *Essays on Freedom and Power*, op. cit., pp. 171-172.

264 A. Maurois: *Storia degli Stati Uniti*, (Italian translation), Milan 1966, p. 193.

265 Ibid. p. 196.

266 Cf. W. H. McNeill: *Editor's Introduction...*, op. cit., p. xv.

267 Cf. J. E. E. D. Acton: "Mr Buckle's thesis and method", op. cit., p. 4.

268 Ibid. p. 8.

269 Ibid. p. 8.

270 Cf. G. E. Fasnacht: *Acton's Political Philosophy,* op. cit., p. 39.

271 Cf. J. E. E. D. Acton: "The History of Freedom in Christianity", in *Essays on Freedom and Power,* op. cit., p. 86.

272 Cf. ibid. pp. 88 ff.

273 J. E. E. D. Acton: "The Protestant Theory of Persecution", in *Essays on Freedom and Power*, op. cit., p. 115.

274 Cf. ibid. pp. 120 ff.

275 Cf. ibid. pp. 123 ff.

276 Cf. ibid. pp. 134 ff.

277 Ibid. p. 136.

278 Cf. ibid. p. 136.

279 Cf. J. E. E. D. Acton: "Mr Buckle's thesis and method", op. cit., pp. 10 ff.

280 Cf. ibid. p. 11.

281 Cf. ibid. p. 13.

282 Ibid. p. 14.

283 Cf. ibid. p. 18.

284 Cf. A. Gasquet: *Lord Acton and his circle*, op. cit., p. 148, Letter LXVI.

285 Quotation taken from P. Alatri: *Introduction* to J. E. E. D. Acton: *Cattolicesimo liberale*, saggi storici, Florence 1950.

286 Ibid.

287 A. Gasquet: *Lord Acton and his circle*, op. cit., p. 3.

288 P. Alatri: *Introduction to ...,* op. cit., p. lv.

289 Ibid. p. liv.

290 Cf. A. Gasquet: *Lord Acton and his circle*, op. cit., pp. 254-255.

291 Cf. J. N. Figgis and R.V. Laurence: *Introduction* to J. E. E. D. Acton: *Lectures on Modern History,* London 1906, p. xv.

292 Cf. ibid. p. xvii.

293 This text is to be found in J. E. E. D. Acton: *Lectures on Modern History*, edited by J.N. Figgis and R.V. Laurence (op. cit.).

294 Cf. Lord Acton: "Inaugural Lecture on the study of History", in *Lectures in Modern History*, op. cit., p. 1.

295 Cf. ibid. p. 2.

296 Cf. ibid. p. 2.

297 Cf. ibid. pp. 3-4. The words between parentheses are my own. (It is hardly necessary to point out that specifically on this latter point, a well-known Catholic scholar of the twentieth century, Gilson, demonstrated that same thesis

of continuity which Acton was unable to identify. In his famous study of Descartes, it was amply shown how much of scholasticism and of mediaeval philosophy it is possible to find in the author of the Discourses. Descartes is presented as a "novelty in continuity").

298 Cf. ibid. p. 5.

299 Cf. ibid. p. 4.

300 Cf. ibid. p. 5.

301 Cf. ibid. p. 6.

302 Cf. ibid. p. 8.

303 Cf. ibid. p. 10.

304 Ibid. p. 12.

305 Cf. ibid. p. 14.

306 Cf. ibid. p. 5.

307 Cf. ibid. p. 17.

308 P. Alatri: *Introduction* to ..., op. cit., pp. xli-xlii.

309 Cf. Lord Acton: "Inaugural Lecture on the study of History", op. cit., pp. 21-22.

310 Cf. ibid. p. 21.

311 Cf. ibid. p. 22.

312 Ibid. pp. 23-24.

313 Cf. ibid. p. 25.

314 Cf. ibid. p. 27.

315 Cf. ibid. p. 27.

316 Cf. ibid. p. 27.

317 Cf. ibid. p. 28.

318 Cf. ibid. p. 28.

319 Cf. ibid. p. 28.

320 L. Kochan: *Acton on History*, London 1954, p. 101.

321 Ibid. pp. 101-102.

322 Ibid. p. 102.

323 Ibid. p. 105.

324 Cf. Lord Acton: *Introduction* to L. A. Burd's Edition of *Il Principe* by Machiavelli, in Acton: *History of Freedom and Other Essays*, London 1907, pp. 25 ff.

325 L. Kochan: *Acton on History*, op. cit., p. 109.

326 Ibid. pp. 109-110.

327 P. Alatri: *Introduction* ..., op. cit., p. xliv.

328 Ibid. p. xlv.

329 J. E. E. D. Acton: "The Beginning of the Modern State", in *Lectures on Modern History,* op. cit., p. 43.

330 Cf. ibid. pp. 49 ff.

331 Ibid. p. 50.

332 Cf. ibid. pp. 50-51.

333 Cf. J. E. E. D. Acton: "The New World", in *Lectures on Modern History,* op. cit., p. 52.

334 Cf. ibid. pp. 63 ff.

335 Cf. ibid. p. 70.

336 Cf. A. Gasquet: *Lord Acton and his ...,* op. cit., p. 221.

337 J. E. E. D. Acton: "The History of Freedom in Antiquity", in *Essays on Freedom and Power,* op. cit., p. 29.

338 A. Gasquet: *Lord Acton and his ...,* op. cit., p. 124.

339 Ibid. p. 224.

340 G. E. Fasnacht: *Acton's Political Philosophy*, op. cit, pp. 187-188.

341 Ibid. p. 85. The two quotations are taken from *The History of Freedom and Other Essays,* op. cit.

342 Ibid. p. 188.

343 P. Alatri: *Introduction ...,* op. cit., p. l.

344 Cf. ibid. p. li.

345 Cf. A. Gasquet: *Lord Acton and his ...,* op. cit., p. 254.

346 Cf. J. E. E. D. Acton: "Political Thoughts on the Church", in *The History of Freedom and Other Essays,* op. cit., p. 205.

347 D. Mathew: *Acton, the formative years,* op. cit., p. 100.

348 Ibid. p. 102.

349 G.E. Fasnacht: *Acton's Political Philosophy*, op. cit., p. 178.

350 J. E. E. D. Acton: *Cavour,* in *Historical Essays and Studies,* London 1907, p. 201.

351 Cf. ibid. p. 202.

352 Ibid. p. 202.

353 Ibid. p. 202.

354 Cf. ibid. pp. 203.

355 Ibid. pp. 200-201.

356 Cf. G. E. Fasnacht: *Acton's Political Philosophy,* op. cit., p. 183.

357 Cf. ibid. p. 89.

358 J. E. E. D. Acton: "Nationality", in *The History of Freedom and Other Essays*, op. cit., p. 288.

359 G. E. Fasnacht: *Acton's Political Philosophy,* op. cit., p. 93.

360 Ibid. p. 89.

361 Cf. ibid. p. 90.

362 Ibid. p. 90. Also the first page of the *Inaugural Lecture,* op. cit.

363 Ibid. p. 93.

364 Cf. A. Gasquet: *Lord Acton and his ...,* op. cit., p. 199.

365 G. E. Fasnacht: *Acton's Political Philosophy*, op. cit., p. 104.

366 Cf. The first chapters of M. D'Addio: *Storia delle dottrine politiche*, Vol. I, Genoa 1984.

367 Cf. J. E. E. D. Acton: "Sir Erskine May's 'Democracy in Europe'", in *The History of Freedom and Other Essays,* op. cit., p. 288.

368 G. E. Fasnacht: *Acton's Political Philosophy,* op. cit., p. 98.

369 Ibid. p. 107.

370 Ibid. p. 108.

371 Ibid. p. 107.

372 Cf. J. E. E. D. Acton: *Lectures on the French Revolution*, London 1910, pp. 342 ff. On this point see also section 14 of this second part.

373 Cf. G. E. Fasnacht: *Acton's Political Philosophy,* op. cit., p. 115.

374 Ibid.

375 L. Kochan: *Acton on History,* op. cit., p. 57.

376 Ibid. p. 63.

377 Ibid. p. 67.
378 Cf. ibid. p. 71.
379 Ibid. p. 85.
380 Ibid. p. 84.
381 Cf. ibid. p. 91.
382 G. E. Fasnacht: *Acton's Political Philosophy*, op. cit., p. 202.
383 J. E. E. D. Acton: "The Influence of America", in *Essays in the liberal interpretation of history*, op. cit., p. 393.
384 Cf. D. Mathew: *Acton, the formative years*, op. cit., p. 79; and in general all Chapter 3.
385 G. E. Fasnacht: *Acton's Political Philosophy*, op. cit., p. 206.
386 Ibid. p. 145.
387 *Il Federalista, Introduction*, edited by M. D'Addio and G. Negri, Bologna 1980, p. 17.
388 Ibid. p. 24.
389 Cf. J. E. E. D. Acton: "Political Causes of the American Revolution", in *Essays on Freedom and Power*, op. cit., p. 178.
390 Cf. ibid. p. 177.
391 Cf. ibid. p. 222.
392 Cf. ibid. p. 182-183.
393 Cf. ibid. p. 192.
394 Cf. ibid. p. 195.
395 Ibid. p. 202.
396 Ibid. p. 215.
397 Cf. G. E. Fasnacht: *Acton's Political Philosophy*, op. cit., pp. 183-184. Cf. also on this issue: J. E. E. D. Acton: "A History of England, 1837-1880" in *Historical Essays and Studies*, op. cit.
398 Cf. J. E. E. D. Acton: *Cavour*, op. cit., pp. 198 ff.
399 This refers to *Nationality*, later reprinted in *Essays on Freedom and Power*, op. cit., pp. 270-300.
400 P. Alatri: *Introduction ...*, op. cit., p. xlviii.
401 Cf. D. Mathew: *Acton, the formative years*, op. cit., p. 77.
402 Cf. J. E. E. D. Acton: *Nationality*, op. cit., p. 146.
403 Cf. ibid. p. 152.
404 Cf. ibid. p. 152.
405 Cf. ibid. p. 144.
406 Cf. ibid. p. 158.
407 Cf. ibid. p. 159.
408 Cf. ibid. pp. 160-161.
409 Cf. G. E. Fasnacht: *Acton's Political Philosophy*, op. cit., p. 130. See also on this issue the essay on *Nationality* cited several times, with particular attention to pp. 288-297.
410 Cf. J. E. E. D. Acton: *Nationality*, op. cit., p. 161.
411 Cf. ibid. p. 165.
412 Ibid. p. 168.
413 Cf. ibid. p. 169.
414 C. Antoni: *Lo Storicismo*, Rome 1968, pp. 151-152.
415 Cf. C. Antoni: *Dallo Storicismo alla sociologia*, Florence 1973, p. 204.

[416] Cf. J. E. E. D. Acton: "Sir Erskine May's 'Democracy in Europe'", in *The History of Freedom and Other Essays*, op. cit., p. 63.

[417] Cf. ibid. pp. 84-85.

[418] Cf. J. E. E. D. Acton: *Lectures on the French Revolution*, op. cit., pp. 109 ff. The definition in parenthesis is found on p. 109.

[419] Cf. J. E. E. D. Acton: "Sir Erskine May's 'Democracy in Europe'", in *The History of Freedom and Other Essays*, op. cit., p. 85.

[420] Cf. ibid. p. 86.

[421] Cf. ibid. p. 88.

[422] Cf. ibid. p. 89.

[423] Cf. ibid. p. 93.

[424] Cf. ibid. pp. 93-94.

[425] Cf. on this issue the essay on *Nationality* frequently cited in the previous chapter.

[426] Cf. G. E. Fasnacht: *Acton's Political Philosophy*, op. cit., p. 117.

[427] Benedetto Croce, in the Preface to one of his famous essays, classes Marx as deserving merit among political scientists because, like few others, he was able to introduce, or rather to restore, the concept of force, among the most determining elements in practical activity. Marx is a kind of Machiavelli of the proletariat because not only did he succeed in understanding the enormous strength of this emerging class, but he gave it a faith to struggle for, and some more or less utopian aims for which to strive. Cf. B. Croce: *Materialismo storico ed economia marxista*, Bari 1961, p. xv. It is perhaps worth noting that Croce wasa to consider Acton as one of those great historical scholars who have contributed no small amount to improving method and rigorous discipline. Cf. for instance: B. Croce: *La storia come pensiero e come azione*, Bari 1938, pp. 54-55.

[428] Cf. G. E. Fasnacht: "Freedom and Socialism", in *Lord Acton on Nationality and Socialism*, London 1949, p. 21.

[429] Cf. L. Kochan: *Acton on History*, op. cit., p. 94.

[430] Ibid. p. 95.

[431] B. Croce: *Materialismo storico ed economia marxista*, op. cit., pp. xiii-xiv.

[432] Cf. G. E. Fasnacht: *Acton's Political Philosophy*, op. cit., p. 201.

[433] Cf. ibid. p. 73.

[434] Cf. Himmerfarb: *Introduction* to J. S. Mill: *On Liberty*, London 1985, p. 48.

[435] Cf. J. E. E. D. Acton: "A History of England, 1837-1880", in *Historical Essays and Studies*, op. cit., pp. 488-489.

[436] Cf. J. E. E. D. Acton: "Sir Erskine May's 'Democracy in Europe'", in *The History of Freedom and Other Essays*, op. cit., pp. 97-98.

[437] Cf. J. E. E. D. Acton: "The History of Freedom in Antiquity", in *Essays on Freedom and Power*, op. cit., p. 56.

[438] Cf. L. B. Namier: *The Revolution of the Intellectuals and Other Essays on Nineteenth Century Europe*, Italian edition, Turin 1957, p. 181.

[439] Cf. ibid. pp. 178-179.

[440] Cf. G. E. Fasnacht: *Freedom and Socialism*, op. cit., p. 26.

[441] Ibid. p. 27.

[442] Ibid. p. 29.

[443] Cf. G. E. Fasnacht: *Acton's Political Philosophy*, op. cit, p. 39.

[444] Ibid. p. 69.

445 Cf. ibid. p. 141 and pp. 161-162.

446 N. Bobbio: *Liberalism and Democracy,* Milan 1986, p. 44.

447 Cf. Karl Popper: *The Open Society and its Enemies.* Vol. II., *The High Tide of Prophecy: Hegel, Marx, and the Aftermath,* Routledge and Kegan Paul, London 1974, p. 364.

448 Cf. G. E. Fasnacht: *Acton's Political Philosophy,* op. cit., p. 114.

449 Cf. ibid. p. 129.

450 Cf. Sections 1 and 4 of the second part.

451 J. E. E. D. Acton: "The history of Freedom in Christianity", in *A History of Freedom*, op. cit., p. 32.

452 Ibid.

453 Ibid.

454 Cf. ibid. pp. 34-35.

455 Ibid. p. 37.

456 Ibid.

457 Ibid. p. 39.

458 J. E. E. D. Acton: "The civil war in America", in *Historical Essays and Studies*, op. cit., p. 125.

459 Cf. Section 14 of the present work, in which Acton's considerations on the French Revolution are dealt with.

460 Cf. J. E. E. D. Acton: "The civil war in America", op. cit., pp. 129-130.

461 Ibid. – both the quotations are on p. 134.

462 On this interpretation, see also pp. 136-137. The quotation in brackets is on p. 136.

463 Ibid. pp. 141-142.

464 J. E. E. D. Acton: "The history of Freedom in Christianity", op. cit., p. 41.

465 Cf. ibid. p. 42. With regard to the position of E. Bloch, see also: *Atheismus in Christentum, zur Religion des Exodus und des Reichs,* Frankfurt am Main, 1968, and especially T. Münzer: *Als Theologie der revolution* Frankfurt am M., 1969.

466 J. E. E. D. Acton: "The history of Freedom in Christianity", op. cit., p. 43.

467 Cf. ibid. p. 46.

468 Cf. Ibid.

469 Ibid. p. 48.

470 J. E. E. D. Acton: "Political Thoughts on the Church", in *A History of Freedom*, op. cit., p. 199.

471 Ibid. p. 202.

472 Ibid. p. 203.

473 Ibid.

474 Ibid. pp. 204-205.

475 Cf. ibid. pp. 208-211.

476 J. E. E. D. Acton: "The New World", in *Lectures on Modern History*, op. cit., p. 67.

477 J. E. E. D. Acton: "The history of Freedom in Christianity", op. cit., p. 52.

478 Cf. ibid. p. 55.

479 Ibid. p. 56.

480 Cf. J. E. E. D. Acton: "Political Thoughts on the Church", op. cit., p. 188.

481 Cf. ibid. p. 189.

[482] Ibid. p. 194.

[483] On the dangers of nationalism, see also Section 8 of the second part of this work.

[484] Cf. J. E. E. D. Acton: "The Rise of the Whigs", in *Lectures on Modern History*, op. cit., p. 211 ff.

[485] Ibid. p. 216.

[486] Ibid.

[487] Ibid. p. 217.

[488] Ibid.

[489] J. E. E. D. Acton: "The English Revolution", in *Lectures on Modern History*, op. cit., p. 231.

[490] Ibid.

[491] Ibid. p. 230.

[492] J. E. E. D. Acton: "The Influence of America", in *Lectures on the French Revolution*, op. cit., p. 20.

[493] Ibid. p. 24.

[494] J. E. E. D. Acton: "The Constitutional Debates", in *Lectures on the French Revolution*, op. cit., p. 109.

[495] Cf. ibid. pp. 115-116.

[496] Ibid. p. 121.

[497] Cf. J. E. E. D. Acton: "The Reign of Terror", in *Lectures on the French Revolution*, op. cit., p. 270.

[498] Cf. J. E. E. D. Acton: "Sieyès and the Constitution civile", in *Lectures on the French Revolution*, op. cit., p. 173.

[499] Cf. J. E. E. D. Acton: "The Heralds of the Revolution", in *Lectures on the French Revolution*, op. cit., p. 16.

[500] Ibid. p. 17.

[501] Cf. J. E. E. D. Acton: "The Influence of America", in *Lectures on the French Revolution*, op. cit., pp. 36-37.

[502] Cf. J. E. E. D. Acton: "The Fourth of August", in *Lectures on the French Revolution*, op. cit., p. 104.

[503] Cf. J. E. E. D. Acton: "Mirabeau", in *Lectures on the French Revolution*, op. cit., pp. 157-158.

[504] Cf. J. E. E. D. Acton: "The Fall of the Gironde", in *Lectures on the French Revolution*, op. cit., pp. 257-258.

[505] J. E. E. D. Acton: "The American Revolution", in *Lectures on Modern History*, op. cit., p. 314.

[506] Cf. ibid. p. 305.

[507] Cf. ibid. p. 309.

[508] Cf. Ibid.

[509] Cf. J. E. E. D. Acton: "The Heralds of the Revolution", in *Lectures on the French Revolution*, op. cit., pp. 4-5.

[510] Cf. ibid. pp. 6 ff.

[511] Ibid. p. 13.

[512] Cf. J. E. E. D. Acton: "The Influence of America", in *Lectures on the French Revolution*, op. cit., p. 23.

[513] Ibid. p. 32.

[514] Cf. ibid. p. 33.

515 Ibid. p. 35.

516 Cf. J. E. E. D. Acton: "The Summons of the States-General", in *Lectures on the French Revolution,* op. cit., p. 75.

517 J. E. E. D. Acton: "The Tennis-Court Oath", in *Lectures on Modern History,* op. cit., p. 75.

518 It was Lord Acton himself who described this mass society hiding behind its own "majestic hypocrisy", in his *Lectures on the French Revolution.* The description is repeated in all its polemical force by Hannah Arendt in her famous work *On Revolution.* Arendt, who quotes Acton's classical study several times in her work, holds, however, that Acton had somewhat exaggerated the influence of the American Revolution on that in France. When the men of the American Revolution came to France and found themselves materially faced with the social conditions of the continent, those of the poor and those of the rich, they could no longer believe with Washington that the 'American Revolution seemed to have opened the eyes of almost all the European nations'. But Arendt's position, too, seems too hasty, vis-à-vis Acton, and does not take account of other aspects of the American Revolution which inspired the French one, such as, for example, the initial idea of decentralizing power.

519 H. Arendt, op. cit., p. 117, of the Italian translation, Milan 1989.

520 Cf. ibid. p. 282.

521 Cf. J. E. E. D. Acton: "The Fall of the Bastille", in *Lectures on the French Revolution*, op. cit., pp. 79.

522 Ibid. p. 88.

523 Cf. J. E. E. D. Acton: "The Fourth of August", in *Lectures on the French Revolution*, op. cit., p. 96.

524 J. E. E. D. Acton: "The Feuillants and the War"*,* in *Lectures on Modern History,* op. cit., p. 195.

525 Cf. J. E. E. D. Acton: "The Catastrophe of Monarchy", in *Lectures on the French Revolution*, op. cit., pp. 238-239.

526 Cf. J. E. E. D. Acton: "The European War", in *Lectures on the French Revolution,* op. cit., p. 320.

527 Cf. the middle part of Section 7 of Chapter 1.

528 A. Capecelatro: *Gli effetti dei decreti vaticani; Considerazioni,* Florence 1875, p. 7. The source to which the author refers is "Le Français" of 6.II.1986.

529 Ibid. p. 12.

530 Ibid. p. 45.

531 Ibid. p. 47.

532 Cf. ibid. p. 56

533 Cf. ibid. p. 57 ff., when the Council of Constance is discussed.

534 A. Capecelatro: *Newman e la religione cattolica in Inghilterra, ovvero l'Oratorio inglese,* Vol. I (the work is in two volumes), Naples 1859, p. 141.

535 Ibid. p. 255.

536 Ibid. p. 256.

537 Ibid. p. 257.

538 Ibid. p. 263.

BIBLIOGRAPHY

1. Writings by Lord Acton:

    a) Collections and anthologies
    b) Lectures and articles published separately
    c) Reviews
    d) Works published, translated or introduced by Lord Acton
    e) Correspondence.

2. Studies on Lord Acton's thought

3. Principal English works on Christianity and Catholicism of the nineteenth century.

1. Writings by Lord Acton.
a₁) Collections and anthologies (in English)

Lectures on Modern History, with an introduction by J. N. Figgis and R. V. Laurence, London, Macmillan, 1906. There are numerous additional editions of this work (1907, 1912, 1918, 1920, 1921, 1930, 1956 and 1960). The 1956 edition was published by St Martin's Press, New York.

Historical Essays and Studies, with an introduction by J. N. Figgis and R. V. Laurence, London, Macmillan, 1907. There are a further three editions of this work (1919, 1926 and 1967). The last of these was published by Books for Libraries, Freeport, New York.

Lectures on the French Revolution, with an introduction by J. N. Figgis and R. V. Laurence, London, Macmillan, 1910. There are three further editions of this work (1920, 1932 and 1969).The 1969 edition was published by AMS Press, New York.

The History of Freedom, and other Essays, with an introduction by J. N. Figgis and R. V. Laurence, London, Macmillan, 1907. There have been three other editions of this work (1909, 1922 and 1967). The 1967 edition was published by Books for Libraries, Freeport, New York.

Essays on Church and State, introduced and edited by D. Woodruff (Writings, Collected Edition, Vol. I) London 1952. A further two (American) editions of this work exist. The first, dated 1953, was publihed in New York by Viking; the second in 1968, also in New York by Crowell.

Essays on Freedom and Power, with an introduction by G. Himmelfarb, Beacon Press, USA. This work appeared with a new introduction by Himmelfarb in a new edition, also published in the USA in 1956, in Meridian Books, and has been reprinted several times, up to the 7th edition of 1972.

Essays in the Liberal Interpretation of History: selected papers, with an introduction by W. H. McNeill. Classical European Historians, Chicago 1967.

Lord Acton – the decisive decade, 1864–1874; essays (written by Acton) and documents, (mainly by Lord Acton (ed); compiled by D. McElrath, in collaboration with J. Holland and W. White, Bibliothèque de la Revue d'histoire ecclésiastique, Louvain, 1970.

Lord Acton in America, Shepherdston, Patmos Press, 1979. These are selected writings on American questions.

Renaissance to Revolution, Schocken Books, New York 1961.

Lord Acton on Papal Power, compiled by H. A. MacDougall, Sheed & Ward, London 1973.

Lord Acton and the First Vatican Council, Catholic Theological Faculty, Sydney, Aus. 1975.

Longitude 30 West, New York 1969.

Lord Acton on Nationality and Socialism. Two lectures, with an appendix on Burke based on the Acton manuscripts, compiled by G. E. Fasnacht, London 1949.

a₂) Collections and anthologies (in other languages)

Cattolicesimo liberale: saggi storici. Translation and introduction by P. Alatri. Le Monnier, Florence, 1950

Antologia degli scritti politici dei liberali vittoriani, edited by O. Barié, Il Mulino, Bologna 1962. In this anthology there are three excerpts taken from *The History of Freedom and other essays*.

Ensayos sobre la libertad y el poder: Selection and introduction by G. Himmelfarb, translated into Spanish by E. T. G., Madrid, Instituto de Estudios Políticos 1959.

Briefe Lord Acton über George Eliot, ed. R. Imelmann, in *Probleme der englischen Sprache und Kultur*, Heidelberg 1925, pp. 195-207.

Especially in German, (but also in other languages) there are many translations of articles, lectures, letters, etc., published separately or in anthologies or reviews. Alongside the English originals, existing translations in other languages will be listed in the section below.

b) Lectures and articles published separately.

The Borgias and their latest historian, in North British Review, No. 106, January 1871.

Conflicts with Rome, in Home and Foreign Review, No. 8, April 1864.

Döllinger's historical work, in English Historical Review (EHR), No 20, October 1890.

German Schools of History, in EHR January 1886. There is a German translation of this article by J. von Imelmann, Berlin, R. Gaertner, 1887.

The history of freedom in Antiquity, and the history of freedom in Christianity. These are two speeches given before the members of the Bridgnorth Insttiute, at the Agricultural Hall on 26th February and 28th May 1877. There is a French translation of these two speeches by L. Borguet, with a preface by E. de Lavaleye, Paris, Sandoz & Fischbacher, 1878.

A lecture on the study of history, lecture held at Cambridge on 11th June 1895, and published by tghe University Press. There is also a second edition of the lecture, dated one year later. A German translation by J. von Immelmann also exists. Berlin R. Gaertner, 1897.

The Massacre of Saint Bartholomew, in the North British Review, No. 101, October 1869. A translation of this article exists in Italian by T. Gar, with an introduction and addendum, published in Venice in 1870.

The Munich Congress, in Home and Foreign Review, No. 7, January 1864.

The Pope and the Council, in the North British Review, No. 101, October 1869.

The Vatican Council, in the North British Review, No. 105, October 1870.

Zur Geschichte des vaticanischen Cônciles, Munich, M. Rieger'sche Universitäts Buchhandlund, (G.Himmer), 1871.

The Waldensian forgeries, in Home and Foreign Review, No. 4, April 1863.

The War of 1870. Lecture given at the Bridgnorth Literary and Scientific Institution on 25th April 1890.

Wilhelm von Giesebrecht, in EHR, April 1890.

George Eliot. Eine biografische Skizze. German translation by J. von Immelmann of an article which appeared in the Nineteenth Century Review; Berlin 1886.

c) **Reviews**

The American Commonwealth, by James Brice, in EHR April 1869.

Democracy in Europe: a History, by Sir T. E. May, 1877, in The Quarterly Review No. 289, January 1878.

George Eliot's Life as related in her Letters and Journals, arranged and edited by J. W. Cross; 3 volumes, in Nineteenth Century, March 1885. There is a

German translation of this essay with an introduction by J. von Imelmann, Berlin, R. Gaertner, 1886.

A History of England, 1837–1880, by F. F. Bright, in EHR, October 1888.

A History of the French Revolution, by H. M. Stephens, Vol. II, in EHR April 1892.

A History of the Inquisition of the Middle Ages, by H. C. Lea, in EHR October 1888

A History of the Papacy ..., by J. M. Creighton, Vols. III and IV; in EHR July 1887.

Letters and Papers, foreign and domestic, of the reign of Henry VIII, arranged and catalogued by J. S. Brewer, M.A., Vol. IV; Introduction and Appendix, London 1875, in The Quarterly Review No. 285, January 1877.

The Life of Lord Houghton, by T. Wemyss Reid, in Nineteenth Century, December 1890.

Mr Burd's Machiavelli, in Nineteenth Century, April 1892.

A short history of Napoleon the First, by J. R. Seeley, and *The First Napoleon*, by J. C. Ropes, both in EHR July 1887.

Talleyrand's Memoirs, in Nineteenth Century, April 1891.

Tocqueville's Souvenirs, in Nineteenth Century, May 1893.

The British Review, Nos. 101-106, October 1869 to January 1871. These contain numerous reviews and writings by Lord Acton. They bear witness to a moment of great difficulty in the life of the English historian. These are the years in which the 'Roman Question' was becoming more and more difficult, until it finally degenerated. These writings also witness to the isolation and disillusionment felt by Acton and by the English Catholics. Many of these articles were republished in the 20th century in various anthologies.

d) Works published, translated or introduced by Lord Acton.

JAMES II King of England, *Letters ... to the Abbot of La Trappe*, published by Lord Acton in Philobiblion Soc., Miscellanies, Vol. XIV, London 1872–1876, 1877.

MACHIAVELLI, NICCOLÒ: *Il Principe*, edited by L. A. Burd, published with an introduction by Lord Acton, Oxford 1891.

Home and Foreign Review (the continuation of the *Rambler*), articles never published, collected and edited by Lord Acton, London 1862–1864.

HARPSFIELD, NICHOLAS: *Harpsfield's narrative of the divorce,* published by Lord Acton, London 1876.

GOOCH, GEORGE PEABODY: *Annals of Politics and Culture (1492–1899)*, with an introduction and notes by Lord Acton (published after the editor's death).

FREDERICK THE GREAT, King of Prussia: *Les matinées royales, ou l'art de régner,* small previously unpublished work, published under the editorship of Lord Acton, London 1863.

The Chronicle, March 23rd 1867 – February 15th 1868, (articles never published) edited by Lord Acton with other collaborators, 2 volumes, London 1867–1868.

The Cambridge Modern History, planned and compiled by Lord Acton, edited by (with the collaboration of) A. W. Ward, G. W. Prothero, S. Leathes, composed of 13 volumes plus an Atlas, Cambridge 1902–1912.
Of this work there are:
– beginning in 1907, a first reprint which was concluded in 1912;
– also from 1907 another reprint which was concluded in 1929, but contained a new edition of the Atlas;
– between 1902 and 1911, there was a partial publication of the work, with Volumes 6, 9, 11, 12, 13, and a reprint of the first volume. From this edition, Volumes 2, 3, 4, 5, 7, 8 and 10 are missing;
– the whole work was reprinted in 1929 (Cambridge) but with one volume less (12);
– again edited by the Cambridge University Press, in 1934 there was a new and definitive edition, which unfortunately appeared without bibliographies. The publication in a cheap edition was resumed in 13 volumes: *The Cambridge Modern History, planned by Lord Acton*, edited by Sir A. W. Ward, Sir G. W. Prothero and Sir S. Leathes (Cheap edition without bibliographies, 13 volumes, Cambridge 1934).

e) Correspondence

in English:

GASQUET, FRANCIS AIDAN: *Lord Acton and his Circle (Letters of Lord Acton),* edited by Abbot Gasquet, George Allen: Burns and Oates, London, 1906. This is certainly one of the most frequently read and quoted texts by scholars dealing with the life and work.

The Vatican Decrees: Four letters by Lord Acton to the Editor of the Times, Edinburg 1906.

Letters of Lord Acton to Mary, daughter of the Rt. Hon. W. E. Gladstone, edited with an introductory memoir by Herbert Paul. With a preface by Mary Gladstone, afterwards Drew, and a portrait. George Allen, London, 1904. There is a second edition of this text, dated 1913.

Selections from the Correspondence of the first Lord Acton; edited with an introduction by John Neville Figgis and Reginald Vere Lawrence; Vol. I, Correspondence with Cardinal Newman, Lady Blennerhassett, W. E. Gladstone, and others. Longman & Co., London 1917.

The Correspondence of Lord Acton and Richard Simpson, edited by Josef L. Altholz and Damian McElrath, in 3 volumes, Cambridge University Press, London 1971–1975. The same collection was also published by the University Press, New York, 1971–1975.

Gasquet and the Acton–Simpson Correspondence, edited by J. Watin and H. Butterfield, in the Cambridge Historical Journal, No. 10, 1950

Selected Letters 1864–1875, in Damian McElrath: *Lord Acton,* in Bibliot. de la Revue d'histoire ecclésiastique, p. 51, Publications universitaires de Louvain, 1970.

Lord Acton and his Letters, edited by Peter Byrne, in the Irish Ecclesiastical Record, Dublin 1918, Series 5, Vol. 11, pp. 89-103.

The Letters of Lord Acton, edited by James Bryce, in the North American Review, Vol. 178, pp. 698-710. This and the previous study contain some passages from Acton's letters and both are cited among Acton scholars.

In German:

Römische Briefe vom Concil, von Quirinus (i.e. Lord Acton, J. J. I. von Döllinger, J. Friedrich and others). Munich 1870. There is an English translation of this dating from the same year: *Letters from Rome on the Council*, by Quirinus (i.e. Lord Acton, J. J. I. von Döllinger, J. Friedrich and others); authorized translation, London 1870.

Sendschreiben an einen deutschen Bischof des Vaticänischen Concils, Nordlingen, 1870.

Ignaz von Döllinger, Lord Acton: Briefwechsel, 1850–1890, Bearb von V. Conzemius, Vol. I, Munich 1963. This first volume was intended to be part of the complete correspondence of I. von Döllinger.

2. Studies on Lord Acton's thought.

In English:

AUCHMUTY, JAMES J., *Acton as a member of the House of Commons*, Bulletin of the Faculty of Arts, Farouk I University, Alexandria 1953.

AUCHMUTY, JAMES J., *Lord Acton's Morality, Theory and Practice,* Bulletin of the Faculty of Arts, Farouk I University, Alexandria 1953.

BARRY, WILLIAM, *Lord Acton, a study,* Dublin Review, London 1918, Vol. 162, pp. 1-24.

BLENNERHASSETT, W. L., *Acton, 1834–1902*, Dublin Review, London 1934, Vol. 194, pp. 169-188.

BRINTON, CRANE, *Lord Acton's Philosophy of History*, Harvard Theological Review, Cambridge, Mass., 1919, Vol.12, pp. 84-112.

BRYCE, JAMES, *The Letters of Lord Acton,* North American Review, Vol. 178, pp. 698-710.

BRYCE, JAMES, *Lord Acton* (in this collection the following studies are also to be found): *Acton as a Cambridge Professor*, by W. A. J. Archbold; *Lord Acton as a book collector*, by H. R. Tedder). Proceedings of the British Academy, I, London 1903–1904.

BUTTERFIELD, HERBERT, *Acton, his training, methods and intellectual system,* Sarkassian, Arshag Ohan, publisher, London 1961, pp. 169-198.

BUTTERFIELD, HERBERT, *Lord Acton,* London Historical Association 1948. This is a pamphlet of 24 pages of which there is also an Italian translation for the Publishing Company Vita e Pensiero.

BYRNE, PETER, *Lord Acton and his Letters,* Irish Ecclesiastical Record, Dublin, 1918; Series 5, Vol. II, pp. 89-101.

CHADWICK, OWEN, *Lord Acton and his Letters,* Athlone Press, London 1976.

DREW, MARY, *Acton and Gladstone,* Fortnightly Review, New York, 1918, Vol. 113, pp. 838-851.

DREW, MARY, *Acton, Gladstone and others,* London, Nisbet 1924.

ENGEL–JANOSI, FRIEDRICH, *Reflections of Lord Acton on historical principles,* Catholic Historical Review, Lancaster 1941, Vol. 27, pp. 166-185.

FASNACHT, GEORGE EUGENE, *Acton's Political Philosophy; an analysis*, London, Hollis & Carter, 1952.

FISHER, HERBERT ALBERT LAURENS, *Studies in history and politics*, by the Rt. Hon. Herbert Fisher; Oxford, the Clarendon Press, 1920. In this work there is a chapter dedicated to the historical works of Lord Acton.

HIMMELFARB, GERTRUDE, *Lord Acton, an intellectual biography*, Chicago 1950.

HIMMELFARB, GERTRUDE, *Lord Acton, a Study in Conscience and Politics*; Chicago, Chicago University Press 1952.

HOHL, CLARENCE L., *Lord Acton's visit to America*, American Catholic Historical Society of Philadelphia, Records, Vol. 71, No. 3/4 (Sept/Dec. 1960), pp. 73-84, Philadelphia 1960.

KETTENACKER, L. L., *Lord Acton and Ignatius von Döllinger*, A study in Anglo-German Intellectual Relations, Oxford 1968.

KOCHAN, LIONEL, *Acton on History*, London, A. Deutsch, 1954.

LALLY, FRANK EDWARD, *As Lord Acton says ...*, Newport, R. I., R. Ward, 1942.

MACDOUGALL, HUGH A., *The Acton–Newman relations: the dilemma of Christian liberalism*, New York, Fordham University Press, 1962.

MATHEW, DAVID, *Acton, the formative years*, London, Eyre & Spottiswoode, 1946.

MATHEW, DAVID, *Lord Acton and his Times*, University of Alabama Press, 1968.

McELRATH, DAMIAN, *Lord Acton*, Bureau de la R.H.E., Bibliothèque de l'Université, Publications universitaires de Louvain, Louvain 1970.

POLLOCK, FREDERICK JOHN, *Lord Acton at Cambridge*, The Independent Review, Vol. II, No. 7, April, London 1902.

POOLE, REGINALD L., *John Emerich, Lord Acton*, English Historical Review, London 1902, Vol. 17, pp. 692-699.

SCHUETTINGER, ROBERT LINDSAY, *Lord Acton, historian of liberty*, La Salle/Open Court, (U.S.) 1976

SHAW, WILLIAM ARTHUR, *A bibliography of the historical works of Dr Creighton, Dr Stubbs, S. R. Gardiner and Lord Acton*, edited for the R. H. S. by W. A. Shaw, London 1903.

SULLIVAN, WILLIAM KIRBY, *University Education in Ireland; a Letter to Sir J. D. Acton*, Dublin, W. B. Kelly, 1866.

281

TEMPERLEY, HAROLD, *Lord Acton on the origins of the war of 1870, with some unpublished letters from the British and Viennese archives,* Cambridge Historical Journal, London 1926, Vol. 2, pp. 68-82.

VENCE, JOHN G., *Professor Bury and Lord Acton: a critique of Professor Bury's "History of Freedom of Thought",* Mont. 1914, London, Vol. 1123, pp. 225-239.

WATKIN, A., *Gasquet and the Acton–Simpson correspondence,* Cambridge Historical Journal, London 1950, Vol. 10, No. 1, pp. 75-105.

WHITE, W., *Acton and Gladstone: their friendship and mutual influence: a dissertation.* Catholic University of America, Washington D.C., 1972.

WOODWARD, E. L., *The place of Lord Acton in the liberal movement of the nineteenth century,* Politica, London 1939, Vol. 4, pp. 248-265.

To all these works on the thought of Lord Acton should be added all the introductory studies to collections of his writings, composed by the editors. These essays are listed in the previous section: "Writings of Lord Acton", under the heading a) Collections and anthologies. We should also add a further more recent text to these: *Essays in the history of Liberty,* by J. Rufus Fears, (*Selected writings of Lord Acton*) Vol. I, Liberty Classics, Indianapolis, 1985.

In other languages

In this section only monographic studies are listed. For introductory studies or the prefaces to translations of the writings of Lord Acton, see the appropriate section.

BANASCHEWSKI, PETER, *Macaulay und Acton; ein Beitrag zum Freiheitsbegriff in der englischen Geschichtschreibung,* Werk–Verlag, München–Gräfelfing 1960.

BLENNERHASSET (LADY), *Lord Acton 1834–1902,* Deutsche Rundschau, vol. 122, pp. 64-92, Berlin 1905.

BUTTERFIELD, HERBERT, *Lord Acton,* Conferenza tenuta all'Università Cattolica di Milano e pubblicata a cura della Società Editrice Vita e Pensiero 1962.

IZQUIERDO, GONZALO, *La libertad política en el liberalismo del siglo XIX,* Fasciculos para la comprensión de la ciencia, las comunidades y la tecnologia, 18, Editoriál Universitaria, Santiago del Chile 1979.

KETTELER, WILHELM EMMANUEL BP. OF MAINZ, *Die Minorität auf dem Concil, Antwort auf Lord Acton's Sendschreiben an einen deutschen Bischof des vaticanischen Concils,* Mainz 1870.

NOACK, ULRICH, *Politik als Sicherung der Freiheit; nach den Schriften von John Dalberg–Acton, dem Historiker der Freiheit, 1834–1902*, G. S. B., Frankfurt am Main 1947.

ID., *Geschichtswissenschaft und Wahrheit; nach den Schriften von John Dalberg–Acton, dem Historiker der Freiheit, 1834–1902*, G. S. B., Frankfurt am Main 1935.

ID., *Katholizität und Geistesfreiheit; nach den Schriften von John Dalberg–Acton*, G. S. B., Frankfurt am Main 1947.

OLIVAR, BERTRAND RAFAEL, *Dos Católicos frente a frente: Lord Acton y Ramón Nocedal*, Ateneo, Madrid 1955.

PETANDER, KARL, *Lord Acton och hans kritikav Leopold von Ranke*, KF. b. i. d., Stockholm 1955.

ZIRNGIEBL, EBERHARD, *Das vaticanische Concil mit Rücksicht auf Lord Actons Sendschreiben und Bischof v. Kettelers Antwort kritisch betrachtet*, München 1871.

3. Principal English works on Christianity and Catholicism of the nineteenth century.

In this section, apart from the principal works on religious themes of the C19 in England, a few studies are also listed on the work and thought of Cardinal Newman. The listed texts, however, are only those which have some reference to issues dealt with in the present research.

ABERCROMBIE, N. J., *The Life and Work of Edmund Bishop*, London 1959.

ADAMSON, J. W., *English Education, 1789–1902*, Cambridge 1930.

ADDERLEY, J. G., *In Slums and Society*, London 1916.

ALINGTON, C., *A Dean's Apology*, London 1952.

ALTHOLZ, J., *The Liberal Catholic Movement in England*, Burns and Oates, London 1962.

AMHERST, W. J., *The History of Catholic Emancipation*, 2 vols., Kegan Paul and Trench, London 1886.

ANSON, P. F., *The Call of the Cloister*, 2nd ed., by A. W. Campbell, London 1964.

ID., *Fashions in Church Furnishings, 1840–1940*, 2nd ed., London 1965.

ARMYTAGE, W. H. G., *Four Hundred Years of English Education*, Camb. University Press 1964.

ID., A. J. *Mundella, 1825–1897; the Liberal Background to the Labour Movement*, London 1951.

ATKINSON, T. D., *English and Welsh Cathedrals*, London 1912.

BASSETT, B., *The English Jesuits from Campion to Martindale*, Burns & Oates, London 1967.

BATEMAN, C. T., *Campbell, Pastor of the City Temple*, London 1903.

BAX, E. BELFORT, *Reminiscences and Reflections of a Mid and Late Victorian*, London 1918.

BECK, G. A., (ed. by), *The English Catholic, 1850–1950*, Burns & Oates, London 1950.

BELL, G. K. A., *Randall Davidson, Archbishop of Canterbury*, 3rd edn., London 1952.

BENNETT, F., *Chester Cathedral*, Chester 1925.

BENSON, A. C., *Life of Edward White Benson, sometime Archbishop of Canterbury*, 2 vols., London 1989.

BEST, G. F. A., *Bishop Westcott and the miners*, London 1967.

BILL, E. G. W. (ed. by), *Anglican Initiatives in Christian Unity*, London 1967.

BLAKISTON, N. (ed. by), *The Roman Question: Letters of Odo Russell*, London 1962.

BOREHAM, F. W., *My Pilgrimage: an Autobiography*, London 1940.

BOWEN, D., *The Idea of the Victorian Church*, Montreal 1968.

BOWEN, W. E., *Contemporary Ritualism: a Volume of Evidence*, London 1902.

BRIDGE, J. F., *A Westminster Pilgrim*, London 1919.

BROWN, A. W., *The Metaphysical Society. Victorian Minds in Crisis, 1869–1880*, New York 1947.

BROWN, C. K. F., *A History of the English Clergy, 1800–1900*, London 1953.

BROWNE, G. F., *The Recollections of a Bishop*, London 1915.

BUMPUS, J. S., *A History of English Cathedral Music, 1549–1889*, 2 vols., London 1908.

BUTLER, C., *The Life and Times of Bishop Ullathorne, 1806–1889*, 2 vols., Burns, Oates & Washbourne, London 1926.

BUTLER, J. R. M., *H. M. Butler, Master of Trinity College*, Cambridge 1925.

BYRT, G. W., *John Clifford, a Fighting Free Churchman*, London 1947.

CAMPBELL, R. J., *A Spiritual Pilgrimage*, London 1916.

CAPECELATRO, A., *Newman e la religione cattolica in Inghilterra, ovvero l'Oratorio inglese*, 2 volumi, Napoli 1859.

ID., *Gli effetti de' decreti vaticani. Considerazioni*, Firenze 1875.

CARPENTER, E. F. (ed. by), *A House of Kings: The History of Westminster Abbey*, London 1966.

CARPENTER W. B., *The Permanent Elements of Religion*, London 1899.

CATHOLIC BARRISTER, A., *The New Departure in Catholic Liberal Education*, Burns & Oates, London 1878.

Catholic Emancipation, 1829–1929: Essays by Various Writers, Longmans, Green & Co., London 1929.

CATHOLIC LAYMAN, A., *University Educations for English Catholics: a Letter to the Very Rev. J. H. Newman*, D. D., Burns & Oates, London 1864.

CHADWICK, H., *The Vindication of Christianity in Westcott's Thought*, Cambridge 1961.

CHADWICK O., *Edward King, Bishop of Lincoln*, Lincoln 1968.

CHAMPNEYS, B., *Memoirs and Correspondence of Coventry Patmore*, 2 vols., London 1900.

CHAPMAN, R., *Father Faber*, Burns & Oates, London 1962.

CHURCH, R. W., *The Church, the Census and the People, by a Priest of the Church of England*, London 1882.

CLARKE, B. F. L., *Church Builders of the Nineteenth Century*, rev. Ed., London 1969.

CLARKE, W. K. L., *Chichester Cathedral in the Nineteenth Century*, Chichester 1959.

CLAYTON, J., *Father Döllinger: a Memoir*, London 1902.

CONZEMIUS, V., *J. J. I. Döllinger: Briefwechsel, 1850–1890*, München 1963.

CORCORAN, T., *O'Connell and Catholic Education: Two Papers Published in Ireland for the Centenary Year of Catholic Emancipation*, Talbot Press, Dublin 1929.

CORNISH, F. W., *A History of the English Church in the Nineteenth Century*, 2 vols., Macmillan, London 1910.

COULSON, J. (ed. by), *Theology and the University: an Ecumenical Investigation*, Darton, Longman & Tod, London 1964.

COX, G. V., *Recollections of Oxford*, Macmillan, London 1868.

COX, G. W., *The Life of J. W. Colenso, Bishop of Natal*, 2 vols., London 1888.

COURTNEY, W. L., *The Diary of a Churchgoer*, London 1904.

CRUICKSHANK, M., *Church and State in English Education: 1870 to the present day*, London 1963.

CURRIE, R., *Methodism Divided*, London 1968.

DARK, S., *Mackay of All Saints*, London 1937.

DAVIES, H., *Worship and Theology in England*, London 1963.

DAVIES, E. T., *Religion in the Industrial Revolution in South Wales*, Cardiff 1965.

DAVIDSON, R. T. and BENHAM, W., *Life of A. C. Tait, Archbishop of Canterbury*, 2 vols., London 1891.

DE MADAUNE, C., *Ignace Spencer et la renaissance catholique en Angleterre*, Paris 1875.

DIGGLE, J. W., *The Lancashire Life of Bishop Fraser*, 3rd edn., London 1889.

Do we believe? A correspondence in the Daily Telegraph, 1904, introd. by W. L. Courtney, London 1905.

EDWARDS, A., *A Handbook of Welsh Church Defence*, 3rd edn., London 1895.

ELLIOTT–BINNS, L. E., *English Thought 1860–1900: in Theological Aspect*, London 1956.

EVENETT, H. O., *The Cambridge Prelude to 1895*, in *The Dublin Review*, n. 218, 1946.

ID., *The Catholic Schools of England and Wales*, Camb. University Press 1944.

ID., *Catholics and the Universities*, in The English Catholics. A Century of Progress, London 1950.

Facts and Figures about the Church of England, 3 vols., London 1959–1965.

FITZGERALD, P., *Fifty Years of Catholic Life and Social Progress*, 2 vols., Fisher Unwin, London 1901.

FITZSIMONS, J. (ed. by), *Manning: Anglican and Catholic*, The Catholic Book Club, London 1951.

FLEMING, D. H., *J. W. Draper and the Religion of Science*, Philadelphia 1950.

FOTHERGILL, B., *Nicholas Wiseman*, Faber & Faber, London 1963.

GILLOW, J., *Bibliographical Dictionary of the English Catholics, from the Breach with Rome in 1534 to the Present Time*, 5 vols., Burns & Oates, London 1885–1902.

GLOVER, W. B., *Evangelical Nonconformists and Higher Criticism in the Nineteenth Century*, London 1924.

GORMAN, W. G., *Converts to Rome: A Biographical List of the More Notable Converts to the Catholic Church in the United Kingdom During the Last Sixty Years*, Sands, London 1910.

GOTT, J., *Letters of Bishop Gott*, A. J. Wortledge (ed.), London 1919.

GRANT, B., *The Dissenting World*, 2nd edn., London 1869.

GRANT, J. W., *Free Churchmanship in England, 1870–1940, with Special Reference to Congregationalism*, London 1955.

GREENSLADE, S. L. (ed. by), *The Cambridge History of the Bible*, 2 vols., Cambridge 1963.

GRUBER, J. W., *A Conscience in Conflict*, Columbia University Press, New York 1960.

GUEDALLA, P., *The Queen and Mr. Gladstone, 1845–1898*, 2 vols., London 1933.

GWY, R. E., *The Synods in English: being the Text of the Synods of Westminster*, Translated to English, London 1986.

GWYNN, D., *Lord Shrewsbury, Pugin and the Catholic Revival*, Hollis & Carter, London 1946.

ID., *O'Connell, Davis and the Colleges Bill*, Cork University Press 1948.

HARFORD, J. B. and MACDONALD, F. C., *H. C. G. Moule, Bishop of Durham*, London 1922.

HAW, G. (ed. by), *Christianity and the Working Classes*, London 1906.

HEARNSHAW, F. J. C., *The Centenary History of King's College*, London 1828–1928, London 1929.

HEASMAN, K., *Army of the Church*, London 1968.

HELMORE, F., *Memoir of the Rev. Thomas Helmore*, London 1891.

HEMPHILL, S., *A History of the Revised Version of the New Testament*, London 1906.

HENNESSY, J. P., *The Failure of the Queen's Colleges and Mixed Education in Ireland*, Bryce, London 1859.

HERON, D. C., *The Constitutional History of the University of Dublin, with some Account of its Present Condition and Suggestions for Improvement*, McGlashan, Dublin 1847.

HICKEY, J., *Urban Catholics: Urban Catholicism in England and Wales from 1829 to the Present Day*, Geoffrey Chapman, London 1967.

HOLLIS, C., *Newman and the Modern World*, Hollis & Carter, London 1967.

HOOYKAAS, R., *The Principle of Uniformity in Geology, Biology and Theology*, Leyden 1963.

HORNE, C. S., *Nonconformity in the Nineteenth Century*, London 1905.

HOUGHTON, W. E., *The Art of Newman's Apologia*, New Haven 1945.

HOW, F. D., *A Memoir of Bishop Sir Lovelace Tomlinson Stamer*, London 1910.

HOWSON, J. S. (ed. by), *Essays on Cathedrals*, London 1872.

HUGHES, T., *James Fraser, second Bishop of Manchester. A Memoir*, new edn., London 1888.

HUNTINGTON, G., *Random Recollections of some noted Bishops, Divines and Worthies of the 'Old Church' of Manchester*, London 1893.

HUTTON, R. H., *Aspects of Religious and Scientific Thought*, ed. by E. M. Roscoe, London 1899.

HUTTON, W. H., *William Stubbs, Bishop of Oxford*, 1825–1901, London 1906.

INGLIS, K. S., *Churches and the Working Classes in Victorian England*, London 1963.

JASPER, R. C. D., *Prayer Book Revision in England, 1800–1900*, London 1954.

JONES, C. A. and APPLETON, R., *A History of the Jesus Lane Sunday School*, Cambridge 1877

JONES, P. D'A., *The Christian Socialist Revival, 1877–1914*, Princeton 1968.

KELLY, H. H., *No Pious Person: Autobiographical Recollections*, ed. by G. Every, London 1960.

KENNY, T., *The Political Thought of John Henry Newman*, Longmans, London 1957.

KENT, J. H. S., *From Darwin to Blatchford; The Role of Darwinism in Christian Apologetics, 1875–1910*, London 1966.

KING, E., *The Love and Wisdom of God*, ed. by B. W. Randolph, London 1910.

KIRK–SMITH, H., *William Thomson, Archbishop of York*, London 1958.

KITCHIN, G. W., *E. H. Browne, Bishop of Winchester. A Memoir 1895; Ruskin in Oxford, and other Studies*, London 1904.

KNOX, W. L. and VIDLER, A. R., *The Development of Modern Catholicism*, London 1933.

LANGLEY, A. S., *Birmingham Baptists, Past and Present*, London 1939.

LEETHAM, C., *Luigi Gentili: a Sower for the Second Spring*, Burns & Oates, London 1965.

LESLIE, S. (ed. by), *Letters of Herbert, Cardinal Vaughan, to Lady Herbert of Lea, 1867–1903*, Burns & Oates, London 1942.

ID., *Henry Edward Manning: his Life and Labours*, Burns & Oates, London 1921.

ID., *Cardinal Gasquet: a Memoir*, London 1953.

MACAN, R. W., *Religious Changes in Oxford during the Last Fifty Years*, revised ed., Oxford 1918.

McCLELLAND, V. A., *Cardinal Manning: his Public Life and Influence, 1865–1892*, Oxford University Press 1962.

McCORMACK, A., *Cardinal Vaughan*, Burns & Oates, London 1966.

McGRATH, F., *Newman's University, Idea and Reality*, Longmans, Green & Co., London 1951.

McPHERSON, R. G., *Theory of Higher Education in Nineteenth-Century England*, University of Georgia Press, U.S.A. 1959.

MacLAGAN, W. D., *The Church and the People*, London 1882.

MacNUTT, F. A., *A Papal Chamberlain*, London 1936.

MAISON, M. M., *Search your Soul, Eustace: a Survey of the Religious Mind in the Victorian Age*, London 1961.

MALLET, M., *Life with Queen Victoria: Marie Mallet's Letters from Court, 1887–1901*, ed. by V. Mallet, London 1968.

MALLOCK, W. H., *Atheism and the Value of Life*, London 1884.

MANNING, H. E., *Miscellanies*, 3 vols., Burns & Oates, London 1887.

ID., *The Office of the Church in Higher Catholic Education*, Easter Pastoral Letter, London 1885.

MARSH, P. T., *The Victorian Church in Decline*, London 1969.

MARTINDALE, C. C., *Bernard Vaughan, S. J.*, London 1923.

ID., *Catholics at Oxford*, Basil Blackwell, Oxford 1925.

MATHEW, D., *Catholicism in England*, London 1948.

MATTHEWS, W. R. and ATKINS, W. M. (ed. by), *A History of St. Paul's Cathedral and the Men associated with it*, London 1957.

MAYNARD, T., *Orestes Brownson: Yankee, Radical, Catholic*, Macmillan, New York 1943.

MAYOR, S., *The Churches and the Labour Movement*, London 1967.

MEACHAM, S., *The Church in the Victorian City*, in *Victorian Studies*, March, 1968, pp. 359 ff.

MEARNS, A., *The Statistics of Attendance at Public Worship*, London 1882.

MORAN, P. F. (ed. by), *The Pastoral Letters and Other Writings of Cardinal Cullen*, 3 vols., Browne and Nolan, Dublin 1882.

MORLEY, J., *Life of William Ewart Gladstone*, 3 vols., Macmillan, London 1903.

MORRIS, J., *Catholic England in Modern Times*, Burns & Oates, London 1892.

MOULE, H. C. G., *The Evangelical School in the Church of England*, London 1901.

MUDIE–SMITH, R., *The Religious Life of London*, London 1904.

MURPHY, T., *The Position of the Catholic Church in England and Wales during the Last Two Centuries*, Burns & Oates, London 1892.

NEILL, S. C., *The Interpretation of the New Testament, 1861–1961*, Oxford 1966.

NEWSOME, D., *The Parting of Friends. A Study of the Wilberforces and Henry Manning*, Murray, London 1966.

NIAS, J., *Flame from an Oxford Cloister: the Life and Writings of P. N. Waggett*, London 1961.

NORMAN, E. R., *The Catholic Church and Ireland in the Age of Rebellion*, Longmans, London 1965.

OAKELEY, F., *The Question of University Education for English Catholics, Considered Principally in its Moral and Religious Bearings, a Letter to the Right Rev. the Bishop of Birmingham*, Burns & Lambert, London 1864.

ID., *Appendix to a Letter on University Education for English Catholics*, suggested by an article in *The Dublin Review*, Burns & Lambert, London 1864.

O'FAOLAIN, S., *Newman's Way*, Longmans, Green & Co., London 1952.

O'REILLY, B., *Life of John MacHale, Archbishop of Tuam*, 2 vols., Fr. Pustet & Co., New York and Cincinnati 1890.

OXENHAM, H. N., *Short Studies in Ecclesiastical History and Biography*, Chapman & Hall, London 1884.

PAGET, S. and CRUM, J. M. C., *Francis Paget, Bishop of Oxford*, London 1912.

PARKER, J., *Paterson's Parish: a Lifetime among Dissenters*, London 1898.

Pastoral Letter of the Archbishop and Bishops of the Province of Westminster in Provincial Council Assembled, September 20th, 1873.

PATTISON, M., *Memoirs, 1885; Suggestions on Academical Organisation with Especial Reference to Oxford,* Edinburgh 1868.

PERKINS, J., *Westminster Abbey: its Worship and Ornaments*, 2 vols., London 1938–1940.

PEROWNE, J. J. S., *Report of the Commissioners appointed by the Lord Bishop of Worcester to inquire into the Needs and Resources of the Church in the Rural Deaneries of Birmingham and Northfield,* Birmingham 1898.

PETRE, W., *Catholic System of School Discipline*, Burns & Oates, London 1878.

ID., *The Position and Prospects of Catholic Liberal Education*, Burns & Oates, London 1878.

ID., *The Problems of Catholic Liberal Education*, Burns & Oates, London 1877.

ID., *Remarks on the Present Condition of Catholic Liberal Education*, Burns & Oates, London 1877.

PICK, J. A., *G. M. Hopkins, Priest and Poet*, 2nd ed., London 1966.

POLLOCK, J. C., *A Cambridge Movement*, London 1953.

PURCELL, E. S., *The Life of Cardinal Manning*, 2 vols., Macmillan, London 1896.

RAWES, H. A., *Cui Bono? University Education: a Letter to a Catholic Layman*, Burns & Lambert, London 1864.

RICHTER, M., *The Politics of Conscience*, London 1964.

RICKARDS, E. C., *Bishop Moorhouse*, London 1920.

ROBBINS, W., *The Newman Brothers*, Heinemann, London 1966.

ROCHE, J. S., *A History of Prior Park College and its Founder Bishop Baines*, Burns & Oates, London 1931.
ROSKELL, M. F., *Memoirs of F. K. Amherst, Bishop of Northampton*, London 1903.

ROTHBLATT, S., *The Revolution of the Dons: Cambridge and Society in Victorian England*, Faber & Faber, London 1968.

ROWAN, E., *Wilson Carlile and the Church Army*, London 1905.

RUPP, E. G., *Thomas Jackson, Methodist Patriarch*, London 1954.

SANDAY, W., *Divine Overruling*, Edinburgh 1920.

SIMPSON, R., *Bishop Ullathorne and The Rambler: Reply to Criticisms Contained in 'A Letter on the Rambler and The Home and Foreign Review' (by the Right Rev. Bishop Ullathorne)*, Williams & Norgate, London 1862.

SMITH, P. VERNON, *The Law of Churchwardens and Sidesmen in the Twentieth Century*, London 1903.

SMITH, W. SYLVESTER, *The London Heretics, 1870–1914*, London 1967.

SNEAD–COX, J. G., *The Life of the Cardinal Vaughan*, 2 vols., Burns & Oates, London 1910.

SPARROW, J., *Mark Pattison and the Idea of a University*, Cambridge University Press 1967.

SPENCER, P., *Politics and Belief*, Faber & Faber, London 1953.

STEPHEN, L., *An Agnostic's Apology, and other Essays*, 2nd ed., London 1903.

STOCKLEY, W. F. P., *Newman, Education, and Ireland*, Sands, Edinburgh and Glasgow, s. d.

Synodal Letter of the Archbishop and Bishops of the Province of Westminster Assembled, August 1874.

TAYLOR, I. A., *The Cardinal Democrat: Henry Edward Manning*, Kegan Paul, London 1908.

TEMPLE, F., *The Relations between Religion and Science*, London 1884.

ID., *Memoirs of Archbishop Temple*, by Seven Friends, ed. by E. G. Sandford, 2 vols., London 1906.

TEMPLE, W., *Life of Bishop Percival*, London 1921.

The Irish University Question: The Catholic Case: Selections from the Speeches and Writings of the Archbishop of Dublin – W. Walsh – with a Historical Sketch of the Irish University Question, Browne & Nolan, Dublin 1897.

THOMSON, E. H., *William Thomson, Archbishop of York: Life and Letters*, London 1919.

TILLYARD, A. I., *A History of University Reform from 1800 to the Present Time*, Cambridge 1913.

TREVOR, J., *My Quest For God*, London 1897.

TREVOR, M., *Newman, Light in Winter*, London 1962.

Universities' Catholic Education Board: a Report of its Work from 1895 to 1897, privately printed, London 1897.

Universities of London: Historical Record (1836–1912), University of London Press, 1912.

VARIOUS, *Catholicisme Anglais*, Les Editions du Cerf, Maubourg, Paris 1961.

VARIOUS, *Les catholiques libéraux au XIX siecle*, Presses Un. de Grenoble 1974.

WAGNER, D. O., *The Church of England and Social Reform since 1854*, New York 1930.

WALSH, W. J., *Trinity College and the University of Dublin*, privately printed, Dublin 1902.

WARD, B., *The Dawn of the Catholic Revival in England, 1781–1803*, 2 vols., Longmans, London 1909.

ID., *The Eve of Catholic Emancipation, 1803–1829*, 2 vols., Longmans, London 1911.

ID., *The Sequel to Catholic Emancipation*, 2 vols., Longmans, London 1915.

ID., *William George Ward and the Catholic Revival*, Macmillan, London 1893.

ID., *The Life and Times of Cardinal Wiseman*, 2 vols., Longmans, Green & Co., London 1912.

ID., *The Life of John Henry, Cardinal Newman*, 2 vols., Longmans, London 1912.

WARD, W. R., *Victorian Oxford*, Cass, London 1965.

WEBB, C. C. J., *A Study of Religious Thought in England from 1850*, Oxford 1933.

WHITE, W. H., *The Autobiography of Mark Rutherford, Dissenting Minister*, London 1981.

WICKHAM, E. R., *Church and People in an Industrial City*, London 1957.

WILLS, A., *A Treatise on the Powers and Duties of Parish Vestries in -Ecclesiastical Matters*, London 1955.

WILSON, J. A., *The Life of Bishop Hedley*, Burns, Oates & Washbourne, London 1930.

WILSON, J. M., *Six Lectures on Pastoral Theology*, London 1903.

WISEMAN, N., *Essays on Various Subjects*, Thomas Baker, London 1888.

ID., *Recollections of the Last Four Popes*, Hurst & Blackett, London 1858.

ID., *Sermon*, T. Richardson, London 1852.

WORDSWORTH, J., *The Church and the Universities*, Oxford 1880.

ID., *The One Religion*, Oxford 1881.

YEO, S., LEECH, K., RECKITT, M. B., AND WOODIFIELD, R., (ed. by Maurice B. Reckitt), *For Christ and the People: Studies of four Socialist Priests and Prophets of the Church of England Between 1870 and 1930*, SPCK, London 1968.